GULF of MEXICO

Puerto Juarez
Merida • Isla Mujeres
Uxmal △ Chichén Itzá
YUCATAN
Ciudad del Carmen

Quintana Roo

[BRITISH HONDURAS]
Tikal • Belize
Flores BELIZE
Livingston
Cristobal Puerto Barrios
s Casas
Huehuetenango
Cobán San Pedro Sula
△ Copán Lake Yojoa
Guatemala
Chichicastenango Tegucigalpa
Atitlan
Antigua
San Jicaro Galán
San José Salvador
Sonsonate Sta. Maria de Ostuma
EL SALVADOR Matagalpa
Lake Managua
León Managua
Granada Lake
Nicaragua Bluefields

Bay Islands
HONDURAS

NICARAGUA

Corn Islands

COSTA RICA
Limón Colón
San
José Panama City
Puntarenas Balboa Darién
Palmar David Jungle
Goffito Yaviza

PANAMA COLUMBIA

End of Inter American Highway

The Road to PANAMA

The Road to PANAMA

SELDEN RODMAN

drawings by

Bill Negron

HAWTHORN BOOKS INC., Publishers, New York City

To
Lucy Sturgill
Guatemalan-American
without whom this book could never
have been written

First Edition, March, 1966

7860

INTRODUCTION

LEAST KNOWN but most rewarding of
the trips an American can take in his
car without going overseas is the road
to Panama.

The deserts of the north, the bull
rings of Mexico City, and the fleshpots
of Acapulco are familiar to millions.
Thousands upon thousands have recognized, or thought they recognized,
Assisi in Taxco or Avignon in Guanajuato. But how many have let the good
road take them to Tula or Salto de
Meca, Metepec or Uruapan, Monte
Albán or San Cristóbal de las Casas?
And how many are even aware that
it is now possible to drive in comfort
all the way to the Panama Canal,
and that off this highway lie such incomparable gems as Tikal and Chichicastenango, Zunil and Esquipulas,
Copán and Guanaja, Santa María de
Ostuma and the unspoiled reservation
of the Cunas?

Seven countries, eight counting

Belize, each of them totally unlike anything in the "American heritage" —can there be a more convenient, delightful, adventurous way of multiplying one's horizons?

Someday the Pan-American Highway will stretch from Alaska to Cape Horn. But until the Darién Gap is penetrated, in the next decade, there will be no way of driving to South America. That section of the Highway known as the Inter-American, however, is complete. From Texas to Darién, all but a fraction of it is paved, and that fraction—short stretches in Guatemala, Costa Rica and Panama—is "all-weather," meaning passable to the most conventional, low-slung models, except in the rainy seasons of late spring and fall. It is now possible, in other words, to drive a car without hardship from the United States border through Mexico, Guatemala, El Salvador, Honduras, Nicaragua, Costa Rica and Panama, to a point in the Darién jungle 574 miles from the junction point with the Pan-American system in Colombia.

Since long ago the concept of the Highway shifted away from a single road linking the various capitals, the word "system" is operative. There are four trunk highways, for example, leading from our border to Mexico City. Strictly speaking, the one from Laredo, Texas, through Monterrey and Ciudad Victoria, is the Inter-American. But since the parallel Route 57 through San Luis Potosí and Querétaro is just as interesting, and since no one driving from California would think of going any other way than by Route 15, which hugs the Pacific until it turns eastward through Guadalajara to the capital, those alternatives are as worthy of description. Similarly, the Inter-American Highway proper runs *south* of Tegucigalpa, but to drive through Honduras without visiting its capital and all of the other attractions of that country would be as pointless as to bypass the Yucatán peninsula in Mexico, or the Petén and Belize (British Honduras), accessible by air from Guatemala City.

The road to Panama, in other words, is conceived in this travelogue as a means rather than an end. Not every motorist, obviously, will want to diverge from the Mexican capital to Zihuatanejo on the Pacific, or to Tampico and Veracruz on the Gulf; nor to the Bay Islands, Great and Little Corn, and the San Blas Archipelago off the Caribbean coasts of Honduras, Nicaragua, and Panama respectively. Nor to such magnificent lakes as Pátzcuaro, Atitlán, Coatepeque and Yojoa, necessarily. Nor to Tula and Yaxchilán, Tikal and Quiriguá and Copán, unless art and archaeology are primary compulsions. Yet all of these places are at least as interesting as anything to be encountered on the main roads. Those who diverge to savor them will perhaps be grateful for more background than the standard guides supply; and those who don't may enjoy reading about them, and sampling one man's view of the adventures, difficulties and rewards involved. But before I go on to explain what method there is in the apparent madness of these excursions, a word about the history of the Highway.

WHAT THE PIONEER TOURISTS ENCOUNTERED

Four hundred years elapsed between the time Cortés' farsighted emperor, Charles V, contemplated a road to link the countries of the isthmus, and 1923, when the Pan-American Union took the first practical steps to build it. It was not until 1929, however, that the American Congress appropriated $50,000 toward the cost of reconnaissance surveys, and that a general plan for the whole "system" was adopted. And it was 1936 before a binding agreement was entered into by all the American republics concerned. In the same year the first big link, from Laredo to Mexico City, was actually completed. By 1940, only twenty-two per cent of the distance to Panama City still consisted of impassable trails. Spurred by World War II's strategic needs, millions of dollars were appropriated by the American Congress to complete the difficult sector through Costa Rica—appropriations that by 1962, when all the thirty-one bridges in this area had been completed, came to $170,703,000.

Although no one has ever yet pushed or carried a car through the Darién Gap, several intrepid adventurers managed somehow to force their way through the roadless terrain north and south of it in the 1920s and '30s. One of these pioneers, José María Barone, spent two years (1927–29) driving a car from Rio de Janeiro to Darién and from Panama City to New York. He hacked his way through jungles, rebuilt his truck from wrecked pieces after plunging over a precipice north of Quito, improvised rafts and bridges to cross swamps, took time out to circle guerrilla war in Nicaragua. Another Brazilian party took *nine years* to drive to Washington —by way of the Mato Grosso jungle! One of the two cars in which this party traveled turned over eight times, the other six. In 1935, Miguel Divo, an Argentine sportsman, made the trip on a bet, living on monkey meat at times, and once taking sixteen days to raise his Model T Ford from Costa Rica's Colorado River where it had sunk. The trip was made on horseback at least once; and on foot by Richard Tewkesbury of Charlotte, North Carolina, who in 1940 penetrated the Darién Gap to the Colombian border, thus disproving the legend that the savages who still live there are unfriendly and cannibalistic.[1]

Soon after the war, Roger Stephens, an American newspaperman, covered the Inter-American span, Laredo to Panama, by *bus*, walking or riding only where he had to. It took him thirty-two days to cover the 3,231 miles (bus fares: $140.14), and his account of the various "gaps" and the time it took to pass them is fascinating. There were no real problems in Mexico by that time, until San Cristóbal las Casas was passed. "It's a physical impossibility," wrote the author, "for any wheeled vehicle to get through from Comitán, either to Huehuetenango, Guatemala, or to Tapachula, Mexico." One had to backtrack through Tuxtla Gutiérrez to Arriaga, where cars could be transferred on flatcars by the national railways of Mexico, to Tapachula. Across Guatemala, El Salvador, southern Honduras, Nicaragua and northern Costa Rica, the roads were far from good, but they were passable—in season. But beyond San José, Costa Rica's capital, Stephens' problems began. It was easy to understand how, when a rice famine struck that country some years earlier, it was found less expensive to transport food in ship bottoms from Indochina via Hamburg, Germany, than by muleback one hundred miles over the mountains from Panama.

During the war it had taken seven days of tough horseback riding to cover the hundred kilometers between San José and San Isidro General; the beginnings of the present road now made this stretch negotiable in five hours. But from San Isidro to David (from which there was a fifteen-hour bus service to Panama City) the time spent by Stephens on "truck, horse, station wagon, taxi, and shanks' mare" totaled forty-four hours—to cover a distance of only 172 miles! Even when Stephens was traveling "comfortably" by bus in Guatemala, the condition of the roads must have been fearful by present-day standards. It took him sixteen hours to traverse the 175 miles between Huehuetenango and the capital, fifteen and a half to drive the 165 miles from there to San Salvador via Asunción Mita. Both of these trips today are easy five-hour drives.

---

[1] *The Pan-American Highway System*, a pamphlet published by the Pan-American Union, contains the best survey of problems and distances. The volume referred to in the paragraphs that follow, *Down that Pan-American Highway*, by Roger Stephens, was privately printed c. 1948.

To experience anything like the adventures encountered by Stephens as recently as 1948, it is necessary to branch out from the Highway proper. But even those who do not relish adventure, or bad roads, or no roads at all, will be obliged to forsake macadam briefly if they wish to see half the things worth seeing and reported in this book.

Since road guides and maps are everywhere available, and because prices and accommodations and signs (and even distances) are in a constant state of flux, I have tried to keep such information to a minimum, and to concentrate rather on three less common ingredients of a travelogue. The first of these is history, but history in terms of where things happened, and how they might have looked and seemed at the time of their happening. Mexico and Central America are rich in great events, from pre-Columbian, Conquest, and Colonial times, down to the present. But none of the high tragedy and low comedy is readily available, and little of it has ever been dramatized in its changeless setting.

The arts are a second ingredient that receives short shrift in both the histories and the travel books. Morley, Thompson and the other archaeologists write eloquently of the pre-Columbian past but have little to say about the living residue—which is aesthetic. Guidebooks have a way of cataloguing the contents of every church and local museum, but passing over such a stupendous sight as the Alameda at Morelia in a sentence. The frescoes of Orozco and Rivera have never been adequately described or evaluated; from monographs in preparation on both artists, I have drawn whatever might interest the general reader. And that same reader, if contemporary art intrigues him, will be able to extend his own explorations from clues and names included here. Similarly with the folk arts, in which Guatemala and Mexico yield to no other nation: without attempting to be exhaustive, this book alone (I believe) pinpoints the places where the best of it is still to be found.

The third ingredient is harder to describe, and no author can possibly know whether he has managed to bring it off. I speak of those elements —personal anecdote, thumbnail characterization, humor—which give some concreteness and memorability to the *moments*, often trivial, which make traveling fun. Some of this, inevitably, is at the expense of "natives"— who fare no worse, I hope the reader will realize, than bystanders, bureaucrats, bunglers and bores would on a trip from New York to Los Angeles;

and some is at the expense of myself and my friends, who blunder, complain and goof as travelers always will. If there is less of this byplay in the first half of the book than in the second, that is partly because I have covered Mexico anecdotally before,[2] and partly because the wit of William Negron, who accompanied me on the Central American trip in 1965, gives to the last five chapters a special flavor.

The three Mexican chapters are a composite of things experienced on four trips to Mexico—1937, 1956–57, 1960 and 1963–64. I spent the fall and winter of 1964–65 in Guatemala, following a shorter trip there with Negron the year before. Negron and I drove from Guatemala City to Panama in February of 1965, and spent a week thereafter in the western highlands of Guatemala. Beyond my major debt to him and to his drawings, I would like to acknowledge (or re-acknowledge) my appreciation of the humor, knowledge and fortitude of such other traveling companions as Donald Demarest, Linton Baldwin, Don Bloom, Maja Wojciechowska, Oriana Rodman, John Booth, Arnold Belkin, Francisco Icaza, Amy Freeman-Lee, Antonio Gonzales de León, Jorge Ibarra, Bart Henson, Lucy Sturgill, William and Roz Brister, Joan Negron, David and Cynthia Jickling, Joya Hairs, Susan Miles, William Dwyer, Ramón Osuna, Lyell Ritchie, Niels Halbertsma, Bob Oliver, Bud Siegel, James Zonnevylle and Daniel Schafer. To the Centro Guatemalteca de Turismo which supplied the Volkswagen from which most of the things described in the last seven chapters were seen, and to Joe Skinner, the Hertz agent in Guatemala City, who was kind and thoughtful on the few occasions when anything went wrong with this rugged vehicle, I owe special debts of gratitude. And beyond all these, for everything that made writing this book possible and unfailingly enjoyable, to Carole, my wife.

SELDEN RODMAN

Oakland, New Jersey
September, 1965

---

[2] *Mexican Journal: The Conquerors Conquered*, Devin-Adair, 1958; University of Southern Illinois Press (paperback), 1965. Some of the historical commentary in the first two chapters of the present book, and the trip to Yucatán in the third chapter, are adapted from the earlier travelogue.

CONTENTS

1   MEXICO EAST:
SOUTH TO
THE CAPITAL

As everyone knows, northern Mexico, like the southern United States across its border, is mostly desert. Culturally as well as physically, some would say—on both sides. Whether you cross over from Texas, Arizona, or Southern California, the landscape will not change much; and the Mexican traveling north will have the same depressing experience: it will be a long time before he sees, or hears, anything he will want to remember. It seems, in a sense, as though both countries are deliberately showing each other their worst face. Many Americans, perhaps a majority, never get any farther than the honky-tonks across the line— Tijuana, Mexicali, Juárez, Matamoros; it is almost as if the Mexicans were saying: this is what you are asking for, so this is what we'll give you —cheap jewelry, gambling, liquor, whores. And the Mexican who crosses into Texas and is offered "Foot-Long

Hot Dogs," or passes the California graveyards with their "Jesus Saves!" signs in winking neon, can bitterly console himself for the unprecedented affluence that accompanies all this mindless vulgarity, by recalling that the land was once his and that those who stole it built the purgatory they deserve.

Since in every educated Mexican's mind there smoulders not far beneath the surface the injustice and humiliation of 1836–1848, it cannot be too highly recommended that those who wish to understand our neighbor pass through the city of San Antonio before crossing the desert into Mexico's heartland. The 2500-kilometer trip down the Pacific coast from San Diego to Guadalajara will be described at the beginning of the next chapter. But for Easterners the city of the Alamo, from which five highways fan out to the border, is a day's drive from Monterrey, the capital of northern Mexico.

San Antonio is one of the lovelier American cities. Perhaps because of its historical associations, its proximity to Mexico, and its considerable admixture of Mexican-Indian blood, it has a leisurely style of its own, and some pretension to being a cultural melting pot. The way a part of the old downtown section hugs the winding San Antonio River, with palm-shaded lawns and stone footbridges, is almost Venetian in its charm. Here, at the Casa Ría Mexican Restaurant, it is possible to charter a boat and dine on it while floating up and down the river; the gift shop La Sirena displays and sells some of the finest Mexican folk arts; and at The Landing local businessmen have formed a Dixieland band good enough to be invited to Mexico. But turning a corner to confront the picturesque Alamo, the prospective visitor to Mexico must be warned to bring his own historical perspective with him. How much of the old fortress remains in the many restorations it has undergone, is hard to determine. The grounds are well kept, and ivy creeps gracefully along the yellow walls. Inside are cabinets of mementoes, and bronze plaques bearing the names of the 183 heroes who fell before Santa Anna's legions. But one would never guess from reading a sixty-four-page booklet sold on the premises that Texas in 1836 was a province of Mexico. Nor that the army sent to keep it from falling into American hands consisted of brave men doing their duty.

There is no denying, of course, that Travis, Crockett, Bowie, and the other Texan adventurers were brave men too. They died heroically for what they deemed ideals of independence and justice. The oft-told tale of Travis drawing a line in the dirt, giving those who did not choose to cross it the opportunity to make their escape, and of the stricken Bowie demanding that he be carried across the line in his bed—all this is stirring. There is no denying, either, that Santa Anna was a scoundrel; if he was cast in the role of a patriot at the Alamo, he cut a sorry figure shortly thereafter at San Jacinto, and an even sorrier one a decade later at Chapultepec, when he might have annihilated General Winfield Scott's invaders and, instead, stood aside to let the *niños heroes* fall and a third of his country be snatched away.

Perhaps the truth is that both sides, between 1836 and 1848, acted with thorough immorality, but that even if the Mexicans had been ruled by patriots or even saints, we would still have found "just" reasons to take what we coveted and, being the stronger, would have gotten it. That being the case, it is *we* who should bend over backward in acknowledging our real motives and, especially in such a shrine as the Alamo, attempt to tell the truth.

MONTERREY, AND TWO "CAMINO REALS" SOUTH

The most direct road from San Antonio to Monterrey crosses the Rio Grande at Laredo; and at Nuevo Laredo, beyond the river border, it becomes the first link of the Inter-American Highway that leads to Panama.

Monterrey is the most American of Mexican cities—modern factories, motels, quick-lunch rooms and curio shops, hotels with swimming pools and TV, broad avenues clean to the point of sterility. The setting is grandly dramatic. Stone mountains ring the valley, one of the peaks (Silla de Montar) carved by the howling winds at eight thousand feet into a profile of haunting intensity. There are many things to do in this city as big as Baltimore. The Cuauhtemoc Brewery, which makes Carta Blanca and Bohémia (both superior to any American brand), serves free beer to visitors. There are theaters and vaudevilles worth visiting. Caves, cannons and fishing streams abound in the nearby hills.

Institutions like the Cervantes Library, and public-spirited citizens like the families Roel and de Perez and Joannidis, and Doña Rosario Barza Sada de Zambrano, give the impression that Monterrey is ready to sponsor a cultural renaissance of its own. When I visited Monterrey in 1963, I had a show of paintings to judge for Romelia de Rangél, patroness of the little local museum, Arte, A.C. As in the United States, where New York has a monopoly, Mexico City drains the talent from the provinces; Monterrey's stay-at-homes were still fighting with (or against) the social realism of the 'twenties and 'thirties. It was only when we visited Carapán, shopping center for the local folk arts, that we saw something to remind us of our own frenetic decade. The proprietor, Umberto Arellano y Garza, employs a dozen Huichole Indians to make eye-catching abstractions out of colored yarns on waxed wood. The smaller squares-within-squares ("Eyes of God") made by these peyote-eating primitives from the states of Nayarit and San Luis Potosí use exactly the same color tricks exploited by Josef Albers, the father of op art. But of course the Indians are not playing visual tricks.

I remember a fifty-cent vaudeville I had attended on Avenida Madero ten years earlier, and how a series of skits spoofing the metropolis' modernity had culminated in a question addressed to the audience—"What's wrong with Monterrey?" My Spanish-speaking wife had responded "Too many gringos!" but instead of the laugh we expected there had been a dead silence. I thought about this afterward and came to the conclusion that they had spotted us as Americans; being Mexicans, gallant and considerate of the feelings of others, the last thing they would want to do was show us that they joined in (or even approved) an expression of anti-Americanism—even if they felt it themselves. Mexican intellectuals, most of whom (we were soon to discover) are Marxists, have no such compunction in ascribing most of their country's troubles to malevolent *Yanquis*.

At Monterrey there is a choice of roads south. Route 57 through Saltillo and San Luis Potosí approaches the capital by way of Querétaro and the noble hill towns of Dolores Hidalgo, Guanajuato and San Miguel de Allende. Route 85, paralleling it to the east, is the Inter-American Highway proper, and it passes through Ciudad Victoria, Tamazunchale and Pachuca, providing easy access to such ports of the Caribbean as Tampico, Papantla and Veracruz, and to the great pre-Columbian ruins of Tula which most tourists miss, and of San Juan Teotihuacán which nobody misses. Let us take this second route first.

JUNGLES, WATERFALLS, BEACHES, RUINS

The place to stop after Monterrey is Ciudad Valles, 320 kilometers down Route 85 and about halfway to the capital. It has an inexpensive inn (the Casa Grande) with rustic cabins, good food and a large swimming pool. A stay of three nights here is recommended, for both Tampico and Salto de Meca are worth a day's excursion. When I visited the latter in 1962, it was one of the world's spectacular swimming holes. Over a cliff a hundred feet high, a river thunders into a deep pool from which it then descends, in steps, from one turquoise basin to another, the rim of each garlanded with daisies. Climbing to the deep pool, one may dive from basin to basin, while in the background the giant cataract fills emerald thickets and stands of bamboo with sun-drenched spray. I visited Salto de Meca with the young Mexican artists Francisco Icaza and Arnold Belkin, and a friend of theirs from the diplomatic corps, together with our combined dozen children. Salto de Meca is the sort of place where the pretensions of adulthood haven't a chance. Sober Mexicans of the poorest class were coming in by the truckload and going wild. American tourists, apparently, had not yet discovered this uninhibiting wonder; and reports now have it that they may never discover it, for an electric company from the capital is reputed to have diverted its entire glory into their efficient turbines.

I visited Tampico the following day in the same company. I'd been suffering from stomach cramps—known variously as *turistas,* or The Mexican Complaint—and Icaza had said: "Don't pamper it." I took his advice. At some unsanitary booths on the beach, I had a lunch of two dozen raw oysters in chili sauce, half-a-dozen crabs fried in bread crumbs, a *corbalo* sandwich, two bottles of Moctezuma XX beer, two bags of peanuts, a chocolate bar and a double scoop of vanilla ice cream. Icaza's advice was good.

The beach, miles long and with a very shallow sandbar over which the breakers roll, was flanked that day by hundreds of cars, side by side, no more than a car's length from the water. My friends wanted to get as far away from this traffic jam as possible, with the result that both of their cars sank wheel-deep into the sand. One car was pulled out by a chain, and the other by an ingenious prying up of the rear end with two logs at right angles to each other and then inserting boards under the tires—an enterprise in which a huge crowd of good-natured bathers participated.

Directly behind the beach, the sand slopes gradually up to a horizon of enormous rippled dunes, dotted with clumps of driftwood and beach grass. As the sun sank behind the highest of these dunes, long shadows were cast, the sand becoming mysteriously gray in patches, but glittering elsewhere with millions of microscopic shells.

The road south from Valles, through the orange groves and papaya plantations of Tamazunchale, begins to rise in fields of red earth. Out-

croppings of bare rock counterpoint the glistening leaves and bright blue larkspur. We were in the clouds, doubling back and forth without any sense of direction. But if the interminable hairpin turns hadn't brought us down to earth, a crowded bus that careened past us on a narrow precipice would have. It bore on its front the legend "ILUSIÓN SIN GLORIA," which seemed to sum up in its carefree cynicism the philosophy of a people that has suffered the brave slogans of a century of promissory revolutions. The monolithic party (P.R.I.) that has now given Mexico stability and a measure of prosperity for almost forty years, solved the problem by "institutionalizing" violent change: it celebrates revolution continuously in poems, proclamations, parades, paintings and songs—but if anybody revolts, off with his head!

At Zimapán, halfway to the capital from Valles, there is another memorable hostelry, the Posada del Rey, spacious, aristocratic, black-beamed, illuminated by candles. This is the place to stay for side trips eastward to Papantla (if you happen to be passing on the weekend preceding Corpus Christi when the famous *voladores* "fly" around their pole) and the Totonac ruins of El Tajín near the oil city of Poza Rica; westward and south lie

Tula and Teotihuacán. But not to be missed before branching off to Tula at Actopan, is the Otomi Indian village of Ixmiquilpan, where it is still possible to buy for a few cents the most elegantly patterned woolen bags north of the Guatemala highlands.

Tula and Teotihuacán are the most spectacular pre-Columbian ruins north of the Maya area—Tula for its sculpture, Teotihuacán for its architecture and painting.

Tula is on a branch road connecting Routes 85 and 57, a few miles north of the capital. Discovered in the 'thirties, the ruin is believed to have been the capital of the Toltecs, a highly civilized tribe that preceded the Aztecs in Central Mexico, and eventually migrated south to take over the Maya "Late Empire" ceremonial center at Chichén Itzá, in Yucatán. On the pedestal of a truncated pyramid stand six twelve-foot-high stone gods (or are they demons?) staring inscrutably over the sulphuric desert. Only at Karnak, perhaps, has stone been worked so monumentally. Originally these figures were carved to support a temple, but in their present isolation they are more formidable, looming against the living blue sky like black shadows of death.

San Juan Teotihuacán is on Route 85, some forty kilometers north of Mexico City, and its vast complex of temples and pyramids is the principal repository of one of the four "classic" or "medieval" civilizations that antedate Tula—the other three being the Totonac (El Tajín), the Zapotec (Monte Albán, near Oaxaca), and the Maya. The site covers more than six square miles and has been systematically (but far from exhaustively) excavated by Gamio, Vaillant, Caso, Bórbolla and many less famous archaeologists. The people who built it deliberately destroyed it in A.D. 658, centuries before the Toltecs, who were once presumed to have been its builders, moved in.

The principal Toltec deity had been Quetzalcoatl, the Feathered Serpent, also worshipped by the Toltec-Mayas in Yucatán and Guatemala and, by some accounts, reputed to have been bearded and *white*, and to have left Mexico around the time of the Toltec migration southward, on a raft, heading east. Moctezuma and his predecessors on the Aztec throne had neglected Quetzalcoatl, a god of culture who abhorred human sacrifice. Having given the primacy in their pantheon to Huitzilopochtli, the god of war, who demanded blood sacrifices insatiably, the Aztecs had made bitter enemies of the vassal tribes that surrounded them, especially of the Tlaxcalans, whom they had never been able to subjugate. And it was partly because Moctezuma felt a sense of guilt over the neglect of Quetzalcoatl, whom the Tlaxcalans continued to worship, and because he half suspected that Cortés was this injured god's reincarnation, that the Aztec emperor made the indecisive maneuvers that led to his destruction. (The serpent heads on the so-called Temple of Quetzalcoatl here were actually carved many centuries before the Toltecs came, and so presumably have nothing to do with the Feathered Serpent.)

It has always surprised me that Bernal Díaz, that excellent reporter of the Conquest, makes no mention whatever of the Pyramid of the Sun, which is larger than the Great Pyramid of Egypt and must have been the most considerable edifice in Mexico, though he passed directly by it. It is 210 feet high. It covers 55,000 square yards. And its mass, formed of some 3,000,000 adobe bricks faced with stone, is estimated to weigh 2,980,000 tons.

To climb to the pyramid's summit (especially if one looks back) is rather frightening. I had climbed it on my first visit to Mexico in 1937, but thereafter I've found excuses to avoid the ordeal. On a more recent visit I spent my time poking around the *subterráneos*, where some of the ancient frescoes are being restored. Many of the originals were lying in big chunks in corners. When we picked up a piece to inspect it, it crumbled at a touch. Outside, less authentic but more durable pre-Columbiana was being hawked. A muchacho tried to sell us an obsidian arrowhead. "Original, señor!" He wanted eight pesos for it, and we finally bought it for two, whereupon a second muchacho came up, looked at it scornfully, and said: "Copy, patrón; look here: *mine* is an original," and proceeded to try to sell us an identical smaller one for three pesos. The first muchacho laughed at him, and we laughed at them. Both, of course, laughed at us as soon as we had left. Near the Quetzalcoatl serpent heads and Tlalocs (effigies of the rain god that look like World War I gas masks) a third muchacho was playing a flute. I had heard that these boys could imitate the sound of a coyote stealing chickens. I asked him to. "No coyotes any more, Señor, and no chickens either!"

IN THE FOOTSTEPS OF CORTES

Veracruz looks much too sleepy and seedy to have harbored such hero-villains as Cortés, Santa Anna, Winfield Scott and Maximilian, yet this is where they marched from in the days before the airplane put Veracruz out of business. Even at the time of my first visit to Mexico twenty years ago, this was the main port of entry, and the ascent to Mexico City by rail—through the jungles, past Orizaba's snowy peak, and into tunnels crowded with gangs of peons tidying up the latest landslide—was a memorable experience. At every whistlestop tequila was served, the stations doubling as bars.

If you are bent on following in Cortés' footsteps—and this is something every American should do once—the place to start is Cempoala, where the wily conqueror found his first native ally. This chieftain of the Totonacs, whom the Spanish soldiers called "the fat *cacique*," has not, understandably, become a national hero. The Spaniards owed him a great deal. Coming here directly from their landfall on the island of San Juan de Ulúa in Veracruz harbor, they found the first direct evidence of dissension within Moctezuma's empire. Two ambassadors had just arrived from Tenochtitlán (the Aztec capital, now Mexico City) and were about to depart with their usual quota of sacrificial victims for the altar of Huitzilopochtli. Cortés insisted that the fat *cacique* seize them and put them in a cage. But then he showed the first of those strokes of genius that rank him with the great captains. "I recall," he wrote Charles V, "that passage of the Evangelist which says, 'Every kingdom divided against itself is brought to desolation.'" He had his men *release* the caged ambassadors, secretly of course, and speed them to Moctezuma with gifts. Thus he was able to pose as the "friend" of both rulers, laying the ground for the confusion, suspicion, and treachery-among-allies that would eventually give him Mexico. Further evidence, say the Indianists of today, of the man's unprincipled conduct. But Cortés, among the "civilized," had been frank about his motives from the outset. When they had offered him a hacienda in Haiti after his arrival from Spain at the age of nineteen, he had spurned it. "I came here," he said, "not to till the soil like a peasant, but for gold." The surprising thing about him was that, unlike any other of the conquistadors except the hapless Cabeza de Vaca, he quickly came to the conclusion that nothing but fair treatment of the conquered, alliance with them in administration, and *intermarriage*, could lead to a stable future in New Spain. It was not to be. The second wave of invaders, armchair generals, the real "exploiters," had other ideas; and they soon succeeded in getting Cortés recalled.

The ruins of Cempoala are well off the highway and not easy to find. Archaeologists discovered them only late in the nineteenth century, and the tourists have yet to come. The temple platforms, composed of river-rounded boulders, are a poor man's Tula. But at the top of one, we found traces of rose-colored frescoes; and in the rubble of another, a small, intricately reliefed stone seal. The road down to Veracruz is lined with these miniature cities of the dead that rival Mexico's cities of the living for color and setting. Occasional sky-blue and terra-cotta tombs make the predominantly white ones the more dazzling, and many are decorated with chaplets of lilies or big rosettes of straw. Drunk with this heady visual liquor, and the dense perfume of frangipani that accompanied us all the way from jasmine-scented Jalapa, we decided to stop pursuing Cortés for awhile and try to find Manga de Clavo, Santa Anna's fabled hacienda. It was to this hideway, feigning sickness, that the dictator would periodically retire from one or another of his dozen presidencies when accused of larceny; and it was from Manga de Clavo he would return in "triumph" to the capital, to oust the honest but incompetent Gomez Farías, or to oversee the ceremonial embalming of his leg, blown off in one of the comic-opera "defenses" of Veracruz, and its solemn consecration in a national shrine in Mexico City. No one we spoke to had heard of Manga de Clavo; and the fact that the once-great name of Antonio López de Santa Anna touched no responsive chord anywhere struck us as happily fitting.

The alternate route back to the capital by way of Córdoba, Orizaba, Puebla, Cholula and Tlaxcala, was the path the Conqueror took for his assault on Tenochtitlán. Córdoba is a city of flowers; orchids hang from the live oaks, and every housefront, no matter how humble, is decorated with a score of tiny cans, each with its individual fern or geranium. Orizaba, where Orozco holed up (with Dr. Atl and other *Carranzistas* evading Pancho Villa during the bloodiest phase of the 1910–20 Revolution), contains one of that great painter's earliest works, but the fresco is in an advanced state of deterioration. Why, we asked an attendant at the Industrial School, couldn't glass be put over the window that exposes "Revolution" to the sun and rain? "Because nobody," he replied, "would clean the window, and then nobody could see the *view*." Puebla is big and prosperous, its architecture Spanish Colonial embellished with the tiles for which (along with Talavera pottery) the city is justly famous. Here also is the secret convent of Santa Monica, where nuns went into hiding after Benito Juárez' "Reform" went into effect in 1857; and a blocks-long market which sells everything from food and clothing to complete suits of armor and life-size paper clowns. But Cholula with its (reputed) 365 churches, pre-Toltec pyramid, and air of faded glory, is much more intriguing.

CHURCHES ON TOP OF CHURCHES

The churches, they say, were established by the Conquerors on the sites of the pagan *teocali* then serving a population of 100,000. The dominant one, housing a doll-like image of the Virgin of Los Remedios, stands on the top of the massive "Pyramid of Quetzalcoatl." The latter, we were told by a pleasantly drunken guide who had taken us over, had been deliberately buried in rubble by the Cholulans when they heard Cortés was approaching from Tlaxcala.

The Cholulans would have been better advised to flee the accursed city. They gave Cortés a royal welcome with flowers and music and the perfume of aromatic turpentine from swinging censers. But in the night Malinche came to her master and informed him of a plot to ambush the Spaniards on their way to Tenochtitlán; and Cortés, "determined to surprise rather than be surprised," as he wrote his king, took her word for it and butchered every last one of his hosts. This Malinche, whom the Spaniards called Marina, is one of the tragic and mysterious figures of the Conquest. Her profound understanding of the Indian soul, even more than her services as interpreter of the Nahuatl language,[1] was the key to Cortés' diplomatic triumphs. The Indians throughout Mexico venerated her as a goddess, according to Bernal Díaz. But in the centuries to follow, her name became synonymous with witchcraft and evil, and is used to this day to frighten children. Was it love for Cortés that made her betray her people? (Cortés made her his mistress while it served his purpose, later turned her over to an underling.) Was it a prophetic sense of Mexico's destiny? Or was it merely the human penchant to be master rather than slave?

The scene of the massacre is dominated by the great pyramid. Like the temple of Teotihuacán that also takes its name from Quetzalcoatl, it is misnamed, having been built in pre-classic times by the same race that built the Pyramid of the Sun, and out of the same materials. The Cholula pyramid is broader than the one at Teotihuacán, but not so high. In 1931 the Mexican government did some extensive excavating. It wired five miles of passageways for electricity, connecting the superimposed pyramids of different epochs. In one position in these catacombs, it is possible to look

---

[1] She had picked up Spanish, before Cortés captured her, from a sailor shipwrecked on the Caribbean coast during one of the post-Columbian, pre-Cortesian probes.

up a vertical shaft to the apex, hundreds of feet above. In an adjoining tunnel, frescoes in red and black of the serpent god whose worship the Toltecs did finally introduce, are fairly well preserved.

The church atop is a renovated horror encased in gold leaf (from Philadelphia, we were told); but a small altar to the right of the entrance is filled with some remarkably surrealistic *retablos* [2]: a woman being pulled out from under a speeding train; a man clambering from a wrecked plane that looks as though it had been built by the Wright brothers; a young woman on her deathbed "saved" by a combination of two doctors, five relatives, a priest, two small angels, and at least a dozen half-emptied bottles of patent medicine.

As one faces north to Tlaxcala, Mount Malinche lies to the right and Iztaccihuatl (the Sleeping woman, Popocatépetl's snowy mate) to the left. The ramps to the apex of the pyramid are bordered by rows of small, leaf-less trees with star-shaped, crimson blossoms. Our weaving "guide," who wasn't making much sense by now, muttered that the tree was called *colorín* and that its petals are cooked and eaten. He smacked his lips. As we stood there surveying the awesome panorama, bestial cries and roars ascended to us from an insane asylum at the base, mingled now and then with the hardly more reassuring shouts of a Mexican soap opera on the radio. Still another incongruity was an ice chest in the chapel bearing the image of Disney's Donald Duck.

There was nothing incongruous, imported or meretricious about the poet-craftsman with whom we spent the rest of that day in Cholula. Rafael Zerón makes fiesta figures—bulls, eagles, bicycle riders, Judases that carry firecrackers in their bamboo understructure—a self-destroying "art" that gave pleasure to simple people long before Jean Tinguely's suicidal machine titillated world-weary sophisticates in the garden of New York's Museum of Modern Art.

DOWN THE MIDDLE TO THE HEARTLAND

If Route 85 from Monterrey is rich with Conquest and pre-Conquest sites, Route 57 which parallels it to the west leads inexorably to that part of the country in which Mexico gained its revolutionary reputation between 1810 and 1910. The first and longest leg of the 950 kilometers to the capital is a no man's land which, if it hadn't existed, might have insured the union

---

[2] *Ex-votos*, popular paintings on tin or wood.

of the United States and Mexico—something that could have rounded out the incomplete personality of each, but which both peoples, I'm sure, devoutly thank God never happened. This is the vast, semi-arid part of Mexico where old Zachary Taylor bungled and blundered his way to victory in 1847 against an army even less prepared for war than our own. Here Pascual Orozco's cavalry burned up the countryside in the early "Wild West" phase of the 1910 revolution; and here, a little later, Pancho Villa's irregulars gave the slip to "Black Jack" Pershing's ill-conceived punitive expedition, singing their song:

> If I must be killed tomorrow
> Then let them kill me today.

Across this cactus land, Madero, the aristocratic idealist, fled north to keep the fires of the 1910 uprising alive from New Orleans; and fifty years earlier Benito Juárez, "Mexico's Lincoln," traversed it in a more unimpassioned dignity to set up his headquarters in the same American city and direct the resistance against the hapless Hapsburg Maximilian, Napoleon III's candidate for empire abroad. Over the whole area broods the huge spirit of Hidalgo, the heretical priest, who started it all in 1810 by turning rebellion against Old Spain into the first proletarian revolution.

San Luis Potosí, at the apex of this Revolutionary Triangle, is the largest, most industrialized, of the cities that comprise it, but the least interesting. Prosperity makes conservatives, and conservatives are generally dull people. I spoke to several solid citizens who remembered Madero in their childhood. The aging dictator, Porfirio Díaz, had imprisoned the young idealist here, only to have him escape to Texas and carry the revolution to success from there. Our friends thought the intellectual Madero, with his high-pitched voice and pear-shaped black beard, completely crazy, and said that his revolution had succeeded only because the middle classes and peons were attracted by Madero's promise of the right to vote and of more of a Mexico for Mexicans. "But they are worse off now—for all the reforms of Carranza, Obregón and Cárdenas—than they were when beer was twenty centavos a bottle instead of five pesos. Even under Díaz there was less political corruption than there is now."

Everybody in San Luis Potosí remembers the final episode of the 1910 revolution, which also took place here. Saturnine Cedillo was the last of the landed, Catholic generals to hold out, and in 1938 President Cárdenas came here to get him, showing that bravado which endeared him to the courage-worshipping mestizos quite as much as his concern for their social welfare. Disdaining the protection of files of soldiers who lined the approach to the rebellious state capital, Cárdenas stepped alone into the crowd of thousands of fanatical Cedillistas and, to their astonishment, accused the former cabinet member of treason, demanding his surrender. Cedillo was forced to flee into the trackless mountains where the Huicholes gather their peyote. Few followed him. Cárdenas, the new-style revolutionary, had more to offer than the old-style bandit. He had broken up forty-eight local haciendas and given the land to the very peasants who had been recruited by Cedillo. On December 1, 1940, the radical Cárdenas, first president in Mexican history to retire from office voluntarily, turned over the reins of government to Ávila Camacho, a conservative.

GUANAJUATO AND PADRE HIDALGO

Halfway down the 200-kilometer paved road to Querétaro, a left turn leads to the three hill towns of Dolores Hidalgo, Guanajuato and San Miguel de Allende. It would be easy to write about all four of these towns in terms of their settings in a wild terrain, their beauty, their picturesqueness, their antiquities—easy but unprofitable. The guidebooks cover that, and for those who don't like guidebooks it is all there to see. I could write of romantic Guanajuato at night, its streets, narrow as machete blades, illuminated by iron lanterns on wall brackets. Or of the day passed there with Harry Brown, the poet, and John Nevin, the painter, two of the colony of Americans who have restored suburban Marfil into a little paradise of their own, Brown purging himself of Hollywood by studying the less changeable stars through his telescope, Nevin chewing peyote and making enigmatic drawings to symbolize the revelation that "Mexicans, unlike Americans, who are a race of zombies, *feel*, and therefore *exist*." I could describe San Miguel in terms of its delightful thermal baths, or its bullfights, or its art school and artists' colony, which have perhaps contributed to keeping it as mellow as it is. But three things I saw on my last visit to these hill towns make me prefer to muse upon the tide of violence that made them what they are.

When he was teaching at San Miguel some years ago, the late Rico Lebrun left one of his great drawings at the home of Professor James Pinto. A bandaged, crippled beggar is facing a wall poster which says something to the effect that the popular arts are now incorporated in a "total aesthetic explosion." A caption underneath says: "Thank God he can't read!" Contemplating it anew, I thought back two days to our endless drive down the paved speedway through the desert, and of the tiny speck in the middle of the simmering road, which turned out to be—a seated campesino reading a *book*. Then I read the sinister inscription on the monument to the revolutionary martyr, Pípila, overlooking Guanajuato: "THERE WILL BE MORE ALHÓNDIGAS TO BURN!"

The Alhóndiga de Granaditas is a handsome, blocky palace in the middle of Guanajuato. It was here, on September 28, 1810, that Pípila, protecting himself with a gravestone slung on his back, fired the gates when Father Hidalgo decided that the Spanish royal garrison inside wouldn't listen to reason. The governor and his garrison were slaughtered, and a few days later the defenseless prisoners. In a matter of months, the heads of Hidalgo and his three associates, Allende, Aldama and Jiménez, were displayed in cages at the four corners of the building. Later still, the heads were removed to the cathedral in Mexico City, and finally to the Independence monument there.

The storming of this "granary" marked the turning point in Mexico's post-Conquest history. Up to that point, Mexico had rounded out three centuries as a colony of Spain. "New Spain," as she was called then, stretched from Panama to northern California without a break. She was the largest colony in the world, and the richest; her output of silver had doubled the world's supply in 150 years, creating many millionaires, yet her annual per capita income, according to Wilhelm von Humboldt's estimate, was fourteen pesos! Excepting Russia, New Spain was the most extensive single territory under one administration on earth. She was also, probably, the most unstable, badly governed, and oppressive such entity anywhere. Of her six million people, considerably more than half (Indians) were slaves in everything but name. A million and a half mestizos (mixed bloods) filled the poorer occupations and had just enough education and freedom to resent bitterly the foreign domination of Church and State. Six hundred thousand creoles (people born in Mexico of Spanish parentage) were one step further up the social ladder, with considerable education and wealth, but were in turn looked down upon and discriminated against by the real rulers, the Old Spaniards, numbering not more than fifteen thousand. These were the high Church dignitaries, hacienda owners, and businessmen, who held almost every office of importance in the colony and were known to all the others by the hated name of *gachupines* (spur wearers).

Hidalgo, Allende, and the other leaders of the insurrection were creoles.

Hidalgo was a parish priest from nearby Dolores: brilliant, humanitarian, fanatical, his head filled with theories of liberation smuggled out of revolutionary France and America. Allende, from San Miguel, was a young soldier and bullfighter. When they led a mob of fifty thousand Indians armed with scythes, machetes, and old muskets on this city, it was not (at first) to promote social revolution, but to protest the outright looting of the colony which had followed Napoleon's invasion of the mother country, and to demand not independence but a viceroy responsible to the deposed House of Castile.

The sack of Guanajuato, however, marked a turning point in Mexico's history in another sense than the liberation from Spain which it finally led to. Before the mob marched in, Guanajuato was a prosperous silver-mining town of sixty thousand inhabitants. When the burning, looting, and killing were over, the population had been reduced to six thousand, and the city never recovered. It was a pattern that was to be repeated, with variations, for a hundred and twenty-five years. Hidalgo, though he was and deserves to be the hero of the Independence, and the first great leader of the social revolution that ultimately released the Indians from peonage, was personally responsible for the pattern of anarchic uprisings under irresponsible *caudillos* that was to bedevil Mexico until the time of Cárdenas. With the "justification" that the Spaniards had originally dispossessed the Indians, Hidalgo sanctioned pillaging and murder by his followers—over the protest of Allende.

Dolores Hidalgo, a few miles east of Guanajuato over a rough road, is where it all began. Here, in the church on the north side of the plaza, Hidalgo rang the bell [3] and gave his famous *grito:* "Long live the Virgin of Guadalupe! Death to bad government! Death to the gachupines!" There is a legendary symbolism in that cry. In recognizing the Virgin who had appeared to Juan Diego, a humble Aztec Indian, outside Mexico City in 1531, Hidalgo was instinctively making the choice that has been made by millions of poor Mexicans ever since—that had been made, in fact, ever since Cortés kicked over the native idols and enforced Christianity at the point of the sword. The smartest man in Christendom was the man who recognized the fact that this miraculous appearance of the Virgin to a poor Indian was the only possible means of affording a transition from the

[3] The bell itself is now in the National Palace where the president rings it every September 15 at 11 P.M.

old religions to the new—and of reconciling, through religion, the native with his fate as a conquered beast of burden. When Hidalgo rang the bell, strode out of his crowded church here, and seized a banner of the Virgin of Guadalupe as his battle standard, he was not only subtly reconciling religion and revolution; he was perhaps unconsciously attempting to justify his own defection from the Roman hierarchy.

As far back as 1800, when he had been rector of the University of Valladolid (now Morelia), Hidalgo had been brought before the authorities for "Jansenist" heresies. Jansenism was only a pretext for indicting unorthodoxy, for no one could have been less a puritan than the pleasure-loving padre. The easygoing Church of that time might condone Hidalgo's moral lapses—his dancing, his cardplaying, his bowling in the streets, even his mistress and his four illegitimate children. After he had received mild censure and taken over the parish of Dolores, they could accept his benevolent camaraderie with the Indians; the brick kilns, pottery workshop, beekeeping and silk industry he developed for them. (It was the civil authorities who tore up his mulberry trees.) What the Church could *not* accept was Hidalgo's "liberal enlightenment" philosophy, his surreptitious reading of Voltaire and Rousseau, his calling the Church scholars "a pack of donkeys," his denial of the absolute authority of the Pope, his questioning the existence of hell.

I thought of this in the great square in front of Dolores' cathedral. I thought also of Emperor Maximilian, the Hapsburg usurper who, by a curious stroke of irony, stood in the same place to address a wildly cheering throng of royalists half a century after Hidalgo. Both were kindhearted men, and courageous, and both met death before a firing squad: Hidalgo because he was a little ahead of his time, Maximilian because he was a little behind it. Both "failed" because of being naïve in the ways of power; and so did Madero, a greater spirit than either, for the same reason in 1913. The men who understood power—Iturbide, Díaz, Obregón—"succeeded." Or did they? Who but the visionaries have given Mexico what makes it Mexican. . . .

MAXIMILIAN AT THE HILL OF BELLS

On the surface, who could ever have been *less* Mexican than the blond, fussy aristocrat, Maximilian? He had no right to be in Mexico at all. Mexico had been in desperate straits after the Hidalgo break-away, desolated by civil strife, impoverished. Benito Juárez had been close to restoring order in 1857–61 with his reform laws curtailing the privileges of the military and the Church, when France, England and Spain invaded Mexico to protect their "interests." England and Spain soon withdrew, but Napoleon III, hoping to re-establish a French colonial empire in the New World, imposed this Austrian Archduke on the divided Mexicans. With the end of the American Civil War in 1865, however, President Johnson issued an ultimatum to France and dispatched a crack army under General Sheridan to the border. Napoleon promptly withdrew his troops, and Maximilian, abandoned, fell back on Querétaro. Clearly his cause was hopeless; Mexico was with Juárez; the "Empire" was a farce.

One has to visit Querétaro and relive the drama that culminated here in 1867 to think otherwise. The drive from San Miguel de Allende is through a dry, spacious valley enclosed by dust-colored mountains. Soon maguey gives way to peach orchards and, near Celaya, to rice paddies. Celaya doesn't have the massive, ornamental doors that are the glory of San Miguel, nor the flowery gardens that grace the four-square stone houses of that hill town. It does have a monument to a local architect, with an inscription that made us wonder whether it had been financed where finance is taken seriously. "This monument," the first words read, "cost $57,000. . . ." But the church at Apaseo el Alto, where we stopped for lunch, is crowned with a row of golden angels that look as though they had just alighted from heaven. It was the Hill of Bells, outside Querétaro, however, that brought us down to earth. Peons were skinning a huge bull that had died, they told us, in the act of mounting its first cow. Not much of a bull, they said scornfully, showing us its equipment to prove their contention. A row of children's faces, watching this scene over the top of the wall of the chapel erected to mark the spot where Maximilian and his generals were shot on Juárez' orders, made me think of Goya's children watching a bull's death, and of Manet, who had borrowed the motif in his great picture of the Emperor's execution.

Juárez, the righteous, puritanical and (some say) Americanized Indian, in his little black carriage, is the father figure of modern Mexico. Maximilian, loving Mexico no less, was kind, pleasure-loving, and pitifully unprepared for the role in which Napoleon III cast him. Yet at Querétaro it is Maximilian who comes out well, and Juárez poorly. For one thing, Juárez was not here while the siege was going on. He preferred to leave the military operations to others—Escobedo, Riva Palacio, Porfirio Díaz.

When he does appear, it is at a distance, like some grim, inflexible school-master, watching in stony silence as the beautiful Princess Salm (American wife of one of Maximilian's officers) throws herself at his feet and offers to die in the Emperor's place. "I am grieved, Madam, to see you on your knees before me, but if all the kings and queens of Europe were in your place, I could not spare that life. It is not I who take it; it is the people and the law. . . ."

There is no doubt that the people of Querétaro, at least, took the kind, well-meaning Maximilian to their hearts. Not here the frigid reception of the Emperor's landing at Veracruz, or the cynical apathy of the capital so inured to the mock heroics of the Iturbides and Santa Annas. The bells rang, and the belles hung over the balconies of this royalist stronghold when he entered it on February 19 with his army of eight thousand. A month later, when Juárez' besieging force had swelled to forty thousand, and the aqueduct had been cut, and they were serving cat pie at the best tables (including the Emperor's), the townspeople still loved him, taxed themselves to pay his army's wages, thought nothing of melting down the church bells for cannon and shot. They loved especially Maximilian's reckless bravery—his walks in the convent courtyard within plain view of the enemy gunners, while shot rained about him—and his democratic behavior, as he promenaded the streets without a guard and asked strangers for a light when his pipe went out. He endeared himself to the common soldier, too, by checking on his rations and pay, which the cruel Márquez, "The Tiger of Tacubaya," was too indifferent to care about, Miramón above thinking about, or Mendes and Mejía, the two full-blooded Indians, too busy quarrelling with each other to attend to. On their own, the soldiers decorated him for bravery.

But it was at the inevitable end, when Colonel López had betrayed the citadel to the Juaristas for a handful of silver, that Maximilian looked best. Here on the Hill of Bells, on the seventy-first day of the siege, he surrendered to Escobedo's men with his staff, including the gallant Salm, who almost effected his escape. (Agnes Salm even offered her body to the prison commander when she thought that the genuineness of Maximilian's bribe was questioned.)

Maximilian's last two messages to Juárez—one a request that Miramón and Mejía be spared, the other a letter urging the Liberal leader to reconcile all Mexicans without bloodshed—make one forget the Black

Decree he was duped into signing the year before, and the hours spent composing his ridiculous court ceremonial. As he passed to the firing squad, the people of Querétaro again appeared on their balconies, in mourning, weeping openly. He gives the place of honor in the center to the brave Miramón; comforts Mejía, who is scarcely well enough to stand up, handing him his smelling salts; gives what little gold remains to the execution party, with the injunction reminiscent of Hidalgo's, fifty years before: "Muchachos, aim well; aim right here." Then a few words to the onlookers: "I forgive everybody. I pray that everybody may also forgive me. And I wish that my blood, about to be shed, may be for the good of the country. Viva México! Viva la Independencia!"

As the body was carried back through the town from the Hill of Bells, a well-dressed woman forced her way past the cordon, stabbed an officer to the heart, and escaped in the crowd, which refused to let her be pursued. There remains the ugly story of the embalming of the Emperor's body by quack undertakers who turned it black and hung it for weeks, by the flesh, on a butcher's hook. And finally of Juárez, creeping back into Querétaro months later to remark smugly, after a long, satisfied look at the remains of his enemy: "It doesn't smell too bad after all."

MEXICO CITY

With its five-million population, Mexico City is the third largest city in the hemisphere and the largest in Latin America; but what enables it to rise above this serious drawback—expressed in noise, smog, traffic jams, slums, monstrous housing developments, pretentious public buildings, and driving-distances that dwarf anything outside of Los Angeles—is that Mexico City is by far the *oldest* city of the hemisphere[4] and that its artistic creations in the twentieth century hold their own with the monuments of the pre-Columbian past. At 7,350 feet, Mexico City is also one of the highest of the world's cities, and considering its subtropical latitude, the coldest; but its situation, on a fertile plateau within sight of the volcanoes of Popocatépetl and Iztaccihuatl, is inspiring.

Eight leagues from this city of Cholula [Cortés reported] there are two marvelous high mountains whose summits still at the end of August

[4] Tenochtitlán, the Aztec capital with an estimated 300,000 population, was built on an island in Lake Texcoco. The ceremonial center was on the site of the Zócalo, the central square where the cathedral and National Palace are now located. The lake was drained in this century, with the result that Mexico City has a chronic water shortage, is sinking into the marshy ground, and when the winds blow is covered with white dust.

are covered with snow, so that nothing else can be seen of them. From the higher of the two both day and night a great volume of smoke often comes forth and rises up into the clouds as straight as a staff, with such force that though a very violent wind continuously blows over the mountain range yet it cannot change the direction of the column.

Those who try, as I did once, to drive between the mountains in the Conquistadors' route, will envy Cortés his horses, but admire most his foot soldiers who thought nothing of this trek through boulders, desert sand and volcanic ash; and especially the intrepid de Ordás and his ten men who scaled "Popo" with nothing but sandals to protect their bare feet against the fire and ice—just to convince the Cholulans that the Spaniards were masters of whatever gods might dwell in that terrible crater. Down in the plain at Ixtapalapa, site of the ceremony to which the Aztecs would repair every fifty-two years to see whether the sun would rise as usual or remain set forever, Cortés and Moctezuma first met. At the approach to the causeway, Bernal Díaz got his first good look at the complex of temples on the island, dedicated to such dread deities as "Smoking Mirror" and "Hummingbird on the Left"—a sight "we could compare," he says, "to nothing but the enchanted scenes we had read of in Amadis de Gaul . . . making us doubt whether we were asleep or awake."

TEPEYAC: THE TEN TRAGIC DAYS

Coming into the capital from the *north*, the Inter-American Highway passes the Basilica of the Virgin of Guadalupe at Tepeyac, a site just as crucial to the making of modern Mexico. The time was 1531, just ten years after the Conquest. It was still touch and go whether the Indians would submit to the new faith or be exterminated, as they had been in Haiti and Cuba. Cortés' successors were well on the way to exterminating them when the Aztec peasant, Juan Diego, came to Bishop Zumárraga and told him of his vision. Because Zumárraga accepted the miracle, and the Virgin's "command" that a great shrine be built here, Mexico as we know it was preserved. The Dark Virgin's image is everywhere—in the buses and taxis, in stores, on postcards, in the homes of rich as well as poor, tattooed on arms, woven into matadors' hats, chalked on mountainsides, flowered in public parks, outlined in neon. Politicians have acknowledged her as the only unifying force in a country immemorially divided by geography, language, revolution, poverty, persecution. Indianists have conceded that nothing else could have arrested the cultural disintegration that overcame the Indians elsewhere. Above all, the very fact of the survival of Roman Catholicism in Mexico—a

survival in the teeth of the most virulent and systematic antireligious campaign of modern times outside the Iron Curtain—must be attributed to the efficacy of this symbol.

The crowds in the innumerable churches of Mexico, even on weekdays, testify to it. The solitary Indian before his tiny shrine along the loneliest road, his arms outstretched in the sign of the cross, bears witness. But here at Tepeyac one December, I saw the extraordinary spectacle of thousands of pilgrims from all over Mexico, many sleeping in their serapes in the angles of the badly listing basilica, many making the last lap of hundreds of miles on their knees, while ambulances, their sirens screaming, carried away the fallen. We joined the crush of penitents pushing their way gently (or not so gently) in and out of the nave, over which hung a dense and stinking silence. We were literally catapulted out of the darkness on a wave of bodies. Up and down the floodlit ramps we continued, buying hot meat-filled rolls and soft drinks at the candle-lit booths; then, in the great plaza, watching the Aztec dances in costume to savage drum rhythms, wherever a clearing could be found.

If one were to pick a third site where Mexico emerged out of violence to become what it is, it would have to be the Ciudadela. For between this old, moldering fortress in downtown Mexico, and the Zócalo a dozen blocks northeast, was waged the bloody fighting of the Ten Tragic Days of 1913. One would never guess it in the capital's showplace of luxury hotels, embassies, restaurants and art galleries a few blocks north. The Paseo de la Reforma, one of the noblest avenues in the world, stretches from beyond Chapultepec Castle to the statue of Charles IV (El Caballito) in the circle from which Avenida Juárez starts. Juárez, after passing the park of the

Alameda and the Bellas Artes Museum, narrows into the street now named after Francisco I. Madero. This in turn leads to the Zócalo, the plaza of Aztec Tenochtitlán, which now contains the cathedral and the Government Palace. The Paseo, Maximilian's principal legacy to Mexico, embellished later by Porfirio Díaz with fountains and rows of diminutive statues, is as it was. José Vasconcelos, who had been a leading figure in the 1910 revolution and who later, as Obregón's Minister of Education, launched the mural renaissance by sponsoring the first murals of Rivera and Orozco, once took me on a tour of the Ciudadela. Inside the portal he showed me the spot where the triumphant conspirators had thrown Madero's brother to the mob, picking out his one good eye with a sword's point, shattering his lower jaw amid jeers, and finally burning the body. The president and vice-president were murdered later.

When the conspiracy began, President Madero was in Chapultepec Castle at the far end of Reforma. Following the flight of the aged dictator Porfirio Díaz, the gentle Madero had been spending most of his time trying to steer Mexico on a moderate, democratic course. Extremists of the Left, like Zapata and Villa, were driving to revive the Hidalgo storm of a hundred years before, their aim to end private ownership in land and business. But it was the extremists of the Right, like Porfirio Díaz' nephew Felix, and the brutal Huerta, who took it upon themselves to liquidate the popular middle course. Disdaining the danger, when General Díaz and Reyes seized the Government Palace in the Zócalo, Madero summoned his household and guard, mounted, and rode down the Paseo as far as the Caballito. Meanwhile, loyal forces under General Villár recaptured the Government Palace, forcing the conspirators to hole up in the Ciudadela. Unfortunately, Madero at this juncture made his great mistake: he replaced the wounded Villár with Victoriano Huerta, although Gustavo, the President's more realistic brother, had warned him that Huerta was not to be trusted.

During the ten days that followed, the city became a battlefield. Cannon and machine-gun fire raked the area between the Ciudadela and the Zócalo. All stores closed down. Electrical and gas services were knocked out, turning the darkness into a nightmare of fires and looting. Piles of bodies were burned in the streets to try to check the epidemics already raging. And through it all, Huerta would slink out of the palace for his clandestine meetings with Felix Díaz at the pastry shop El Globo, and then report back to Henry Lane Wilson, the infamous American ambassador who was pulling every wire at his command to bring the government, the revolution, and Madero down in ruin. How well he succeeded, the walls along Bálderas and Arco de Belém, still chipped and bullet-pocked from that murderous crossfire, hardly tell. But no Mexican has forgotten the lesson. The hundreds of thousands of wildly cheering citizens who jammed the approaches to the Zócalo in 1937 to cheer Cárdenas for his expropriation of the American oil properties were not cheering for cheaper gasoline.

The real hero of the Mexican revolution is the martyred Madero. The others, with their sanctioning of various forms of social extermination, only did the obvious in terms of self-interest. Madero alone acted *against* his personal interests, believing in the rights of all men, and in principle. As the son of a millionaire *hacendado*, he had every reason to support Porfirio Díaz and the status quo. As the leader of the revolution, he had every interest in executing his enemies—which he consistently refused to do. As a politician, he would have remained in power indefinitely, had he brushed aside constitutional government and given the roughriding Zapatistas what they demanded without legal procedure. But as a genuine democrat, Madero opposed the extremism of both camps. His downfall and death have all the elements of Greek tragedy. Fate (the times, Mexico's immaturity) overcame him. Morelos and Juárez had as much integrity, but the one was cruel and the other righteous. Madero is of the order of Lincoln and Ghandi.

REVOLUTION IN PAINT

That sunburst in fresco painting without parallel outside of Renaissance Italy, took place in Mexico City in two decades (1924–1944), and all of its major achievements—with the exception of the cycles at Guadalajara and Cuernavaca described in the next chapter—are to be found in the metropolitan area. Its master painters—Rivera, Siqueiros, Orozco, Tamayo —were children of the revolution of 1910, the first two expounding its mystique didactically or symbolically, the last two reacting against its excesses with as much spirit. I was singularly fortunate to have visited Mexico when these painters were on their scaffolds; later I got to know most of them, and still later their heirs, a generation of young humanists revolting against both the propagandistic "social realism" into which the mural tradition had degenerated, and the uncommitted abstract modes imported from Paris and New York. I was also fortunate to have been with the architects O'Gorman, Barragán and Candela at that time in the 'fifties when University City and the nearby Pedregal development were taking shape; and no survey of the wonders of Mexican art can be complete without a glimpse of O'Gorman's library mosaics and cave-like home, Barragán's spacious private patios, and Candela's public innovations in poured concrete.

Sculpture, for some reason never explained, failed to take hold in modern Mexico. Monuments to the revolution in stone or bronze, from one end of the country to the other, are without exception uninspired. Perhaps the sculptors were inhibited by the unflagging inspiration of the anonymous pre-Columbians. For wherever picks are dropped in Mexico, masterpieces in a hundred distinctive styles keep emerging from the earth. The place to see the best of this exhaustless lode is in the collections of Rivera and Tamayo, or in the National Museum of Archaeology, which contains such monumental stones as the frightening "Coatlicue" and the circular 60,000-pound Aztec calendar. The museum also contains a full-scale reproduction of the very sophisticated Maya frescoes discovered at Bonampak, Chiapas, in 1946; had these been exposed in the 'twenties, the painters too might have been inhibited!

Fortunately they were inhibited by nothing, past or present; and least of all by back-breaking work at little or no pay. The place to appreciate this, and to spend the first of three days required to see the best of the murals in the capital, is in the National Preparatory School on San Ildefonso, and at the Ministry of Education and the National Palace a few blocks distant. Vasconcelos started things off in 1923 by turning over to Diego Rivera the Bolívar Theater in the Preparatory School. Rivera, who had spent years in Europe, as a *bon vivant* in Spain, a Cubist in Paris, and an antiquarian in Italy, made an unpromising beginning in the theater— ponderous nymphs in gluey encaustic. After a trip to Tehuantepec and Yucatán, which opened his eyes to the riches of Mexican folk art, landscape and native types, he moved to the lower court of the nearby Ministry of Education and began painting his way upstairs through three enormous arcaded patios, at a pace and with a gusto for documentation that has never been equalled. Vasconcelos, meanwhile, turned José Clemente Orozco, David Alfaro Siqueiros, Jean Charlot and a number of lesser talents loose in the arcaded courts of the Preparatory School. Charlot introduced them (and Rivera) to true fresco. Siqueiros didn't take to this technique and experimented inconclusively elsewhere. But Orozco, off and on during the next five years, produced the first masterpiece of Mexican painting.

As an artist Orozco had led a double life. He had been a classical draftsman and also a caricaturist for the revolutionary "trade papers." He began painting the lower court as a classicist. Then, after the "Damas Católicas" and other reactionary elements had defaced and threatened to destroy these murals, he had his revenge on the second floor in a series of the most savage cartoon "strips" ever painted. But in the stair well and on the third floor he began to synthesize the two styles, and painted with emotional depth and compassion. From his revisions of the early murals, Orozco's pessimism about the course the revolution had taken was already clear. Under President Calles, who had succeeded Obregón, a new wave of exploiting *hacendados* and industrialists were moving into the ascendancy, and the "proletarians"—on whom the doctrinaire Marxists like Rivera and Siqueiros counted—were too deeply involved in corrupting power struggles of their own to save the revolution from Calles and his fellow generals.

Under Calles (whom he exempted from attack at the time), and under many later presidents, Rivera continued to expound his naïve interpretation of the Mexican past on the staircase and adjoining patios of the National Palace. The dimensions of this work are even more staggering than the Ministry of Education frescoes, and Rivera's talent for storytelling and composition receive greatest scope, but the painting is no longer lyrical or inventive, and in the last panels it becomes illustration hardly less sentimental than Maxfield Parrish or Norman Rockwell.

Rivera himself is thus in part responsible for the low estate to which his reputation as an artist has fallen outside of nationalistic Mexico; but not entirely. Most guidebooks do not mention, and very few foreigners (or even Mexicans) ever see, what is incomparably his finest work. This is the little chapel in the government's Agricultural School at Chapingo, a few miles north of the city. It was painted in the late 'twenties when the artist was at the height of his powers. I had visited it with Rivera in 1939; but in 1964 it took Bill Negron and me the better part of a day to find it—and get the attendants to unlock it for our inspection. This is one of the miracles of mural painting, and the most perfect blossoming of the revived art of fresco (apart from Guadalajara's Hospicio) in the Americas. It is pure poetry, a hymn to sensuous female beauty, and intellectually a dazzling solution of the most complex of spatial problems.

The last of the three days I suggested devoting to the arts in the capital could be spent in the center of the city, visiting Rivera's "Sunday After-noon in the Alameda" in the Del Prado Hotel, Siqueiros' "The Trial of Fascism" in the headquarters of the Electrical Workers' Union, and the murals by all of the Big Four in the Bellas Artes palace on the Alameda.

The Rivera is a fun mural, but beautifully painted. It depicts a nostalgic memory of walking in the park during the artist's childhood in the Porfirio Díaz period. In the center of the throng, one of the artist's wives, the surrealist painter Frieda Kahlo, fully grown, holds the little boy by the hand; a frog (which the artist resembled) is stuffed in one pocket; and they are flanked by Posada, the great engraver of the revolution, who was Rivera's and Orozco's preceptor, and by Death in a floppy Victorian hat.

There is nothing amusing about Siqueiros' 1939 mural which depicts Hitler and the democratic Big Three as demons. The children of Republican Spain are innocent angels being screwed into a press "powered" by a dive-bomber. Republican justice is a Greek temple with *Liberté-Égalité-Fraternité* on its pediment; it is going up in flames which issue from a moneybag. The overall effect, with high-lighted black machine forms against flame, is exciting and maddening, like an early Eisenstein film. There are other similarities: the crude humor (one of Hitler's three hands holds a pansy) and the use of photo-montage to keep hammering the message at the spectator's ("guilty") conscience.

Here, and in his Bellas Artes mural glorifying Cuauhtémoc, the rebellious Aztec prince whom Cortés tortured and hanged, Siqueiros may be seen at his infrequent best. Tamayo's two big murals, "Mexico Today" and "The Birth of Nationality," facing each other across another court in the Bellas Artes, are among this more introverted and subtle artist's best work. Where Siqueiros' protagonists are suffering from the conspiracies of malign forces working upon their exposed bodies, Tamayo's Man (he is always alone, accompanied at most by his shadow) is suffering inside from his inability to reconcile his instinctual, primitive self with a uni-verse no longer answerable to magic or religion. It is worth noting that Tamayo is a Zapotec Indian from Oaxaca, an internationally famous figure who has worked his way to the top, not only in artistic but in social and financial terms, and that he is still bitter over the rejection of his art by the dominant social-realist bureaucracy. He made it in the Bellas Artes—but lately.

Two huge frescoes by Orozco and Rivera also face each other across a stair well in this museum. Rivera's, in his most didactic manner, is a 1934 copy of the 1933 "Man at the Crossroads," which Nelson Rockefeller destroyed in New York's Rockefeller Center when it was discovered to contain the figure of Lenin. Orozco's "Catharsis" is a thunderous answer to Rivera's simple-minded faith that Utopia will arrive, once the honest day laborer gets his hands on the controls. In Orozco's apocalyptic vision, total war is about to engulf the world—as indeed it soon did. Amid flames over stacks of murderous weapons, the "honest day laborer" is fighting his comrade to the death, while at the bottom of the pile, naked, bejeweled whores are grinning insanely at the holocaust. To drive home the point that this state of affairs is not a local aberration but a sickness of all mankind, the figures on the outer slopes of Armageddon face away from each other. Horror, in other words, is compounded by the realization that one is looking at only one isolated focal point of an action that is endless and permanent. The four figures above the blasted safe on the right may be too stricken to get to the next bloodletting, but they are doing their best to make it. Only the title "Catharsis" (Purgation) suggests that there is anything of value to come from all this destruction, but the Greek word— as applied to such a spectacle as Oedipus "atoning" for his crimes by putting his eyes out—referred mainly to a dramatist's capacity to make his audience accept its mortality.

For the first and last time, while these two murals were being painted, Orozco and Rivera confronted each other—in their works and *at* work. A story of that confrontation, which I had from an eyewitness, reveals as much of their personalities as the two frescoes do of their ideas and art. One day, as they were working on their scaffolds back to back, a dozen art students came in and called up to Diego that they had sketches to show him. He lumbered down, ordered drinks for all of them, called their sketches "very promising," and even bought one. Then they turned to Orozco. "Maestro. . . ." Annoyed at being interrupted in what to him was a matter of life and death, Orozco looked down at them and their sketches and said: "Art, gentlemen, is like parachute jumping. Sometimes the parachute never opens. In art, this is almost always the case. You are parachute jumpers. Your parachutes have not opened. You are dead." And back to work he went.

Small wonder that Orozco, whose genius looms larger down the years, was succeeded by no school. Or that Rivera's camp followers still crowd Mexico's public walls with dutiful Marxist sermons—parachutists all.

2 MEXICO WEST: GUADALAJARA, ACAPULCO, CUERNAVACA

MEXICO HAS NOT ONE, but three Pacific coast lines, each more than a thousand miles long. From the Mexican point of view, the only part of the 1848 Treaty of Guadalupe Hidalgo that wasn't disastrous was that she managed to retain possession of all three. It seems that the courier carrying instructions from President Polk to General Scott's State Department aide, Nicholas Trist, died of fever in Veracruz, and his dispatch case got lost. When the Mexicans discovered that the United States must have upper California and New Mexico, "—and Baja California, provided the Mexicans do not hold out too firmly," they did just that, and retained the arid peninsula. For a hundred years it didn't look like much. But today, with roads beginning to penetrate the rugged cactus jungles and ore-rich mountains, irrigation turning the northern deserts into cotton and fruit plantations, and plane service opening such great bays as Concepción and La Paz on the Sea of Cortés to the best deep-sea fishing in North America, Lower California is beginning to look like quite a prize.

DOWN THE THREE COASTLINES

I have driven the paved roads to Ensenada on the Pacific and San Felipe on the Gulf. The lower reaches of the peninsula are accessible only by four-wheel-drive jeep and truck, and driving there without careful planning can be fatal. Deer, antelope, and bighorn sheep are abundant in the ten-thousand-foot-high central range. The farther south one goes, the better the fishing gets: corbina, croaker and perch in the surf: striped marlin, sword-fish, tuna, yellowtail, skipjack and bonito in the offshore waters; giant lobsters among the rocks, oysters to be picked from *trees* (mangrove) at low tide; and at San José del Cabo at the tip, there are fish so plentiful that in fifty feet of clear water the bottom cannot be seen! There's a ferry service from Guaymas on the Mexican mainland to Santa Rosalía, and from Mazatlán to La Paz; and both fishing ports are accessible by air from San Diego and El Paso.

Guaymas and Mazatlán are the places to stop overnight, driving down the Pacific highway (Route 15) to Guadalajara. There is not much to say about either—unless it is fishing and bathing one is looking for. The fishing at Guaymas is almost as good as the fishing at Santa Rosalía across the Gulf. And bathing on the circle of white sand at Mazatlán is as good as any on the Pacific coast. The states of Sonora and Sinaloa, through which one drives on a perfectly straight, flat road to reach these ports, must provide most of Mexico's food; at least this is the only part of Mexico where agriculture is mechanized and where there seems to be unlimited irrigation and electric power. But beyond Guaymas the landscape achieves another dimension—grandeur: distant mountains sculptured in their out-cropped combs by centuries of wind and sand into fierce profiles of witches, priests and warrior-kings. Both harbors are beautifully situated—Guaymas' landlocked, with peaks rising out of a veil of mauve mist on all sides; Mazatlán's ringed with coconut palms, thatched bathing cabañas and impressive bone-white buildings.

Halfway between Mazatlán and Guadalajara is Tepic, capital of the primitive province of Nayarit. Guaymas, and even Mazatlán to a large extent, are Americanized towns; not Tepic. Nestling against an extinct volcano, Tepic is in *tierra caliente*, but though the broad valley in which it lies has plantations of sugar, papaya and bananas, it takes on some of the grimness of the surrounding hills, and I couldn't help wondering whether this harshness might offer a clue to the grotesque pre-Columbian burial statuary for which Nayarit is famous. At any rate, these red-clay Tarascan warriors, with their stumpy legs, hooked noses and bulging eyes, have none of the ingratiating curves of Colima statuary to the south. I wondered, too, whether there could be a connection between these nonconformists of antiquity and the Huichól Indians of present-day Nayarit, who have never been Christianized and who keep their customs and exquisite arts intact in the remote mountains. Later, in Guadalajara, I asked a girl in a folk-arts shop why it was almost impossible to find any Huichól woven work, and she told me that one Huichól had wandered in and held out his hat, begging her for a few centavos. He was wearing a magnificently embroidered scarf, and she suggested that he sell it to her. "I'll give you two-hundred pesos for it," she said. He turned his back on her, spat, and walked out.

The colors with which the Huicholes work are confined to green (fertility), red (blood, the sun), black (night, death), and burnt umber (the cultivated fields). Their religious ceremonies resemble Haitian *vaudou*, in that states of possession are of primary importance, though the Huicholes bring these on, not by communal rhythmic rites, but by drinking or chewing a distillation of the peyote weed. Oddly enough, peyote does not grow in Nayarit, so the Indians make annual pilgrimages in December to the country north of San Luis Potosí, where this cactus flourishes. As in the drug mescalin, which is derived from peyote, consumption of it brings on hallucinations through its effect on the optic nerve.

The Huicholes believe that the peyote plants were deer at one time, and that before this, the deer were corn. So both the weed and the deer (which they hunt as part of the ritual) help the crops. On the pilgrimage, which follows the harvest, important matters are settled by interpretation of dreams. Arriving in San Luis Potosí, the pilgrims' food supply is exhausted, and they live on the peyote. Tired and thin on their return, they must still hunt deer. Then begin the ceremonies, the feasting and drinking, and the end of sexual abstinence. The bud, when put in a drink, is said to make the drinker mad for love, *empeyotado*, and is said to sing when being plucked. The Huicholes, among the most musical of Mexican tribes, make their own violins, guitars and ceremonial drums. But before settling down to music or revelry, the pilgrims take time out to beat their wives, on the likely supposition that they were unfaithful during the months-long pilgrimage.

Not far from Tepic is the black-sand beach of San Blas, memorialized in Longfellow's last poem. In the hotel, when I visited this resort, mimeographed copies were available at the desk; and in the dining room a California oldster was reading it, or rather intoning it, to his grandchildren, pronouncing the name of the town "Sand Blast," and doing full justice to its synthetic banalities:

> But to me, a dreamer of dreams,
> To whom what is and what seems
> Are often one and the same,—
> The bells of San Blas to me
> Have a strange wild melody
> And are something more than a name.

What they were, it seems, was a sad reminder that the power of the priests over Spanish Mexico—

> The vanished days of yore
> When the world with faith was filled

—was vanishing. Longfellow, characteristically, never visited Mexico, basing his poem on an article he had read in *Harper's* in 1822.

San Blas, even with Longfellow's help, will never be a popular resort. The incoming waves are filled with tiny black particles, and the thin curtain of water that finally sweeps up the shingle is dark brown, like mud. There is also a constant wind, and when it subsides, biting gnats. The beach is strewn with wizened coconut rinds, broken shell, and an occasional dead sea bird. I watched a family of middle-class Mexicans busy over a huge sand sculpture. The sixteen-year-old boy most actively; two younger girls when the spirit moved them; the mother prancing back and forth, making occasional comments in an advisory capacity: she had done her creative work. When she marshaled them into the water, I got up and looked at the figure. It had an enormous head, dwarfing the body, grotesque, with bulging eyes and lips, and eyebrows like lintels—precisely like a pre-Columbian Nayarit warrior!

GUADALAJARA: OROZCO'S CITY

If there was any doubt in my mind that Orozco was the great artist of our age, it vanished on my first trip to Guadalajara. In the Preparatory School (see p. 37) there could be a question whether so little deviation, except in subject matter, from the modes of the fifteenth-century muralists,

entitled Orozco to rank with the best of them. But returning here, to the land of his birth, in the late 'thirties, Orozco *invented form* to match his content, creating as he did so entirely new color harmonies, on a scale and with a soaring imagination comparable to Tintoretto or Greco or Goya at their best. And perhaps my first reflection, after the physical shock of coming into sight of the works themselves, was that Orozco was as fortunate as Tintoretto and Greco had been (and more fortunate than Goya) in having had an accepted iconography (or "story line") from which to work. Greco's and Tintoretto's "story line" was the Christian mythos; Orozco's was the Mexican revolution (1810–1939). Like them, he didn't exactly "accept" his mythos, rebelling against its inconsistencies and excesses and inner corruptions as they did; yet it remained for him, as Christianity did for them, the supreme reality through which his own terrifying inner struggle could be projected and dramatized.

Picasso is the only other modern painter whose powers of invention are as awe-inspiring, yet beside the mighty Hidalgo cycle in the stair well of the Palacio de Gobierno here, such a cerebral fantasy as the "Guernica" seems like a game with cutouts. The subject is the same—the horror and pity of war—but whereas Picasso felt compelled to invent visual symbols related to little in the common heritage, Orozco was able to take a number of perfectly familiar historical events (familiar to the Mexicans, that is) and on that "story line" magnify the human material into symbolic images. These images, far from losing their reality in the process, become more personal as they become more heroic.

As one ascends the stairs, one's eyes are carried up and back to the gigantic effigy of the revolutionary priest, brandishing his torch directly overhead. From its flame, the color symphony of the surrounding areas takes shape. Below the white heat enveloping the prophet's head (flying splinters of burnt wood give the head a palpable dimension), are the swirling bodies of the masses that stormed the Alhóndiga. Pípila bearing his gravestone. A towering central figure with arms outstretched, throat pierced by a blade. A child draped over a cross. Dozens of others, less particularized, are perfectly related to the whole; and below them lie the shattered bodies of the dead and dying. To offset the curves of their anguish, stacks of bayonets in one corner bristle like cacti.

And then the side walls! Gradually, as one ascends, they come into focus, perhaps forty feet high and wide. The one on the left is a prodigious still life, dominated by a blocky cross and red bishop's miters against the white-hot sky. On the left is hell itself, snarled and smoking; but a close look reveals that there is nothing literary about the demons in this inferno. The bearers of swastika, fasces, hammer-and-sickle and dollar stomp over the smashed emblems of culture. And at the bottom of this maelstrom of violence, Karl Marx, a pompous bearded head set upon a dwarfed body, is making a speech.

If I had not already seen these Hidalgo frescoes—*not* the later version in the Chamber of Deputies upstairs, which is diffuse and surprisingly mild —the Orozcos in the University Theater would have been enough to persuade me of the artist's stature as an expressionist. The big wall at the back of the stage is another tragic hymn to man's capacity to suffer and endure. The photographs of the concentration camps that shocked the world in 1945 came later; which goes to prove that life follows art—if the artist is bigger than life. With upraised arms, the victims drive their cowering oppressors across a chasm of flame into the "paradise" they have prepared for humanity. The oppressors, as they flee, point to legal precedent in law books spattered with blood. On one of the side walls is a haunting image of a bony father and son standing over the body of a child. On the other, facing this scene, is a brutalized Mexican soldier backing up two bloated, bird-brained revolutionists, their hands on their pistol holsters, their feet on a stack of rifles and law books. These three in their dehumanized grossness are as frightening as any figures Orozco ever painted, but if he had painted nothing else they would entitle him to rank only as one of the world's great cartoonists.

In the shallow dome, high-keyed colors, distortion, and swirling movement contrast most effectively with the somber hues of the stage panels. Here the artist is paying his respects to science—admiringly, most commentators say, but to my mind with tongue in cheek. A five-faced head, a trepanned (empty) skull, entrails receiving shock treatment—these give no very reassuring vision of the miracles the professors have in store for those who put their trust in physical therapy.

But the climax of Orozco's art—and in terms of man-made beauty, of any trip to Mexico—must be the Hospicio Cabañas. I was lucky to visit it, in 1956 and 1964, with Orozco's friend, Ignacio Díaz-Morales; and especially lucky the first time because our architect-friend was then supervising the repair of the dome, which had burst its iron hoop, and it was possible to see the dome murals from close up, as even Orozco had never seen them. The artist, Díaz-Morales pointed out, had been provided with a primitive scaffolding that obscured everything except the area directly in front of his brush. In fact he had never seen the work as a whole, except from the rotunda of the orphanage chapel 106 feet below—and then only when the work was completed. Even in the Sistine Chapel, working conditions could not have been so difficult; and indeed the images of "Wind" and "Water," with fingers not quite touching, can only be compared with Michelangelo's somewhat similarly posed "Creation" group. Nor does Orozco suffer by the comparison. The head of "Wind," its features loosely composed to suggest a blowing apart of the facial structure, could perhaps only have been carried off by the Florentine master—if he had been familiar with El Greco. There could be a reference in this figure to Quetzalcoatl, creator among the Indian gods, who was also a symbol of the wind until the day Tezcatlipoca, god of night, assumed a tiger's form and pulled him down to earth.

Eight years later, when the repair work was over, I again stood under the dome. Surrounded by the orchestration of those seventy intricately modulated frescoes of arch, lunette, squinch and cupola-frame that build up to that climactic coda of blues, reds and grays, Díaz-Morales told me of the visit Orozco had made to Guadalajara a few days before his death in 1948. "We stood in this spot and I said to him, 'Maestro, you should be buried here!' He hated monuments, memorials, panegyrics, praise, but he replied, 'Yes. That would be wonderful.' And then he looked at me with that ironical smile of his and added: 'I would be laughing here for all eternity with my *monos* [monkeys].' "

Díaz-Morales had already told me a story about the image of Philip II of Spain on one of the overhead vaults in the nave. It seems that Orozco had already painted in that panel a centaur, and that our friend had chided him, suggesting that Philip, the very quintessence of the Spanish character, more rightly belonged there. Orozco had grumbled that he was only painting Spain-in-Mexico. But several months later, when leaving for the capital, he had sent a message to the architect, informing him that a present awaited him at the Hospicio. Díaz-Morales had found Philip, larger than life; so, when he encountered the painter the next time, he had asked jokingly how he was expected to take his present home with him. "That's your problem," Orozco had growled, "but if you want it, take it; it's yours."

Díaz-Morales has left a worthy masterpiece of his own to Guadalajara. This is the Plaza de la Liberación. The cathedral and palaces surrounding this focal point of Mexico's second city were of course already there, but it was Díaz-Morales who swept away the clutter between them, planting the trees and designing the fountains. The result is one of the world's fine gathering places. As in the noble concourse of New York's Grand Central Terminal, one never feels lost in it, or overpowered, or friendless.

Guadalajara has many other attractions, of course. It is spacious, clean, progressive; its climate is wonderful; and last but not least, its women are the most beautiful in Mexico. Tonolá and Tlaquepaque, where the Tapatians relax on warm evenings at their summer residences, are pottery towns where descendants of the Tonaltec Indians still make high-glazed and painted earthenware figures, each family handing down its secret formula from generation to generation. But I think the thing that impressed me most, during my first visit to Guadalajara, was the pair of larger-than-lifesize seated sculptures flanking the gates to the city. The one to the right is Mariano Azuela, the pioneer social novelist. The one on the left is José Clemente Orozco. Both heroes of culture had been *alive ten years before*. To Guadalajara, evidently, they were already immortal. Where else could this happen?

CHINESE MICHOACAN

Chapala, Pátzcuaro and Cuitzeo are the great lakes of Mexico, and the country around them is mostly Michoacán, a state that has such a variety of attractions, talented people, and romantic landscape that visiting it is like visiting another country. Chapala, where D. H. Lawrence wrote *The Plumed Serpent* in 1923, and Cuitzeo, a fishing and hunting resort for Michoacán's capital, Morelia, are less interesting than smaller Pátzcuaro. The town of the same name is the place to stay if you are interested in seeing people fish with butterfly nets, glaze plates and pitchers to an incredible emerald-green luster, or weave the finest serapes anywhere; it is also the place to visit November 1 for the fiesta of the Day of the Dead when *calaveras* and candy skulls are sold in the streets, and the little island of Janitzio lights up at midnight with ten thousand candles.

General Cárdenas, a native of Michoacán, endowed Janitzio with a huge statue of Morelos which dominates the lake; and when he was president he also employed Orozco to paint the formidable, mostly black-and-white murals in the Gabino Ortiz library at Jiquilpán, across the street from the house in which Cárdenas was born. For all the five years' work in the three buildings at Guadalajara, Orozco had received no more than four hundred pesos (thirty-two dollars) a month, a salary that could hardly have defrayed the cost of his materials and the wages of the one or two assistants who prepared, each day, the surfaces of the walls to be worked on. The governor of Jalisco allowed the four-hundred-peso stipend reluctantly, it is said, and only because he believed that Orozco was a political radical who might glorify his regime—which of course the artist never did. Cárdenas paid Orozco better, and if *he* expected the revolution to be romanticized, he must have been even more disappointed, for the scenes at Jiquilpán are of firing squads, mounted *caudillos*, and faceless mobs carrying red flags, in the artist's most disillusioned (and convincing) realism.

Between Jiquilpán and Pátzcuaro, the road branches south to Uruapan. I've never been in China, but I had the feeling continuously that this must be what it is like at its best. The terrain rolls sensuously from the gently truncated pyramids of ex-volcanoes, pagoda-shaped and densely green with conifers, that stud the plain, to much higher mountains with sharp peaks purple in the haze of distance. The plain itself varies in texture from the shimmering pale green of wheat to the rich black or contoured umber of fields newly prepared for planting; and among the fields the wind, stimulated by some uneasy turbulence in the huge saucer of varying altitudes, builds twisters, miniature dust devils, of the soil. These swirl crazily like tops until, miles away, attenuating to great heights, they suddenly, like Aladdin's jinni, vanish.

Perhaps the impression of China comes from the stone walls that divide the fields. They average six feet high, with uneven tops, and are built only to the thickness of a single dusty rock; consequently they are full of holes through which the light leaks, giving the appearance, from a distance, of black lace. Perhaps the impression comes also from the houses of the Tarascan peasants. These are built of unfinished logs, or squared timber, with the ends crossing unevenly to protrude at the angles. The walls and high-pitched roofs are shingled black; and the gates in the stone walls are covered with little peaked "hats" of black shingles too, like the garden shelters of the philosophers in Sung painting. The more substantial houses of adobe have red tile roofs with an overhang of almost three feet, delicately dentiled and sometimes gaily painted.

Perhaps, though, the insistent impression of China comes from the Indians themselves, with their broad-brimmed, flat-crowned sombreros and their serapes of black wool, sparsely "jeweled" in deep reds and blues.

UNDER THE VOLCANO

One such peasant, abandoning to a small boy his donkey, which was dragging behind it two thirty-foot timbers, asked us for a ride. I was driving with a friend in search of the buried church of Parangaricutiro, and this was at the point where the road turns off, eight miles from Uruapan, to Angágua. The man's features were Mongolian. Sitting in the back of our Jeep, with a corded cylinder of faggots between his knees, he looked like some Tartar hetman of Genghis Khan. When he had reached his destination, short of ours, he asked us to stop, and alighted. I asked him if I might take his picture.

"If you like," he grunted with a toothy grin, "but the price is ten pesos."

"And what of *our* price for bringing you here?" I countered.

"You pay the ten pesos—you Americanos."

"We Americanos, *verdad*," I said, "but we do not pay ten pesos to photograph our guests."

He shrugged good-naturedly but uncooperatively and plodded off with his bundle. When a boy came running to us and shouted in English, "You want I show you volcano?" I suddenly remembered that only five years back Parícutin was still erupting, and that this whole countryside had been overrun by tourists come to see a show Barnum might have dreamed of. Dr. Atl and his book had already made me familiar with the story of this newest of the world's volcanoes: how it had sprouted without warning on the morning of February 20, 1943, in the cornfield of Dionisio Pulido of Parangaricutiro; and how, later, the church had been buried to its steeple in lava. As we drive into Angágua in a cloud of ashes, another muchacho dashed up to our car and shouted: "You see volcano? I spoken English like perfectly six, seven word. I guide man."

We invited him in, and he led us a tortuous path through the rocky streets to a point where the hillside drops abruptly to the valley of death, Parícutin distinguished from the green peaks behind it by its sinister nakedness. Seeing deep ashes ahead, I suggested we park the car and walk.

"No, no!" said our guide. *"Pasen! No hay peligro!"*

We sank to our hubcaps. I gave the wheel a few frantic turns, and whoof! it spun around in my hands! Getting out, we crawled under the car. Sure enough, the gear cord that controls the front wheels was dangling; and below, where it was supposed to meet the axle, a small, round piece of fractured metal had dropped into the dust. We asked if there was a mechanic in the village.

"No, señor."

"A car, then?"

"Como no?" There were two, in fact, but unfortunately both turned out to be in Uruapan.

"When will they be back?"

"Mañana, señor."

Then our guide had his first brainwave. He would hitch a ride or wait for a bus—"Two pass here almost every day"—and return with a mechanic or a steering gear, or something. There'd be a long wait in any case, so we decided to walk to the volcano, leaving a six-year-old muchacho to guard our stricken vehicle.

We walked for an hour, mostly downhill, arriving finally at the river of solidified lava that surrounds the unburied roof and spire of the church of San Juan. However more dramatic this may have looked in the decade of Parícutin's fury, it remains a sight never to be forgotten. Perhaps in any age but ours it would have been merely a natural curiosity. Today it could be regarded as a symbol of ecclesiastical impotence, or of miraculous survival, or of the dread shape of things to come. We climbed the frozen river of stone, stepping across the crevices, holding on to the jagged edges for support as we advanced toward the buried church. Reaching it at last, we were amazed to see that in addition to the upper third of the façade and side walls, the top of the apse and high altar remained unscathed. The white marble of the latter stood out, quite detached from the nave, like a miniature Greek temple. Ennobled by its isolation in this veritable landscape of hell, it shone with a dazzling radiance in the last rays of the setting sun.

Back at the car, our muchacho was faithfully standing guard. We gave him three pesos and a pile of cookies, and walked into the village in search of more substantial sustenance. On the way, we passed a street in which two old women, twenty feet apart, with wine-red skirts sweeping the ground and black rebozos under waist-length pigtails, were drawing skeins of white wool from pegs attached to the wall. Through an open door I saw a family seated on the ground in a circle around a twelve-year-old girl on a stool. Her mother was combing her hair while her sister gently searched for lice. A girl of about the same age passed us with a baby peeping from the folds of her rebozo—her own?

There was no restaurant in Angágua, but a motherly Indian woman and her daughter were officiating in a booth. A wood fire burned on the earth floor. We bought slices of watermelon, *bollos* hard and soft, bottles of Moctezuma XX, and soon there was delicious hot coffee. In the deepening shadows of the little square, boys were laughing and chasing a ball— not boisterously. The proprietress, seeing us rubbing our cold hands, offered us a place by the fire. Her daughter smiled sweetly as she poured the thick coffee into tiny glasses. Every gesture, every expression among these Indians, I was beginning to realize, is in tune with some profound harmony—time-less, artless, selfless—that has been lost to the rest of us. No doubt there are hidden wells of violence, but that is part of the order of nature too, not a force to be turned off or on deliberately.

It was almost dark now, so we decided to go back to the car while we could still find it. The village, lacking electricity, was preparing for sleep, but by the light of the little kerosene flares I noticed an old man standing erect by the angle of a building. His serape, drawn over his mouth and nose, was of deepest blue. The fretted border was of old rose, and along it at intervals were "diamonds" of yellow and red. It was the most beautiful serape I had ever seen. I walked over to the old Indian and expressed my admiration for it. He was pleased. His wife had woven it for him almost forty years ago, he said.

"They don't make them like that any more," I said.

"Not many," he agreed. "It takes time."

I wanted to add: "and an unspoiled eye for perfection," but lacked the words.

Uruapan—which we reached next morning, after a night curled up in the car under the moonlit shadow of the volcano—is a pretty little town on the banks of the green Cupatizio River. We celebrated our restored mobility by lunching under its cedars and *fresnos*, visiting one of the famous lacquer factories, and buying a guitar down the road in Paracho, the village that has been making the finest instruments in Mexico ever since Bishop Quiroga of Michoacán in the sixteenth century introduced the art here—as he did the weaving of butterfly fishing nets at Pátzcuaro, and the glazing of pottery and featherwork at Tzintzuntzan.

MORELIA: A CADENZA IN PINK TRACHYTE

From the moment one begins to descend from the hills, an awareness creeps over one that there is something special about Morelia. A word like "picturesque" could never be applied to its stately splendor. From the distance, it makes a very beautiful valley more beautiful. Entering, one passes the 254 acres of a ruined eighteenth-century aqueduct. In a little square facing the Church of the Roses, there are ancient trees braided with vines whose roots are as thick as the tree trunks. Bronze effigies of Cervantes and Don Vasco de Quiroga, the noble bishop of Michoacán, face each other in the leafy shade enclosed on all sides by peach-colored palaces with cast-iron balconies. Then walk to the Alameda. . . .

The cathedral, between the two squares of this park, was 104 years a-building, and its intricately carved rose stone façade and organ case brought the plateresque style to full flower. From the 210-foot towers, all the domes and steeples of Morelia march to this climax. But it was not from here, but at eye-level, that the Alameda was designed to be seen. This, surely, is one of the great (and as yet uncelebrated) architectural wonders of the Western World. Everything is of a piece. The broad arcades supported by Doric columns give rhythm to the more static façades of the palaces, their wide areas of simplicity accented by the richness of elaborate balconies, the rows of delicate brackets, the complex dentiled cornices, the funerary urns of stone profiled against the blue sky. Small, widely spaced rosettes adorn the architraves and pendants. Corinthian pilasters do not clash with the severer orders beneath them, nor do the window pediments, decorated with stone drapery, ever seem to sag. Black gutter spouts, two feet long, protruding like cannon (to which in some cases copper pipe extensions have been added) give another note of serial, brazen discipline to the stone symphony that fills the park. The buildings can be seen only one, or at most two, at a time. The planting of the plaza, and its particular furniture, provide still another harmony. The benches are of stone, very long and pierced in the back by clover-leaf "windows." The bandstand, a gift from Cárdenas' brother Dámaso, who was governor of Michoacán in 1952, harmonizes perfectly, being constructed of cream-pink trachyte like the buildings that surround it. It is encircled by miniature Doric columns, set widely apart and beautifully pitted by the weather. There are just enough trees of every height and shape; just enough flowers. The water in the circular marble basins is black and motionless; and along the borders of the grassbeds, cut in elegant patterns, stand rows of very high, square columns crowned by truncated obelisks. The iron lanterns which hang from these columns illuminate—but don't defy—the night.

As we were leaving, a tourist from Texas was loading miniature replicas of these lanterns into his trunk compartment; and under one of the arcades, an Indian in broad-brimmed sombrero, shod with classic huaraches and covered with a serape of deep purple and gold, was examining eagerly a stack of American aluminum ware, overalls, and cheap print smocks.

APPOINTMENT IN TOLUCA

Never buy a piece of living folk art in a gift shoppe—even a Mexican one. By "living," I mean made today or yesterday, by an artist and in a tradition that still flourishes. Mexico and Guatemala are still alive with such traditions and artists. It's not that the gift shoppes necessarily stick you with fraudulent or inferior pieces (though some do, of course), or that a great deal of money can be saved (though it can), but that the better articles are almost always to be found on the artisan's bench. And *finding* that bench, as readers of this book will be reminded time and again, is always an adventure.

Metepec was no exception. I had admired for years the gaily painted candlesticks in red-white-purple-yellow, and even bought one in the Toluca market, but I had never been to Metepec, a few kilometers beyond this city, where they are made. I was driving from Cuernavaca to Morelia with my wife and our year-old baby in 1964, and we thought visiting Metepec in the early morning would be a diversion of minutes. By the time the day was over, we'd barely made it to Toluca. There are no signs, and, taking a wrong turn we suddenly found ourselves in a hot, dusty, and seemingly vast village that appeared to be totally uninhabited. We stopped the car and waited, and finally a child appeared. The name of this place, he informed us, was Santiago Toto. We waved goodbye, I turned the key jauntily—and nothing happened! The starter was *kaput*. It took me an hour to find out that there was no mechanic in Santiago Toto, that the nearest garage was in Toluca, an hour's walk away—"Ah, but *señor*, I think there is an old man at the other end of town who knows cars and has a screwdriver!" In another hour we had found him, and by the time he was poking around under the hood, our car (and especially the baby) was the focus of attention on the part of a crowd that filled the entire street. "There," said the man with the screwdriver, "it goes, but it will never go again, so I advise you to drive straight to Toluca and make it go by the button." We thanked him, drove straight to Metepec. Leaving the car running, we bought for $1.68 two ceramic candlesticks dripping with angels, and a shocking-pink mermaid with a blue crown, playing a yellow guitar, the likes of which I had never seen in Toluca or anywhere else.

Just east of Toluca, at a place called Las Cruces, the government has built a public picnic ground, with artificial rivulets, trout basin, and saddle horses, to commemorate the place where Hidalgo and his army of revolutionaries were turned back, scarcely ten miles short of the capital. The monument says the battle was a "glorious triumph." And in a sense it was. The Spanish federals of Trujillo and Iturbide, numbering only eighteen-hundred men were repulsed by the huge *tumulto* of Allende, but were allowed to retreat in good order. Why Hidalgo with his one-hundred thousand didn't continue to Mexico City, where the viceroy was preparing to flee and the mob was taking to the streets, is still a mystery. My theory is that history was repeating itself. Moctezuma, with all his host, gave way to Cortés with his battalion, not so much because faced (as the military historians always claim) with superior fire-power as because the "gods" had deserted him and he was already psychologically beaten. Could one oppose the Virgin? Were not the Church and State indissoluble? As soon as he began to suffer reverses, the ruthlessness he had shown at San Miguel, at the Alhóndiga, and at Valladolid began to prey on his conscience. God was punishing him for his pride! The thin layer of French Revolutionary confidence left him. He was a priest again—and a wayward priest who must pay for his sins of rebelliousness and his lack of humility. The tragic denouement of Chihuahua and of his anguished recantation was at hand.

What a man, though, what a hero old Hidalgo was. I could see him standing on this huge rock (he *must* have stood on it!) that now supports the commemorative obelisk, haranguing the poorly armed and clothed Indians, wearing his long blue coat, with red cuffs bordered with silver galloon. At that moment, at least, he was more than the Generalissimo— he was Christ's Vicar on Earth! And it was in this spirit that he replied to the charges of the Holy Office two weeks later in Valladolid:

> I am accused of denying the existence of Hell, and at the same time affirming that some Pope is in that place. How can one deny the existence of Hell and yet say that a Pope is in it?

But greater than Hidalgo the logician, or Hidalgo the revolutionist, was Hidalgo the humanitarian, with courage and serenity (at the final scene) to match his humanity. He *had* sinned. He *had* shown pride in the righteousness of his position. He *had* carried off two million dollars in silver bars and coin. He *had* given orders for the massacres and reprisals. But—he had been, for all that, on Christ's side, the side of the poor and the oppressed, of the Indian. It was this certainty, surely, that sustained him in the days that followed his recantation. It was this that brought peace to his spirit as he made the last request—candy for the firing squad—and the sublime gesture of placing his hand upon his heart, both to make clear the target and to receive there one of the stigmata of his Lord.

ACAPULCO: CITY OF PLEASURE

The stubborn muleteer Morelos would not have turned back at Las Cruces, but by the time the brilliant Morelos had disciplined a small band of guerrillas in the west, fortune had temporarily forsaken the revolution. Padre Morelos was able to accomplish no more than a series of textbook delaying actions in the mountains between here and Acapulco before the ambitious Lieutenant Iturbide managed to turn the independence movement to his own account and crown himself Emperor.

The road south from Toluca, though Taxco, Iguala and Chilpancingo, leads directly to Acapulco. Taxco is another Guanajuato, a hill town with winding cobblestoned alleys and tiled roofs, so perfectly preserved that tourists would have overrun it by the thousands even if William Spratling hadn't revived the silver industry and lured them in with his hammered jewels and tableware. My first visit to Taxco was with Spratling, who flew me in with a cargo of silver sheets, landing his tiny open-cockpit two-seater in a cow pasture during a thunderstorm. That was in 1956, and Spratling had just completed a new wing to his home, to display his pre-Columbian "Remojadas" sculptures. This Totonac culture of the Veracruz region flourished, he told me, between A.D. 200 and 600. The figurines have a uniquely humorous air. One smiling face I liked especially had a small hand cupped over the sardonically half-open mouth, as if to say, "Don't believe a word you hear; they're all fakers!" An American dental surgeon, Milton Leof, has an equally distinguished collection of "Remojadas" in Taxco. For those who are not aficionados of sculpture and folk art, however, it will be enough to contemplate the gorgeous pink limestone façade of Santa Prisca. This jewel of the Mexican baroque was financed in the early 1700s by the silver king, José de la Borda, who is reputed to have said, "God gives to Borda, and Borda gives to God."

For those who *are* carried away by sculpture and folk art, there is a roadside stand on the highway just outside of Iguala where one can carry away (at prices ranging from five cents to two dollars) the most off-beat ladies of high fashion imaginable. Moulded from clay in a tiny village of Guerrero, six hours from here over the mountains by muleback, these attenuated female figures, with weirdly sorrowful faces, are painted from base to crown with birds, beasts and flowers in black and terra cotta.

Acapulco is for those who like great beaches, deep-sea fishing, hunting, yachting, fifty first-class hotels and fifty thousand American tourists. Some of the latter look as though they must have been imported from Southern California in flying boxcars. Complaining children. Distracted mothers. Philandering husbands. Fat-flanked teen-agers in skintight bikinis. Gray-haired schoolteachers in rhinestone-studded sunglasses—also in skintight bikinis. Retired businessmen with female companions of every age from nineteen to ninety. During my first visit, one of these paunchy tycoons and his girl friend had just been dredged from the bottom of the bay. They had had rocks attached to their feet. The guide, who took them out in a rowboat and stripped their jewels before killing them, had just been apprehended. Fortunately for Acapulco—because the tourists hadn't been concealing their intentions of going to a "safe" American resort next time—the guide had turned out to be an American.

Quebrada means "cliffside," and this is the word that doubles for the famed divers who now perform at the Hotel Mirador. The cliff on which the hotel stands is at the neck of a narrow inlet. One hundred and fifty feet below, the surf crashes into this pocket and then withdraws with a frustrated bellow, leaving the jagged rocks exposed like teeth. Sitting in the bar waiting for the show fills me with the same sense of guilt I feel at the bull ring: why am I here? is it the possibility of death that really draws me? A diver clambers up the virtually perpendicular cliff across the defile. We watch him kneel and cross himself at a tiny shrine to the Virgin of Guadalupe. Then, to a roll of drums, the diver seizes a flaming torch in each hand and soars out into the velvety night. The incoming wave must be caught exactly at its crest to prevent death on the rocks. He catches it. . . .

Puerto Vallarta, up the coast a long way, has received ample coverage as a hideaway for publicity-crazed lovers; but Zihuatanejo, much closer to Acapulco, is a fishing village with real fish. Bill Negron, who likes to live dangerously, made the round trip from Cuernavaca in 1964 with his eight-year-old son on one of those pensioned relics of the U.S. transportation system, a Flecha Roja bus. A letter from him described the coastal road as "a proving ground for tanks," and the driver who negotiated it at night as having worn sunglasses and scorning to use the bright-dim floor button. "Once, just for the hell of it, he jumped out on a blind turn at the edge of a four-thousand-foot drop to inspect the motor. Satisfied, he pulled a gun out of his belt, fired into the air once, climbed back, and continued driving."

They arrived at noon after the twelve-hour ride, "feeling like two sprung tuning forks," and were immediately spotted by the local welcoming committee and offered a thirty-peso trip across the bay. Dragging their "matrimonial hammocks" out of the bus, they explained that they were only looking for a couple of coconut palms on the beach—"though two dollars American for room and board here certainly beats the tariff at the Acapulco Hilton." In a few minutes they were being offered the same trip for twenty pesos. "Adapting fast to this hot village where no one is in a hurry," Negron wrote me, "I responded, 'See you after we eat, maybe,' whereupon we had a marvelous dinner of fish soup with thick chunks of *huachinango*, followed by deep-fried *ojotones*, a local fish of great delicacy, and the usual tortillas." By the following morning, the price of the fishing boat had come down to ten pesos, and a wonderful time was had by all, the catch including several gigantic sea turtles.

As Bill concluded his report: "The sun beats down heavily here. But in Shangri-La who cares?"

CUERNAVACA: PEOPLE OF LEISURE

I have lived in Cuernavaca longer than I have lived anywhere else in Mexico, but I find it hard to describe. Dozens, perhaps hundreds, of rich Americans, some of them socialites, some celebrities in the theatre, some dilettantes or hangers-on, live here. But Mexican millionaires, and celebrities from the political and art worlds, invariably have second homes in Cuernavaca too. Their worlds never mix, and seldom touch. Nor will they have anything to do with the young artists, Mexican and American, who come to Cuernavaca weekends. Then of course there are the natives, who live off all these intruders—some well, but most poorly; surely detesting their affluent guests, but rarely showing it. Before the 1950s, when the high-speed toll road from the capital knifed into Cuernavaca (and beyond, to Iguala), Cuernavaca was an end in itself. But by the time this highway is completed to Acapulco, Cuernavaca may become only a place where the Jet Set and the tourists stop for lunch, take a quick look at the Riveras in the Palace of Cortés, and pass on. Which will be too bad. For Cuernavaca with its perfect climate, its leisurely pace, and its tropical garden homes sprawling up and down the *barrancas*, is one of the most attractive cities in the Americas.

There are hotels, pensions, and houses-to-rent for all incomes in Cuernavaca, but for reasons too involved to relate, my wife and I spent the winter of '64 in the largest and most bizarre of them, the Casino de la Selva.

This complex of bungalows, bowling alleys, swimming pools, overhead kiddie-cars, and razzle-dazzle art works caters almost exclusively to week-ending Mexicans. Its proprietor is an eccentric Spaniard named Manuel Suarez, who has made a fortune selling concrete water tanks to the Mexicans and would like to resell them Hernando Cortés. He goes about this difficult task by presenting an effigy of the Conqueror (the only one in Mexico) in bronze on a rampant charger. Then he makes his apologies to the Indians by filling a garden with little pre-Columbian replicas, and to the intellectuals by offering a cast of Dr. Atl, larger than life, and filling his recreation halls with nationalistic murals. According to latest reports, Siqueiros has just been hired to paint "the largest mural in the world" around a convoluted pyramid at the Casino. And it seems perfectly predictable that neither Suarez nor the Mexicans will see any irony whatsoever in the fact that Siqueiros' entire life—when not engaged in threatening capitalists (like Suarez) for the Communist Party—has been devoted to making romantic heroes of Cortés' victims.

Angry men of genius like Charlie Chaplin and Erich Fromm come to Cuernavaca to simmer down; but milder eccentrics come here because there is always a receptive audience. Bill Negron and I encountered one of the oddest of the latter on the tennis courts east of the Casino, just before taking off for Guatemala. He was an American named Harry Bennett. His age: 68. His profession: promoter, retired. His avocation: tennis, which he still plays remarkably well. His trademark: a limp cigar butt in the corner of his mouth, which hasn't been lighted for thirty years. We asked him whether it was the *same* cigar butt, and that was his opening. Shifting the butt to the other corner of his mouth, he uncrossed his bow legs, gave us a squinting smile, and whipped a mimeographed document from his hip pocket. "This will answer all your questions," he said briskly, "but I'm running out of copies on this trip and would like it back."

Entitled *Stranger than Friction*, the first paragraph read: "Friction is a physical phenomenon the explanation of which is controversial even among physicists. Since it has nothing to do with this tale, it will be skipped." The six pages following proceeded to tell how a dentist thirty years ago said to him: "Harry, the roof of your mouth would be all right on the bottom of your shoe. . . . Cancer may develop unless you give up smoking." After much anguish, snarling and sneering at friends, etc., our hero went to Havana—of all places—and was urged to just hold a cigar in his mouth.

When he got back to New York it was still there: "My friends were astounded at the change in me. . . ." He visited his dentist: "Egad, cancer had flown from my oral zodiac!" He offered ten dollars to anyone catching him lighting the butt, but once at Parícutin, following inadvertently his guide's suggestion that he light it on the hot lava, a friend demanded payment but got only ten pesos—"Mexican dollars!" The remainder of the article was devoted to technical explanations: "Since, by the process of attrition, lixiviation, and occasional amputation of the soggy stump, the length of the cigar decreases, the observer is puzzled; the logical reason, amputation, does not seem to occur to him." My own reaction, I'm afraid, was exactly that of a passenger on the Grace Line who had watched Harry for six days and finally slipped a note ("in a childish scrawl") under his door. The note said: "WHEN ARE YOU GOING TO LIGHT THAT DAMN CIGAR?"

Robert Brady is at the opposite pole from Harry Bennett. He is a painter—interior decorator who has spent a small fortune restoring a colonial palace on the street called Netzahualcoyotl. The palace is part of the cathedral compound that is believed to have housed Cortés during the building of the more formal palace on the Zócalo. From the exterior, all is Spanish reticence: massive, eyeless walls of tan-pink adobe. But once through the studded oaken portal, patio after patio opens up, disclosing pools, fountains, scarlet and yellow-flowering vines, giant trees, sculpture niches, and a tower in which hangs a giant chandelier that once graced the cathedral at Puebla. Among Mexicans whose homes I have visited, only Tamayo's is furnished with such impeccable taste. Brady paints the low arches and vaulting of the four-foot-thick walls white, and then pierces them with deep niches for back-lighted sculpture. The unpierced walls are hung with handsome tapestries in primary colors, of his own design, or used as a setting for Pátzcuaro plates, Michoacán masks, Guerrero figurines or candlesticks from Metepec. Only in his choice of contemporary paintings— where he seems to prefer the chic Chouchu Reyes and Rafael Coronél to such uncompromising exponents of the great tradition as Sepúlveda, Muñoz, Arévalo, Cuevas, and Góngora—could I find anything to quarrel with in Brady's taste.

It was across the street in the home of Margaret Jessup, ten years earlier, that I had listened to a monologue that could serve as a threnody for Cuernavaca's fading splendor. Eduardo Bolio Rendán, a Mexican of pure Spanish ancestry, was then writing a book to be called *Unworldliness as a*

Fine Art. He expounded his theory of the three "historical disasters" that have kept Mexico from realizing its potential. The first occurred at the time of the Conquest. "If Mexico had been conquered two hundred years earlier," he said, "its conquerors would have been Byzantines, men of the Middle Ages, whose viewpoint would have coincided with that of the great Indian cultures already here. But Cortés, though he came out of the medieval court of Isabella la Católica, was caught up in the belated Renaissance of the epoch of Charles V. Though he tried, at least halfheartedly, to build an independent empire, with free Indians intermarrying with Spaniards, he was recalled and disgraced. Similarly, the Franciscans and Dominicans, true medievalists who sympathized with the Indians' other-worldly culture— their inability to acquire property, measure accurately, think in commercial or scientific terms—lost out to the secular Church, in particular to the Jesuit order, which established the disastrous pattern by which Mexico was gradually 'middle-classed' and shorn of its individuality.

"The second disaster," he continued, "occurred when the 'liberal' Maximilian was ousted by the 'conservative' Juárez. Only Bulnes's interpretation of Juárez' character is to be relied on. Juárez was an Indian, to be sure, but an Indian who had become a petty lawyer, and hence dedicated to solid middle-class ideals such as 'progress' and 'social comfort.' Maximilian, a true aristocrat, at once espoused the Indian cause, thus alienating the secular Church, which had brought him to Mexico in the hope that he would reinstate its lost privileges. Juárez triumphed because he was wholly the tool of American interests. At one point, he even offered half of Mexico's territory to the United States—an offer that your Congress was too embarrassed to accept."

"But, Señor Rendán," I interrupted, "wasn't half of Mexico's territory already ceded to the United States?"

"That came later."

"But wasn't the Treaty of Guadalupe Hidalgo signed in 1848?"

"Perhaps. But dates are not important. I can never remember my own birth date. It is the spirit of history that matters, and if you are interested in the larger picture, I shall continue."

"By all means, do."

"Well, as I was saying, Juárez' acquiescence in American materialism was Mexico's second disastrous failure to realize his destiny. . . ."

"And the third?"

". . . was Ambassador Dwight Morrow, whose reign and diabolical influence I myself saw at first hand here in Cuernavaca."

"Morrow? I thought that Morrow only gave the Palace of Cortés to Diego Rivera, and his daughter to Charles Lindbergh."

"Morrow taught the petty middle-class lawyers, who had hitherto been content with a few hundred or a few thousand pesos, to think in terms of millions. He introduced the legalized larceny of the House of Morgan with his confounded 'liberalism'; and from that point on, the Mexican revolution became the rule (in the name of social benefits, security, industrialization) of Calles, Alemán, Ávila Camacho and Company."

"You leave out Cárdenas?"

"Cárdenas is a rich man, too; but Cárdenas' aim has always been power—to work behind the scenes. Cárdenas is the real ruler of Mexico, even today. He has a home here in Cuernavaca, of course, like the rest of them, and when anything goes wrong he calls a meeting, *sub rosa*, and the orders go out to the puppets who occupy the nominal offices, from the president on down.

"The golden age of Mexico," Rendán continued, "was the age of Porfirio Díaz, but Díaz unfortunately made two mistakes. He failed to democratize the country when he might have, leaving the Indians out of his scheme of things entirely; and he lived too long, losing his grip and thus preparing the way for the decade of anarchy that followed his exile.

"Mexico today," he went on sadly, "has lost its chance to be a great nation. Individuality persists among the sixty or seventy per cent of the people not yet reduced to middle-class status. But the percentage—what with the success of industrialization, social security, and the infiltration of American tourism with its gadget-mindedness—is diminishing rapidly. In fifty years, every Mexican will be an undifferentiated consumer type, like you Americans. Already the country is flooded with cars, radio sets, and Pepsi-Cola—as you can see. Why, I can remember when every woman in this town could cook. And cook well. All they know how to do now is open cans and push the contents in front of you—and they don't *like* to do even *that*."

"The legacy of Zapata?" I said with a smile.

"Do you know John Steinbeck?" he asked.

I said I had known him.

"Well, he was here for some weeks writing the scenario for that absurd movie—*Viva Zapata!* I think they called it. One day at a cafe in the Zócalo, I came up to him at his table and said: 'Why in the name of God don't you hire a taxi just for one afternoon and go out into the countryside and see what your hero really did—how he destroyed all the wealth of this richest of Mexican states, totally destroyed it—instead of writing this absurd rot about his noble idealism?'

"But don't misconstrue my position," Rendán added. "While I'm not a professional radical like Steinbeck, neither am I a hopeless reactionary like Evelyn Waugh. Waugh was here, too, and I said the same thing to him. 'Instead of assuming that the secular clergy is doing good and is being persecuted unjustly, why don't *you* hire yourself a cab and go out and talk to the average Indian, who truly loves God and the saints and his own church, but hates the grasping priests with all his heart and all his soul? But you won't,' I said to him, 'because the truth would interfere with your dogma.'

"No," Rendán said, "the truth is always beautiful—because it is true. How many of us can face it? Mexico will lose, is already losing, its chance to face the truth."

As we were saying good-bye under the blue jacaranda in the garden, he pointed to the hills fading in the twilight. "Do you see that haze?" he said. "I can remember when the atmosphere here, forty or fifty years ago, was absolutely clear—every day, all day."

"You mean it's the smog of the capital, reaching even this far?" I asked.

"Not necessarily," he replied with a smile. "It's more than that. It's creeping all over Mexico. The haze of modernity."

3 MEXICO SOUTH:
OAXACA,
YUCATAN, CHIAPAS

THE INTER-AMERICAN HIGHWAY into
southern Mexico may be picked up at
Izúcar de Matamoros either by driving south from Puebla or east from
Cuernavaca by way of Cuautla. From
that point on to Oaxaca, and beyond
Oaxaca through the Isthmus of Tehuantepec and across the wild mountains
of Chiapas to the Guatemala border,
there is so much hot desert, such a
desolation of bristling cacti, and so
many thousands of hairpin turns, that
every time I traverse it I say to myself fervently: "Never again!" Why,
then, do I come back? Good reasons—
three of them. There is no better way
of getting to Guatemala, and the most
Guatemalan town in Mexico, San Cristóbal de las Casas. There is no other
way of getting overland to Oaxaca—
and if one gets *that* far, why stop?
And . . . hairpin turns, through some
mental quirk which boggles at quantity, become converted by memory into

one hairpin turn. And now there is a fourth reason: it is possible at last to *drive* into the Yucatán Peninsula, by way of Coatzacoalcos, Villahermosa and Campeche.

MITLA AND MONTE ALBAN

On my third trip to Oaxaca, with Bill Negron in 1963, we decided to stop off at Acatlán and visit Herón Martinez. Our difficulty in locating him tells something of the change that has come over even this little-traveled part of Mexico in less than a decade. In 1956 Herón was making a unique kind of unglazed pottery and selling it in Oaxaca—animals with riders and acrobats, candelabra with little figures dangling from wire, all painted with an intricate design in blues, blacks, oranges and greens. Because he was unknown locally, he was easy to find. But in 1963 an urchin took us by a roundabout way to a part of the town I had never seen before. Herón had changed, and his pottery (glazed now) had a Texas look. Puzzled, I questioned him for some time and finally elicited the reluctant information that "up that street" there was "another Herón Martinez." There was, too, and not one, but several! We did find the original artisan, finally, and his work hadn't deteriorated a bit, but he had a huge workshop now and was executing commissions for agents as far away as San Francisco at high prices. The whole town, these days, he explained, was full of "fake Herón Martinezes" and to prove that he was the real one—though we assured him no papers were necessary—he showed us a framed diploma from Adolfo López Mateos, President of Mexico, authenticating his status as Folk Artist of the Republic.

Oaxaca itself hasn't changed noticeably. On my first visit in 1937 I had watched Alfonso Caso and his assistants removing the last of the royal treasures from the newly discovered tombs on Monte Albán. Today the golden necklaces and earplugs are on display at the museum on the Zócalo, and the famous archaeologist, after moving up the political ladder to the Interior Ministry under Alemán, and then heading the Instituto Indigenista [1] which he founded, is now writing his memoirs. The Zócalo, with its jade-green arcades and giant laurel trees full of singing birds, is the same. Its

---

[1] This wonder-working organization, which unfortunately receives little federal support and reaches only a fraction of the Indians it might serve, teaches the primitive tribes the advantages of co-operatives; offers elementary accounting and Spanish if the Indian wants them; supplies free medical and surgical care; installs pure, fresh water; and gives him (for the first time in history) a sense that outsiders respect him for what he is and can do.

dozens of tiny booths dispensing everything but pipe tobacco haven't changed. Nor its army of vendors hawking *serapes;* not the nearby Indian market, largest on the continent, with the famous gray-clay bells from Coyotepec and children's whistles with the blow-hole under the donkey's tail. The stall nearest the market still sells witch's charms and pre-Columbian *copal.* And at the Hotel Monte Albán, *plumados* in sandals and feathered headgear still listlessly go through their ceremonial-dance paces under the dirty skylight. But at Cervantes' curio shop the best *huipils* are now displayed under glass in a "museum," and one has to go to the villages far in the surrounding mountains to find bargains.

Mitla is an hour's drive on the road south, beyond Santa María del Tule where stands the immense *ahuehuete,* 162 feet in diameter, which was ancient when Cortés and his men took shelter under it. Mitla was the shrine of the Mixtec god Xipetotec, a forerunner of the bloodthirsty Aztec idols, and Mitla's appliquéd geometrical abstractions in stone (perhaps symbolizing the birds' feathers and serpents' scales of Quetzalcoatl, who was also worshiped here) are forbidding. Penitents were sealed up alive in these walls, and one legend has it that Fray Francisco de Burgoa in the 1650s sent priests into one of the subterranean passageways until they encountered snakes and evil smells and a fierce wind which caused them to "wall up forever this back door to hell." It was this same good Dominican who secretly watched a pagan confession rite and was horrified to hear the confessor conclude: "Now you can be happy and sin anew."

In the private museum of Howard Leigh near the ruins, there is a most extraordinary Zapotec head of a young man, dating, Leigh told us, from the classical period of this culture—around the second century A.D. Its anguished beauty bespeaks a culture with humane preoccupations, the reverse of those of the Mixtecs—and of most modern nations.

The center of that civilization for several thousand years was Monte Albán, a mountaintop four miles west of Oaxaca. Among the major archaeological sites of Mexico (Teotihuacán, Tula, Palenque in Chiapas, Chichén Itzá and Uxmal in Yucatán) it is the oldest, dating back to at least the fifth century B.C., and the only one continuously occupied until the Conquest.

The site covers twenty-five square miles. The central plaza is 1,000 feet long and 650 feet wide. Monte Albán's hieroglyphic writings, its calendar, its numerals, and its observatory shaped like an arrowhead to face the winter solstice, antedate the Mayas, to whom alone these intellectual feats are usually ascribed. There are also indications of a healthier, less caste-ridden culture. For one thing, the Zapotecs appear not to have become obsessed, as the Mayas were, with measuring time; time and space are identical in their thinking, and the stars were worshiped as symbols of permanence amid the flux of worldly ambitions. The proof of the success of their philosophy is in the centuries of peace and uninterrupted commerce with the lands to the south and north—a unique achievement in the annals of Middle America. No weapons were found in the Monte Albán tombs. The famous Tomb 7, which Caso discovered in 1932 with its nine pounds of jewels, is of a very late date, probably just before the Conquest, and its craftsmen were the ultra-refined, less humane Mixtecs who had by then taken over. To this day the Zapotecs, whose blood sacrifices in the pre-Columbian days went no further than puncturing the lobe of the ear, will have nothing to do with bullfighting.

The serenity of the Zapotec culture is best expressed in the proportions of the great plaza, its nobly stepped temples, and its gentle domination of the huge valley. We were reluctant to leave it and found little to say until released from its magical communion with the heavens.

CHICHEN ITZA AND UXMAL

The people of Yucatán have always been isolationists. The peninsula held out against the Conquest long after the rest of Mexico had succumbed. In the nineteenth century it almost managed to secede. And in the twentieth, the most utopian of the revolutionaries, Felipe Carillo Puerto, was on the way to making the province an exemplary communal state (and taking an American wife) when assassins' bullets cut him down. To this day Mérida, the Yucatán capital, is quite unlike any other Mexican city. It prides itself especially on its cleanliness. "In *their* army," a young man said to us bitterly, "we die of dysentery and other diseases because we have no resistance, never having lived in the filth that they are accustomed to."

In 1956 there was no way of driving to Yucatán. Donald Demarest, a novelist and co-author of *The Dark Virgin*, a study of the cult of Tepeyac, had just flown to Mérida with me, and on the plane, somewhat inebriated from reading Malraux's *The Royal Way*, we decided to see an "inaccessible" ruin—Bonampak if possible, Yaxchilán at least.

When we heard that Ruz Llullier, who had made the sensational discovery of the King's Tomb at Palenque three years before, was in town, we went to see him. We found him at the archaeological headquarters, poring

over maps with an assistant, Hypolito Sanchez Vera. The latter turned out
to have been a collaborator of Giles Greville Healey, the American explorer-
photographer, in the period immediately following Healey's 1946 discovery of the great Maya frescoes at Bonampak. Sanchez told us that
penetrating to Bonampak would require a pack train of mules from
Yaxchilán, and a week's time. Since we had a week before our return-flight
tickets to the capital would expire, fifty dollars apiece to spend, and no
intention of missing Chichén Itzá, Uxmal, and Palenque, it was clear that
we'd never make Bonampak. Ruz threw up his hands when we said we'd
have to settle for Yaxchilán in the three days our schedule permitted. He
himself had yet to get there and was waiting for a government expedition,
complete with plane, guides, mules, and camping equipment. "Impossible!"
he exclaimed. "A trip like that requires months of planning." Sanchez Vera,
more familiar with the madness of Americans, humored us by drawing a
map of the area and suggesting that we wire Paco Villanueva, an exporter
of chicle who lived in Tenosique in Tabasco and who might fly us in to a
mahogany clearing in the jungle, from which dugout canoes could be
procured.

After sending the wire, we saw something of Mérida by the satisfactorily
slow (but not inexpensive) medium of a horse-drawn carriage. The tiny
horses are supposed to be descendants of those which Cortés and Montejo
brought with them from Spain, but their ancestors must have been a lot
larger to have frightened the natives so badly. Our "hay burner," as Don
called him, took us to Ruz's house in the suburbs along perfectly straight
streets bordered by pink-flowering "begonia" trees. Almost every house—
the most attractive are built of white limestone chips imbedded in gray
mortar—is equipped with a Texas-type windmill to tap the shallow wells
(*cenotes*). An abundance of these wells makes possible Mérida's 300,000
population; for Yucatán, being entirely without rivers, is an arid limestone
tableland.

We got a good look at the scrubby countryside, dotted with the sisal
which is Yucatán's money crop, on our way to Chichén Itzá next morning.
The Indians are pathetically poor, but their women, with typically Maya
high cheekbones, receding foreheads, and almost Oriental eyes, have a
token luxury to match the inherited aristocracy of their features. It is an
ankle-length white *huipil* embroidered with red blossoms. A guide, apparently by prearrangement with our driver, seized us the moment we

alighted at the ruins. The word "Maya," he told us, means either "not many"—i.e., "The Chosen People"—or "not much" (water). Here, there are apparently only two subterranean wells. One of them is the Sacred Cenote that lost its "roof" centuries ago and became the place where virgins were first drugged and then thrown in by the priests. Our guide explained that this drowning ceremony was proof of the superior civilization of the Maya in the time before the Toltecs came down from Tula, introducing blood sacrifice. Occasionally, he said, the virgins did manage to revive and swim; and if they swam about all day in the forty-foot-deep pool, they were pulled out "and became heroines," almost goddesses. "Anyway," he added, "those that didn't survive believed that they were being thrown to paradise."

Another way of becoming a hero among these people, apparently, was to score a goal in *pelota*. We visited the court, an enclosure as long as two football fields placed end to end, and when I saw the goals I could believe it. Almost forty feet above the field, they stick out at right angles to the side walls like doughnuts. Through these circular openings no more than a foot in diameter, the contestants tried to propel a ball by motions of their elbows and hips, to which pieces of leather were attached. (The fact that the ball is known to have been made of rubber is cited as one proof that the Mayas were deeply indebted to their Gulf Coast cousins.) Judging by one of the nearby reliefs, losers, instead of being traded or returned to the minor leagues, were executed.

We had paid off our guide by this time and managed to spend the rest of the day in a more leisurely inspection of the ruins. As nearly as I can make out from what has been written on the subject (much of it contradictory and all subject to revision by new evidence), and from talks with Caso, Gamio, Covarrubias, Ruz, and later on Healey, the early history of Yucatán was somewhat as follows. The Maya drifted into the waterless peninsula from their cultural centers in Chiapas, Guatemala and Honduras, some time after the catastrophe that brought their classic period to a close. That catastrophe, whatever its cause—religious, military, economic (infertility, resulting from constant "burning-off" of the corn lands, is most frequently cited)—took place in the year 10.0.0.0.0, correlated by one group of savants as A.D. 830. Settling here, in Uxmal, and at the other nearby sites, they prospered for a time and evolved the architectural-sculptural style known as Puuc. The rectangular palaces of

Uxmal mark the culmination of this Maya culture, but it survives also in the early architecture of Chichén.

Then came the Itzá, sweeping up from the Gulf Coast near the mouth of the Usumacinta River. According to the Chronicle of Chilám Balám, a narrative of surviving legend taken down by the early priests in Yucatán, they were led by a high priest named Kukulkán. Kukulkán—whose name also appears in *Popol Vuh,* a compilation of Quiché-Maya legends preserved by the early priests in Guatemala—is sometimes identified with our old friend, Quetzalcoatl, "culture-hero" of the Toltecs from Tula. All this occurred toward the end of the ninth century, and though it resulted in the introduction of some Toltec ideas, it didn't basically alter the Maya style of Chichén Itzá. The Itzá flourished under the so-called League of Mayapán until driven out of Chichén around the year 1000. Mayapán, the Itzá-Toltec capital, was destroyed in 1461, but Maya culture survived spottily in Yucatán even after the Conquest, the last holdouts being defeated in 1697 at Lake Petén-Itzá in Guatemala (see p. 125), whither they had fled.

Chichén Itzá was known to the early Spanish priests, but ignored by them once pagan religious and cultural activities had been stamped out. The site was rediscovered by John L. Stephens, the American traveler-diplomat, in 1841, on the same safari that led him to Palenque. Early archaeologists then visited it. But in 1900, Edward Thompson, American Consul General in Yucatán, bought the hacienda on which the ruins stood and, employing a diver and a dredge, extracted from the Sacred Cenote a wealth of jewelry, gold and copper plaques, bone and jade ornaments, many originating from as far away as South America and the Valley of Mexico. He sold them to Harvard's Peabody Museum.

While Demarest, to satisfy his thirst for religious symbolism, concentrated on the Temple of Jaguars, the Wall of Skulls, and other Toltec buildings adorned with reliefs depicting the exploits of the Plumed Serpent, I, with six rolls of film to squander, succumbed to such photographers' dreams as the Temple of Warriors, surrounded by its forest of free-standing columns, and a small temple of the Maya period called The Church, that is literally top-heavy with bristling stone masks of the rain god. We ascended El Castillo together. This shapeliest and best-preserved of pre-Columbian pyramids has many unique features. Its temple atop is well preserved; in fact it served as a fort during some of the campaigns the

Spaniards were obliged to wage against the recalcitrant Indians. Inside the outer pyramid with its 365 steps (counting the platform), archaeologists found a smaller pyramid whose temple contained a recumbent rain god (Chacmool) and a limestone throne carved in the shape of a jaguar, painted bright red, with eyes and spots of green jade. Both are to be seen in their original positions, and both struck us as more comic than awesome.

Perhaps we were beginning to tire, but we had strength for one more ruin and staggered to the Caracol. This observatory takes its name (shell) from a spiral staircase inside. Its magnificent silhouette reminded me of Theodoric's Tomb at Ravenna. More knowledgeable explorers at Chichén have been reminded of the Orient. There are lotus designs that could have originated in southern India. For that matter, a tiny Maya head I had picked up the day before in Mérida could be pure Cambodian. Face scarification and nasal distortion, as once practiced here, are common in the South Pacific. A two-way trans-Pacific trade in ancient times is almost as well established a hypothesis among the ethnologists as the Mongol origin of the Indian race.

It was on one of these regal platforms that my old friend Carleton Beals had a talk with Felipe Carillo Puerto in the early 'twenties. The latter had spent seven years in Porfirio Díaz' prisons and had emerged during the 1910 revolution to liberate the Indians from their virtual slavery to the sisal planters. Standing here, he had said: "We have used force. Now we must use love. In the name of Jesus you have been betrayed. In the name of the old gods I declare you free!"

Brave words . . . but the humanitarians like Carillo Puerto and Madero were cut down in their prime, and the only Maya text we have, the *Popol Vuh*, offers no Christ-like compassion. Quetzalcoatl in this bible is not the beneficent abhorrer of human sacrifice that Moctezuma feared. Coming out of the barbarous north, he brought with him the same attitudes of jealousy and suspicion as the gods he supplanted. He brought with him fire—and the fire kept going out. In the cold darkness, the poor Mayas asked him whether he would accept money for his good will, but he replied that he was interested only in blood. So the cycle of sacrifices and wars began again, and the Mayas exterminated one another to keep the altars smoking. Late, but too late, they turned Quetzalcoatl into stone. For then the bloodthirsty Aztecs moved in, and behind them the Spaniards with their firesticks, putting an end to the Quiché-Maya dream of peace, corn, and glory.

The ruins of Uxmal rise out of the plain dramatically, after one crosses a range of very low foothills fifty miles southwest of Mérida. Unlike Chichén Itzá, Uxmal is without water, and its inhabitants had to rely entirely on catchments and cisterns. It is hardly surprising that Chac, the rain god, supplies almost all the decorative motives here. The dryness is forbidding, even today. Some vultures were working over a skunk as we drove in. In the rubble—and, at Uxmal, rubble predominates over ruins—iguanas stared at us dubiously. Pale green, crested with gold and jet, and looking as prehistoric as any of the fallen stelae, they quickly withdrew into their dens. And in the V-shaped burial chambers, whose green, dripping walls are streaked with black and yellow, bats could be heard squeaking in the crevices of the broken combs and merlons.

Uxmal may be closer to "classic Maya," as they say, but it doesn't compare with Chichén in either variety or detail. Some of the flat-topped palaces have been likened to the Greek temples for their simplicity, but such comparisons are misleading; structures like The Church or the Caracol at Chichén need not be compared with anything. The beauty of Uxmal is in ruin itself. It lacks finished sculpture of any quality, all the good pieces having been carted away by the hated Mejicanos to the Archaeological Museum in the capital. The casual disarray of centuries of neglect, the action of wind and sun, and of gravity, have produced a fine conglomeration which, happily, Uxmal's chief explorers, Stephens, Frans Blom, and Sylvanus Morley, did nothing to restore. Only now are the bureaucrats beginning to move in and make their neat card indexes of scattered stone. Meanwhile, adventurous tourists climb the almost perpendicular steps of the Pyramid of the Magician, hanging precariously to a rusty chain as the footing splays out from under their feet; or pose against the orange and black striations of the Palace of the Governor, the triangular shadow of whose opening, punctured by a single brutal column, frowns upon them with an almost sexual emphasis.

YAXCHILAN AND BONAMPAK

The "classic" Maya ceremonial center of Yaxchilán, which lies on the Mexican side of a loop in the Usumacinta River separating Chiapas from Guatemala, was discovered by the British antiquarian, A. P. Maudslay, in the late 1880s. Chiapas was then part of Guatemala, and Maudslay called the ruin Menche Tinamit, and got permission from President Rufino Barrios of Guatemala to remove the most superb of its stone and wood lintels to the British Museum. Then, as now, a dying tribe of un-Christianized Maya Indians, *Lacandones*, visited Yaxchilán periodically to burn copal in their "god pots" and worship the ancient deities whose very names had been forgotten. Ten years later, another great pioneer archaeologist, Teobert Maler, visited Yaxchilán and was told by the Lacandons of "certain ruins, opposite . . . but four leagues inland from the right bank of the river." This, one may suspect, was Bonampak, whose existence was revealed to Healey by the sons of these primitive tribesmen half a century later.

Demarest and I began our flying visit to Yaxchilán by taking a night train from Campeche, a little south of Uxmal, to Tenosique on the Usumacinta. The roadbed through the steaming jungle must have been built in Díaz' day, when the old dictator was saving every centavo to stay in power— or by the British who were saving every cent to *keep* him there. It was like riding a bucking bronco: an accelerating crescendo of jolts, culminating in a thump that tossed one completely free of the berth at the various whistle-stops—and there was one on an average of every ten minutes. A dozen or more inhabitants could be seen at these stations, squatting or standing in the dim, blue light of a single bulb or kerosene flare; and once a couple of ten-year-olds raced us down the tracks for half a kilometer, shouting and laughing.

Early the next morning, Paco Villanueva agreed to fly us to Agua Azul in his Cessna. There dugout canoes might be procured for the ascent of the Usumacinta. Everything went according to plan, and by mid-afternoon we were sitting with Miguel de la Cruz, guardian of the ruins, on a high bluff looking across the mighty river into Guatemala. Soon we were climbing through the complex of broken temples. The terrain has a floor of limestone, sharp and white with black markings, and rotted vegetation—a brown peat moss that looks and smells like that surrounding the roots of laurels in the rocky hills behind my home in New Jersey. It's a slippery footing, and in many places we had to pull ourselves up by roots and lianas. How the ruins have survived the tentacles of this rankness of growth so many centuries is a mystery. Many haven't, of course. We found temple after temple, split by trees, the roof caved in, the gates filled with rubble. But at least four are more or less intact. One has fragments of rose-and-blue frescoes still clinging to its walls. Another still retains its intricately carved lintels. And a third has the center of its three doors blocked by the torso of a gigantic "king." The head of this stone figure has fallen and rolled to

a spot fifty feet below, where it has assumed an upright position. The Lacandons make a pilgrimage here every year, to see if the head of the statue is in its present position. Were it not, they say, the world would come to an end. One of them told Miguel: "But we're not afraid of the world's end. When that time comes, we'll be with all honest men [they never bring their women or mention them] in paradise, the place where men are without fever or consumption and have only two children."

From fragments revealed by Sanchez Vera and Miguel de la Cruz,[2] we were soon reconstructing the drama of Bonampak's discovery. Bonampak (Maya for "painted walls," a name suggested by Sylvanus Morley) remained a secret as long as the Lacandons had a chief. The last of these died in the early 1940s. In February of 1946, Lacandons took a party of Americans headed by Charles (Carlos) Frey to the site, but they missed the temple with the great frescoes. Then came Giles Healey, the American photographer for United Fruit, who on many earlier treks through Chiapas had compiled his own list of sites. He got along famously with the tribesmen. They showed him the murals. He photographed them in color, applying kerosene to the semi-opaque deposit of calcium carbonate which had protected them since their painting some time between A.D. 730 and 820 when classic Maya art was at its height. The kerosene brought out the colors and forms just long enough to permit flash photography. Painted on wet lime, and possibly a whole wall to a single sitting, since no joints show, the frescoes depict religious rites, bands of musicians, court scenes, battles in the jungle, triumphal parades with mutilated captives, and dance festivals. The colors are brilliant, and the handling of action is without precedent in its realism. In a flash, more was revealed of Maya culture than all the temples and sculptures had revealed. The Mayas grew in stature as artists, but no one would ever again describe them as pacific.

By the 1960s an airstrip had been hacked out of the jungle near Bonampak and visitors were flown in, but the murals had disintegrated. The place to see them is the National Museum of Archaeology in Mexico City, where painters have created an exact-scale replica of the three decorated chambers from sketches made on the spot with the aid of infrared and ultraviolet photographs.

Sanchez Vera, who accompanied Healey on several jungle trips, char-

[2] And later by Healey himself, whom I visited in California; though he is in no way to be held responsible for this version of what happened.

acterized the photographer as a chain smoker who carried a ham and a bag of dried beans in a sack over his shoulder. As he trudged through the jungle, with the Lacandons cutting a path ahead of him with their machetes, he would reach over his shoulder from time to time for food. "With his film," the young archaeologist told us, "Healey was generous. But his equipment was personal and sacred. A guide would sooner have touched the face of a Maya image than one of Healey's light meters or filters." The United Fruit Company (the American monopoly in Guatemala which the Communists opposed, to gain whatever popularity they had there under Arbenz) paid the expenses for Healey's various expeditions. But Healey's alliance with United Fruit could not have been, at most, more than a marriage of convenience. Like Maudslay, Maler and the others, he was an eccentric, a dedicated explorer with just the right gifts for the place and the time in which he made his epoch-making discovery.

Miguel de la Cruz is also a dedicated man. He ekes out a subsistence at Yaxchilán, thanks to the $150 a year the government allots him. He is proud of the ruins, knows every inch of them, and loves showing them off. His patch of corn, bananas, and sugar is across the Usumacinta, Guatemala being very possibly ignorant of his existence. Since every planeload into Agua Azul cost 400 pesos for gas alone, how did Miguel make out? Jaguar skins brought 175 pesos. "I bag them at night with a carbide lamp and the coffee spout." "The *what?*" "The coffee spout. I'll show you tonight when it gets dark." But that night, by the time we thought of it, the coffee spout was being put to more domestic uses, and we had to be content with a rank imitation of the way a coffee spout sounds when it's imitating the mating *tigre*.

THE LITTLE GRAND INQUISITOR AND THE DERAILED TRAIN
Our canoe trip up the Usumacinta from Yaxchilán was more eventful than our trip down. We were bucking the current, and without the skilled boatmen we would have capsized in the rapids a dozen times. We also encountered a variety of wildlife: several families of tiny duck; blue and white heron that waited until we approached to within twenty feet; a treeful of medium-size monkeys; flocks of tanagers, parakeets and macaws; and two large crocodiles sunning themselves in the shallows.

Back in Tenosique, we went fishing with Don Paco, and though neither of us had ever been on trolling terms with much more than bass and perch, we landed two twenty-five-pound tarpon in an hour. It must have gone to our heads, for soon we were negotiating for a quiver of Lacandon arrows, and that was almost our undoing. A small evil-looking man accosted us and demanded to see our identification. Resenting his tone, I asked to see his. Never make that mistake, traveler! In no time at all we were in the Immigration Office; José May (for such was his name) was glaring at us over a typewriter in which he was inserting six sheets of blue-and-white forms separated by carbons; and we had settled down to what was obviously going to be a long session. I thought of the railway clerk who had so exasperated Flandrau in 1908—"pausing now and then to lean and look at the ceiling as if in the throes of composing a sonnet." And Don, by the expression on his face, was thinking of our objective, Palenque, which we'd never see if José May decided we'd look better in jail than on the 4 A.M. train going west. He asked for our nationality.

"Americanos? From what country is that?" We responded again.

"Es-ta—dos U—ni-dos." He spelled out every letter of the hated words as he pecked them out fiercely (and as slowly as possible) on his Smith-Corona. The Inquisition had begun; and much as we may have been to blame for precipitating it, I couldn't help feeling that this xenophobia must be a by-product of the regime of the fanatical Garrido Canabál. It was that governor of Tabasco under Calles who had forced priests to marry within ninety days or quit the state, who had named his two sons Lucifer and Lenin, and who had been immortalized as the villain of Graham Greene's *The Power and the Glory*.

Seeing that my tourist card was in order, our inquisitor asked me to sign my name on a blank sheet of paper, ostentatiously covering the signature on the card to make it clear he didn't trust me. Then he turned to Demarest, who confessed that he had no papers with him.

"Ah-han!" José May leered. "No right to be in Mexico at all! How did you get here in the first place?"

I looked at Don apprehensively, fearing an outburst. He had been living in Mexico for years and loved the Mexicans so much he'd adopted one to augment his own family of four. He shifted his heavy frame in the wicker chair. His habitually ruddy face turned a shade redder. But he controlled himself. He explained that he had immigration papers, but that he didn't carry them about for fear of losing them. "We came here," he added hopefully, "on government tickets by courtesy of the Ministry of Tourism."

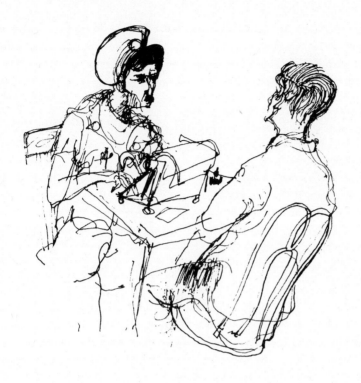

"Writers?" Señor May almost spat the word in his contempt. "And where are these alleged government tickets?"

We'd left them in our room, of course, but I seized the opportunity to inform Don Paco of our plight. I was given permission to fetch them. Don Paco had left his house a few minutes before in his car. His wife had no idea where he'd gone, but would send him to the rescue the moment he returned. At the official's office, meanwhile, the Grand Inquisitor had made a startling discovery. He had asked Demarest in turn to write his name on a blank sheet. After studying it for some time, his face lighted. Grabbing my tourist card he shook it under Don's nose triumphantly.

"So you make a false declaration!" he crowed. "You write 'Demarest' and the card says 'Rodman'!"

Don was trying to explain that we were two different people, when Don Paco arrived and prepared to share our vigil. By the time I got back with the plane tickets, Demarest explained that they wouldn't be needed. Our friend had embarked on a fresh tack. Every time Don explained that his papers were in Mexico, his tormentor would shake a pamphlet under his nose:

"The law says. . . . It says here perfectly clearly. . . . I know *nothing* about Mexico; we are in Tabasco. . . . Read for yourself what it says in the small type."

Technically, of course, he was right. One should travel with all one's papers.

"Where was it you say you live?"

"New Orleans," Don said.

"You mean—*Nueva Orleans?*"

That was too much for Don. "We pronounce it New Orleans," he snapped, "in New Orleans." I signaled him to calm down.

Quite possibly José May could have demanded that we return to the capital at once, or clapped us in jail, but probably Don Paco's disapproving presence prevented him from going so far. He compromised by standing Don against a wall where he pretended to check with a ruler (I noticed that he had the side with the figures turned away from him) the height Don had given him. If he'd had scales, he'd have weighed him. But after another hour, the filing of many more forms, and a veiled threat that we'd be deported the moment we arrived back in the capital, we were free.

I looked at Don Paco. His eyes had been lowered. In Mexico, with the revolution become official, a pervasive fear of soldiers and federal official-dom remains. But later, in a bar, a friend of Don Paco, who had witnessed the farce, exploded. "It's an outrage," he said, "a damnable outrage! My country *lives* on American tourism. Where would we be without it? And this is the way we treat you!" We protested that the fault had been ours and that we had always been treated with courtesy in Mexico; but later, in the train to Palenque, we yielded to the more human reaction—how to put that jackal, José May, in his place. Unfortunately, our one brilliant idea came too late. Don Paco had assured us that what the petty official really wanted was a *mordida*—a bite, a bribe. If we had given him one, with Don Paco as witness, we could have reported him to the Ministry of Tourism with some assurance that he would have been jacked out of that swivel chair. Not that the *mordida* doesn't remain a practice at every level, but that the Ministry is said to be doing its best to protect visitors from its more flagrant abuses.

I said "the train to Palenque," but the train never made it. Thirty

kilometers short of our destination, there was a crunch and a list to star-
board. Our "rapido" had jumped the tracks. Ten of the eleven passenger
cars were still on the rails, but the eleventh, as well as two cattle cars, an
oil tanker, the baggage car and the engine were lying on their sides in a
jumble of rotted ties in the jungle. The hundreds of native passengers were
resigned to their fate—rumor had it that another train would come to the
rescue and pull us back to Tenosique "in about ten hours"—but we were not
resigned. If we stayed here, we wouldn't see Palenque. . . .

First we tried to gain recruits for a forced march overland. Looks of pity,
as though we ought to have our heads examined—nobody wanted to leave
the scene of discomfort. We tried to rent a horse from an elderly peon who
rode by on one. "I must consult my father," he said, disappearing for good.
At the head of the train, a soldier informed us that a repair cab would arrive
shortly from up ahead, with ties to replace the half-mile of soggy splinters.

"Good!" I said to Don, "when he drops them, we'll hitch a ride ahead,
wherever he goes."

"Stupid Americans with their arrows and cameras!" I heard an unkind
civilian remark as I took snapshots of the damaged underpinnings.

But stupid or not, we were the only passengers to leave the wreck that
morning, and a few minutes later we were seated with the repair crew on
the gasoline-powered cab, enjoying a free ride up the wobbly tracks to Lacandon, the next station.

I stood watch over our bags while Don set out to canvas the village for
horses. Palenque, we were told, was some twenty-five kilometers farther
along and might be ridden to in three hours, though no one had in many
years. Reports were coming in that a salvage train was due from Palenque
any minute, and Don thought we ought to wait for it, but I pointed out that
even if it arrived in an hour, it would take another two to load those
sedentary citizens aboard flatcars, and perhaps another to double back to
Palenque. "Surely," I said, "we'll make it in three; we'll be the first to
get to the hotel, and to get out on another train—if there is one."

As it turned out, it took us four hours to ride to Palenque. The horses
were tiny, the saddles kept slipping off, and we were soon so blistered that
we had to stand up in the stirrups. But the rescue train never did come;
and by the time we were heading for Campeche the following day on the
eastbound track, the wreck was still there, and the passengers were still
waiting.

PALENQUE'S TRIUMPH OVER TIME

On his march to Guatemala and Honduras in 1525, Cortés passed within a few miles of the ruins of Palenque without suspecting their existence; they had been ruins for centuries even then, the great civilization that built them long forgotten. I had read the account of Stephens, who visited the site in the 'forties of the last century. Stephens had not been its discoverer—a French antiquarian, Dupaix, had visited Palenque a decade earlier—but Stephens was probably the first to appreciate its romantic beauty, and his traveling companion, the English artist Catherwood, embellished his account with excellent drawings of the Maya sculptures.

Their visit took place during the rainy season. They were devoured by mosquitoes. Their thirty or forty Indian porters refused to spend the night in the ruins, which were reputed to be haunted. Half the population of the village had just been swept off by cholera. Stephens himself became the victim of ticks and had to be carried out of Chiapas in a litter. But the exaltation of the place stayed with him:

> We lived in the ruined palaces of kings; we went up to their desolate temples and ruined altars; and wherever we moved we saw evidences of their taste, their skill in arts, their wealth and power. . . . We called back into life the strange people who gazed at us in sadness from the walls. . . . In the romance of the world's history, nothing ever impressed me more forcibly than the spectacle of this once great and lovely city, overturned, desolate, and lost; discovered by accident, overgrown with trees for miles around, it did not have even a name to distinguish it. Apart from everything else, it was a mourning witness to the world's mutations.

Nations melt
From Power's high pinnacle, when they have felt
The sunshine for a while, and downward go.

It was good to see Palenque in the eerie, ruined light. The jungle setting, the compactness of the temples, the devastating power and purity of the reliefs make a combination that Chichén Itzá with its range, Uxmal with its unity of design, and Yaxchilán with its inaccessible mystery cannot match. One feels that everything at Palenque reached perfection, and that with this thrilling achievement, this absolute aesthetic pitch, things had to fall apart.

"There," I remarked to Don as we stood amid the thunderheads on the peak of the Temple of Inscriptions, watching a tiny native woman draw water from the original aqueduct and disappear in the riot of "elephant ears" on the encroaching jungle's edge, "there goes the last Maya—precisely like the first, in her bare feet, white *huipil,* and pigtails, except that the tin pail would have been an earthenware jug."

But for the likes of her, or her prototype, what use had the aristocrats and sorcerers who built these architectural masterpieces? She planted the corn, bore and raised the children, perhaps carried some of the smaller building blocks. The male slaves carried the larger ones, including the five-ton plinth which our friend Ruz of Mérida raised with jacks and windlasses when he discovered the King's Tomb under this temple. When the worker ants weren't building for the celestial architects, they were providing the cannon fodder.

It was not difficult to imagine Palenque as it must have been. The priests cutting out hearts—but in moderation, this early—at the altars. The king reviewing his feathered division on the banks of the Otolum. And then—panic! A dispatcher rides in (or rather, is carried in by porters, because the pre-Columbians, amazingly, had domesticated no animals) to announce that Yaxchilán and Bonampak have fallen to the barbarians; and that Uxmal and Chichén in Yucatán, still mere aggregations of thatched barracks, have joined with the "primitive" Quichés from Guatemala and even talk of making an alliance with the savage nomads from central Mexico.

The shudder of panic, this first one, the sense that affluence and the convention of centuries of ritual count for more than resistance to aggression, set up its disintegrating rhythm throughout the whole civilization and its institutions. Perhaps it would be farfetched to suppose that the equivalents of minority rioting, pacifist demonstrations, and teach-ins by impulsive men of learning take place. But there is no doubt that the rhythm is accelerated by the hostility of nature. Hills denuded of trees have lost their topsoil and there is a chronic water shortage. There is also a sudden awareness that the men of god—with their claims to be on terms of intimate, daily communion with Chac, the provider of water—are presiding over a desert. Nor will these vibrations cease until the living trees grow through the dead walls, bringing them finally down, and the archaeologists pitch camp with their repair crews to make a safe and orderly attraction for the tourist.

Fortunately, the archaeologists who have worked at Palenque have not gone far with their restoration. Cropping the jungle around the ruins and keeping it cropped (for jungle moves in, almost perceptibly) was of course a necessity, but it has added greatly to the beauty of these hilltop temples, whose steep steps have yet to be excavated; it has provided them with soft, velvety bases, like so many exquisite funerary urns in a museum's cabinet.

In addition, Palenque has had allies in the elements. Limestone deposits have not only preserved many of the low reliefs in stucco but have added a lace fretwork to the portals: stalactites like marble icicles. Water has streaked the graying stone with superb greens and blacks. Emerald moss has filled the cracks. And finally an orange lichen (similar to the one that adorns Christophe's Citadel in Haiti) has covered many a shattered arch and crumbling vault with its magical coloration.

To the question of whether the great arts of pre-Columbian Mexico meant anything to anyone before the restless eclectics of our time, I quote the testimony of Albrecht Dürer, who in 1520 saw jewels and gold figurines which Moctezuma had sent to Cortés the year before. Cortés in turn had dispatched the treasure to Charles V. "These things," the great German artist wrote, "are so precious that they were valued at a hundred thousand gulden. But I have never seen in all my days what so rejoiced my heart. For I saw among them amazing artistic objects, and I marveled over the subtle ingenuity of men in these distant lands." (The Spaniards, more impressed by the gold's monetary value, promptly melted them down.)

For all that, it is difficult, if not impossible, for us to fathom the logic of these arts. What were the Mayans trying to say? The archaeologists tell us little. The pyramids at Chichén and Uxmal and Palenque were probably erected to mark the lapse of time between some remote event and the then present. That much the dated *stelae* indicate. But it isn't much. Apart from numbers, the written inscriptions have not been deciphered. Aldous Huxley, describing the mysteries of Copán, southeast of here on the Honduras-Guatemala border, had this to say about it: "Time is unbearable. To make it bearable, men transform it into something that is not time, that has the quality of space." But he adds: "What causes a people, or at any rate the thinking part of a people, to become as acutely time-conscious as the priestly mathematicians of the Maya Old Empire?" His answer is: a series of personal accidents. "A man is born to whom, for whatever reasons, time is an obsession. It also happens that he possesses the kind of abilities which enable him to solve his problem—the problem of the intellectual mastery and transformation of time—in comprehensible, quantitative terms. Furthermore, as luck will have it, he is in a position to influence his fellows."

It is an answer, but not *the* answer. The mystery remains. Best of all, the art remains. Nor do we have to be obsessed by time to be thrilled by it. The same qualities that appeal to us in Athens, in Chartres, in the Sistine, in the Hospicio, appeal to us here. Perhaps this is the *only* constant in variable history. The wars, the revolutions, the social institutions, the dates, and the names, are swept away. Art remains!

TEHUANTEPEC, CAMPECHE, QUINTANA ROO

Covarrubias, who wrote a rapturous book about the isthmus of Tehuantepec, once told me that I didn't like this part of the country because I had had to change all four of my tires in Juchitán. That may have been part of the reason, but there are others. The matriarchy of tall, haughty Tehuanas with ankle-length skirts, whom Diego Rivera glorified in the Education Ministry, is no longer to be seen—at least in the towns through which the Inter-American Highway passes. Salina Cruz, the port Porfirio Díaz built to capitalize on trans-isthmian traffic, was put out of business when the Panama Canal was opened in 1914; and its beach is a windblown desolation. Since it is now possible to drive between two of the most attractive cities in Mexico—Oaxaca and San Cristóbal—in a day, travelers rarely stop.

A few kilometers beyond Juchitán, Route 185 north now provides access by car to Campeche and Yucatán. For those who like to touch all bases, it is quite feasible to take an early morning dip in the Pacific (Salina Cruz), then jump in the car and have a late afternoon cooler in the Atlantic (Coatzacoalcos). But swimming aside, Coatzacoalcos, on Route 180 from Veracruz, is one of the few obtrusively ugly Mexican towns, oppressively hot under the sludge-dust of booming refineries.

To Ciudad Carmen and beyond, there is a 250-mile stretch where the road leapfrogs two rivers and brackish "Lake" Términos. Four ferries, in all, must be taken (in a high wind think twice about it) but Ciudad Carmen, a shrimping town renowned for its *camarones empanados*, is a lovely place to linger en route to Mérida via Campeche.

Campeche is better taken on the run. Capital of the province of the same name, it still has its original forts to guard the port against pirates, each turret dominated by a scavenger in black—*zopilotes juridicales?* In Campeche, water is conveyed from house to house in blue barrels slung between wheels and drawn by donkeys. And the colors of the houses, mel-

lowed to pastel by the salt spray, are attractive. But the museum has a hideous mural, combining the worst of Picasso and Tamayo—Exploitation and Ultimate Triumph of the Indian—and a glass case containing the bones, in foetal position, of a king of Jaina. "His name is unknown," says the label, "but he was 50 years old and measures 1 metre, 73 centimetres."

Sic transit . . .

Beyond Mérida, Route 180 terminates at Puerto Juárez in the territory of Quintana Roo. For those who like snorkeling and unspoiled seascapes, ocean ferries are available to the islands of Mujeres and Cozumel. For those who like untracked wilderness, Quintana Roo is an end in itself. Almost the entire province, down to Belize, is roadless, covered with scrub jungle, and virtually unexplored. Tulum, a spectacular Maya ruin overlooking the sea, was sighted by early Spanish navigators and then forgotten until Stephens came overland to it from Guatemala in 1842. An aerial survey by Lindbergh in 1929 disclosed other ruins. In 1958 a hardy young Frenchman, Michel Peissel, sailed but mostly *walked* to the Belize border, discovering many unmapped temples, and writing a fine account of his adventures; but (like Healey) Peissel may have to outlive a lifetime before the archaelogists admit him to their club. The interior of Quintana Roo is sparsely populated with the remnant of the Maya tribesmen who in 1847, and again in 1911, almost succeeded in driving the Mexicans out of Yucatán, and returning a part of the continent for the first time to its original owners.

INDIANS' LAST STAND: SAN CRISTOBAL

San Cristóbal las Casas, named for the Conquistadors' priest who became the Indians' fiery advocate and the first bishop of Chiapas, is still a frontier settlement—in the sense that Dodge or Virginia City once were. It is still the most *Indian* city in Mexico, and it it will *always* be the coldest place in the tropics north of La Paz, Bolivia. The women of the Chamula and Zinacantán tribes still pad into town on their leathery bare feet, carrying packs of firewood and babies on their backs, their black homespun *huipils* with rose stitching pulled over their mouths to keep the "consumptive" night air from their lungs. Their men, in white wool shorts and sandals, still come to the market to replace the black-banded flat straw hats with long pink tassels. Señor Humbres' "La Segoviana" still sells the best embroidered shirts, belts, leather bags, sandals and bronze knockers north of Guatemala. And at the pension "Español," three Indian seven-year-olds in woolen burnooses still build an aromatic fire of cedar chips in a corner of your room before you turn in, and another fire first thing in the morning. But when Bill Negron and I came through here in 1963 on our first trip to Guatemala, two things had changed since my last visit in 1956. "Pancho" Blom had died. And the Instituto Indigenista seemed to have abandoned the Indians.

Frans Blom was one of those old-time Americans—like Spratling, Fred Davis, Anita Brenner—who "went Mexican," and in the process saved a bit of Mexico that the Mexicans hardly knew they had. Between San Cristóbal and the Usumacinta River lies the untracked *Selva Lacandones*—The Forest of the Lacandons. Untracked, that is, by anyone but Healey and Frans Blom. Blom tracked it all, mapped it, made friends of the suspicious, miserable Lacandons. Indians from all over Chiapas brought him gifts, treasures dug from the ground—priceless sculptures and iron grave crosses, and with these he made of his handsome, ancient house a museum. I took Negron to see it, recalling the old man's hospitality, and asked an attendant what had happened to Gertrude Duby, the easygoing archaeologist's formidable German wife. He led us over to a box on the wall labeled "Voluntary Contributions" and said pointedly: "She's on her way back." Over the box, before we took flight, we read this much of a printed warning:

> In droves and in herds you come ringing my bell.
> My impulse is always to wish you in hell
> For my peace you disturb,
> My garden you trample . . .
> For all you took and you took and you took
> Leave something more than your name in my book.

Showing a color film he had taken of the Chamulas stamping out a blazing ritual field with their bare feet, Frans Blom had once said to me: "I'm glad I'll be dead when all the Indians are in overalls and all the tourists are in Indian costume." It hasn't happened yet, but a pall of hostility hung over the market place, and the village of Chamula, which was full of color and pride and friendliness in 1956, when the Institute was giving the Indians the feeling that their customs and crafts were worth preserving, had yielded to bureaucracy—and anti-gringoism. The door of that wonderful candle-lit church that had been jammed with worshipers kneeling in the pine needles, seven years before, was locked. A surly attendant (in overalls) impounded our cameras and handed us a form headed—"Voluntary Contributions." Bill gave him a peso and was promptly told that the entrance fee would be five. In Guatemala, we were soon to find out, there is no government of Indian-lovers to turn hot and cold. The Indian has been left alone, to survive the encroachments of business, modern "improvements" and tourism as best he can. He goes about his business, ignoring most interlopers, but responding to those who take a friendly interest, in a like spirit.

Vejron 65

4 GUATEMALA I: THE HIGHLANDS

FROM MEXICO there are two roads into Guatemala and its capital city of the same name. One is the northern or "highland" route that I am about to describe, a link (and at its beginning the worst link) in the Inter-American Highway. The other, a paved road all the way, but passing through less interesting country, parallels the Pacific, and will be described at the opening of Chapter 5, along with the "lowlands" it leads to. The highland route is for lovers of art and nature. The lowland route is for people with myopia, asthma or bad springs. Put another way, the first is for people prepared to savor mountains, lakes, costumes and ceremonial rites as spectacular as any on earth; the second is for people in a hurry.

EL TAPON AND SLUSH
Coming down through Comitán from San Cristóbal de las Casas, the paved Highway ends at the border. A little

more than a hundred miles of unpaved road now lies ahead, divided into two stretches. The first stretch, running from the border to the provincial capital of Huehuetenango, is somewhat longer and in poorer shape than the second, and is known as *El Tapón* (The Plug). The shorter stretch runs south from Huehue (pronounced way-way) to the paved highway, eastward into the heart of Guatemala. There are various theories as to why El Tapón has proved unpavable, but there is no doubt at all that the Highway's engineers blundered in electing to build their road along the Selegua River's steep canyon, clinging to the base of its unstable cliff. Even in the dry season, pebbles and small rocks bounce off the dusty road. In the rainy season, periodic landslides occur and the road is at times impassable. The mountain, we were told, is "young," geologically speaking, and so in a constant state of shifting. Volcanoes abound. Tacaná and Tajumulco, Guatemala's highest, lie fifty kilometers south. Under favorable conditions the El Tapón stretch may be driven in three hours, but Negron and I had an introduction to a Dr. Harold Graves who runs a clinic at La Democracia, so we stopped in that village for lunch.

And what a lunch! Dr. Graves is a Seventh Day Adventist missionary who has made his conversions via kindness and medicare, and he resembles Dr. Schweitzer in other respects, including a capacity to make the natives work for him, and a lordly contempt for sanitation; but his aesthetic tastes are less developed. During our lunch—a remarkable, slushy concoction of locally grown bananas, pineapple, papaya, lemon and honey—the good doctor's mother thumped out "Onward, Christian Soldiers," "Rock of Ages" and other hymns on a spinet that hadn't been tuned in the four years since Graves moved in, while over her bobbing head a color reproduction of the familiar academic painting of "Jesus Praying" looked down upon us in saccharine piety. There is no doubt that Dr. Graves found himself an earthly paradise in this jungle with its rushing river, and we marveled at the ingenuity with which he has diverted the opaline waters half a mile up-stream into a canal that *crosses back over the river* in a wooden trough suspended by cables, and then flows through several hundred feet of em-banked ditch, traversing the flower and fruit gardens and aviaries to a miniature waterfall where a primitive turbine supplies the clinic with all the electricity it needs. But we marveled, too, that no one seemed to be *enjoying* this earthly paradise. Hedonists like Negron and me at once conceived the idea of taking an inner-tube and floating down the whole waterway from the river to the power station. But Dr. Graves' two Filipino assistants discouraged us. No one had ever gone swimming here, they con-fessed, even in the river itself, and such levity on the premises might dis-courage the Indians' hard-won capacity to work. "The clinic is at least self-supporting," they told us. "We have made eighty-six conversions in these four years." But in the next breath they confessed that their consuming hope was to return to the Philippines—their bid for the dubious Nirvana of American citizenship under the quota having been frustrated. Why? "We don't belong here. We want to bring the faith to *our* people."

HUEHUETENANGO, SAN FRANCISCO EL ALTO, MOMOSTENANGO

Huehuetenango is the nexus of four roads. The one we entered by limps on, and on, terminating finally in the highland city of Cobán, far to the east; this is a country of great splendor, and we would be traversing much of it later on. The road south, already mentioned, hooks into the paved highway to the capital. The road north leads to the wild mountain-country of Todos Santos, and a little beyond. Todos Santos is not quite as hard to reach as in 1950 when Maud Oakes went back and forth on muleback, composing her pungent account of primitive Indian life, *Beyond the Windy Place*. Now-adays, buses and trucks with four-wheel drive go back and forth to Todos Santos daily; but there is no inn, and it is cold at 8,200 feet, and at the pass (the "windy place," 11,200 feet) there are sometimes snow flurries. Now as then the men wear pants striped vertically red and white; there are whitewashed houses with high, Chinese-looking thatched roofs, each with its sweat-bath; apple and peach trees sprawl over the stone walls and around the Maya ruins nearby; roosters hang by their feet on All Saints' Day and have their heads yanked off by horsemen galloping by; *chimans* and *brujos* (witch doctors, good and bad) vie for the sacrifices of the faithful; and the eternal Guatemalan conflict between *ladinos* and Indians smoulders apace.

In Huehuetenango, things are much more subdued, and a mile out of town, at the ruins of Zaculeu, the Maya past is so subdued (thanks to the United Fruit Company) that it hurts. Zaculeu is the most sizable pre-Columbian ruin of the Guatemala highlands, but by the time the American fruit company got through tidying it up in 1946–49, planing off the jagged stones, whitewashing the columns and truncated pyramids, and putting sheep to work to crop the surrounding fields as close as a putting green, the site looks as sterile as any exhibit at a New York World's Fair. The little museum, with some good examples of late Quiché-Maya pottery and bones, is more interesting.

Huehuetenango is a clean city without charm, graced by a shocking-pink town hall with fairy-tale towers. It has an excellent small hotel, the Zaculeu, with a menu reading: "Breakfast—Complete; Lunch—4 courses; Dinner—Enough," which sums up the abundance very accurately. We played tennis with the proprietors, Guillermo and Erica Tornoe, and then spent a fascinating evening hearing about Guatemala's ill-fated German colony which, until 1941, was the most enterprising and prosperous part of the Guatemalan economy. When the war came, Tornoe told us, he and all the other Guatemalans of German ancestry were contributing money to the various Hitler fronts. By 1943 the United States was fed up trying to keep tabs on them all and removed them *en masse* to a camp in Texas. Those that wanted to were then permitted to transfer to Germany in exchange for American prisoners of war. Tornoe wanted to return to Guatemala (although the Guatemala government had long since expropriated the exiles' rich estates) but was told he had entered the U.S. "illegally—without the proper papers"(!). He didn't get back to his place of birth until 1948. He showed me a little book printed in Stuttgart in 1938—*Deutschland in der Alta Vera Paz: 1888–1938.* Beautifully printed, and documented with typical Teutonic thoroughness, it listed the family connections in Germany of every member of the Club, originally established in Cobán, with such touching highlights as the visit of the crew of the armored cruiser *Emden,* and the unfurling of the swastika flag over the clubhouse. "By special agreement," Tornoe told us, "every German in Guatemala retained his German citizenship and so did his children. Of course," he added disarmingly, "it worked both ways: Guatemalans in Germany could do the same." . . . If any!

The road south from Huehue finishes its unpaved course in three hours of dusty driving-time at another four-way intersection, San Cristóbal Totonicapán. Here are two unforgettable sights. At the crossroads, a hot spring from the mountainside has been channelled into an oblong tub, or *pila,* perhaps thirty feet long. In the blue, sudsy waters, dozens of peasant women wash their clothes *and* themselves at all hours of the day; nor does the soap seem to bother thousands of minnows. This is the first place in western Guatemala where the traditional costumes of the Indian women may be seen in all their glory and diversity, and Negron and I were busy with our cameras and sketchpads for an hour. The second visual wonder, looking westward, is the view of the town with its magnificent colonial Franciscan church, and the Salamá River winding southward through the valley, with the volcano of Santa María, far beyond Quezaltenango, closing the distance. It is such a view as the Italian painters of the Quattrocento delighted in as background for a sumptuous Madonna or the reverse of a formal portrait.

A fifth road (dirt, but passable in all weather) meanders northeast from this crossroads to the hill towns of San Francisco el Alto and Momostenango. The view from San Francisco, a ten-minute drive, is even more staggering— especially if one applies to the parish priest for permission to climb to the church's roof, from which the town's Friday market, one of the busiest and most colorful in Guatemala, presents an expanse of white sun-shades like the wings of doves. Momostenango, at least an hour farther north over a deteriorating road, boasts three attractions, though two of them are not easy to come upon. The festival of the Eight Monkey (New Year by the Tzolkin-Quiché calendar, which has 260 days) took place in 1965 at midnight on Friday, April 2, ending Sunday noon. It took us four months to find this out. The following festival should start at midnight of December 17; and in 1967, presumably, on September 2. Catch it if you can. The festival attracts as many as 20,000 Indians from all over the country. After a perfunctory Christian ceremony the first night, worshipers repair to Little Broom, west of the town, where they make offerings to the *chimans* and burn *copal* incense before piles of broken pots that accumulate over the years. At nightfall, the faithful move on to Big Broom in the hills beyond, where more prayers to Dios Mundo (God of the World) are chanted. Much *aguardiente* (raw rum) is consumed, to heighten the sense of fraternity and to loosen prophetic tongues.

Momostenango's other two attractions are available any day, but observing and photographing one of them, mixed nude bathing and blanket washing in the hot springs at Rio Paúl, a mile north of town, is not always appreciated. The great soft wool blankets for which Momo is justly celebrated are best seen at the Sunday market, hung from every balcony in the picturesque square, and spread (sometimes still wet, to show that the colors won't run) on the cobblestone streets, where trucks and buses frequently roll over them. Six dollars to eight dollars is a good price for a blanket, ten dollars to twelve dollars for an exceptionally fine one, but prices in the capital, if one is prepared to bargain in Spanish, are about the same.

QUEZALTENANGO: WHERE IT ALL BEGAN

Back at the San Cristóbal Totonicapán crossroads, a very short drive on the southwest fork leads into Quezaltenango, Guatemala's second city. It was near here early in 1524, that Cortés' burly, red-headed twenty-eight-year-old lieutenant, Pedro de Alvarado, swept into Guatemala from western Mexico with 135 horsemen, 300 Spanish footsoldiers and a scattering of Aztec or Tlaxcalan mercenaries. Up the steep gorge from Zunil trudged the armored Conquistadors, dragging their four cannon and sending out scouts to the leaders of the several million Indians, demanding that they give up their "sovereignty, sodomy and human sacrifice" and acknowledge the Catholic Church and the Spanish Crown. The Indians were badly divided among the Quiché, Cakchiquel and Tzutujil "nations," who had been fighting each other in Guatemala since the Maya fade-out six centuries before. In 1524 the Quichés, based in Utatlán thirty miles to the northeast, were the strongest and most warlike tribe, and their chief, Tecúm Umán, elected to fight.

The chief sent an advance-guard of six thousand warriors, clothed in cotton quilting, feathers, and turtle-carapace, into the Zunil pass; but instead of rolling boulders down on the clogged invaders or ambushing them by night, they proceeded to signal their advance in broad daylight with conch-shell trumpets and daemonic drumming. The Indians' wooden swords were edged with volcanic glass, their javelins and arrows were tipped with stone, and their blowguns fired poisoned darts. Against the crossbows, arquebuses, cannon and tempered steel of the Europeans, they were helpless. The horsemen, whom they took for centaurs, terrified them. And (as in Cortés' case five years before) the myth of the white god Quetzalcoatl's vengeful return disarmed them psychologically. They were already referring to their blond adversary as *Tomatiúh* (The Sun).

At Olintepeque on the Rio de Sangre north of Zunil, the decisive battle took place. Tecúm Umán was slain, his army of thirty thousand routed, and Alvarado continued eastward to complete piecemeal the conquest of the demoralized three nations. Padre Las Casas, the pro-Indian priest who came to Guatemala shortly after, from Santo Domingo, summed up what followed from the Indians' point of view:

> Alvarado and his brothers, together with others, have killed more than four or five million people in the fifteen or sixteen years from 1524 to 1540 and they continue to kill or destroy those who are still left. They have destroyed and devastated a kingdom more than one hundred leagues square, one of the happiest in the way of fertility and population in the world.
>
> It was his [Alvarado's] custom when he went to make war on some town or province to take with him as many of the Indians as he could to fight against the others, and as he led ten thousand to twenty thousand and gave them nothing to eat, he allowed them to eat the Indians they captured, and so a solemn butchery of human flesh took place in his army, where in his presence children were killed and roasted. They would kill a man only to eat his hands and feet, which were considered the best bits.

Quezaltenango was named after the *quetzal* bird that once abounded here, the green-tailed trogon that is the freedom symbol of modern Guatemala, as in times past it had been identified with Quetzalcoatl, the Indians' culture hero. The city nestles at the top of the pass. Violence has been its climate down the centuries; and great beauty. Stephens came here in 1840, just after the city and province had declared their independence in support of the great liberal leader from Honduras, Francisco Morazán—"the best man in

Central America." Morazán had promised to break the power of the Church and liberate the Indians, but the Indians rallied behind the fanatic illiterate, Rafael Carerra, and as a result reestablished their serfdom for at least another century. By the time Stephens arrived, Carerra had already taken the eighteen foremost men of Quezaltenango into the plaza and executed them. The American traveler saw what he described as a "whirlwind of fanaticism," daily parades of Indians in "frantic fervor" beside images of Christ smeared with blood, and in the background "the rent volcano constantly emitting smoke," and its creeping lava field "which, if it had taken its course toward the city, would have buried it like Herculaneum and Pompeii."

Forty-two years later (1902), Santa María *did* destroy the city. An entire side of the twelve-thousand-foot cone blew out, hurling white-hot boulders as far as forty miles away into Mexico. People were crushed or smothered in the houses they fled to, and for weeks after the cataclysm men walked about with dishpans over their heads. Out of this infernal labor was born a new volcano, Santiaguito, on the slopes of the old, and the Indians, in respect for its "mother," called it "Niño Jesús." Santiaguito belches fire and smoke to this day, and Jorge Bonifaz, proprietor of the Pension Bonifaz, Central America's best-run middle-size hotel, with a cuisine second to none, takes guests on a midnight tour of the fireworks at the crater's rim.

But an attraction surpassing this in Jorge's plans for the future is Fuentes Georginas—and he is right. To get to this hot spring high on the slope of Zunil volcano, one must drive down the unpaved road through the famous pass as far as the village of Zunil on the Salamá River. This in itself is a voyage of unparalleled beauty. Jungles crowd the mountain slopes, the summits wreathed in clouds. Almolonga, halfway, has hot springs of its own, and beautiful costumes. Zunil has everything. Beds of watercress in the deep gorge. Every kind of fresh vegetable on the sloping, terraced riverbank. High stone walls shaded with calla lilies. Every house of adobe or wood freshly painted, and roofed with orange tiles. A dreambridge of stone. A golden-pink cathedral. Men with long wooden paddles flinging water on their onion- and carrot-patches. Women robed in royal purple to their ankles, their heads wound in multi-colored silk *rupas*, with blue folded towels above to steady the red earthenware pots which they fill at the fountain facing the church.

Continuing through Zunil reluctantly, we turned right and began to
circle the volcano on a one-way track, ever ascending. Rock and jungle to
the left, a fearsome chasm with steam spouting from fissures down its
sides to the right. Not a human being in sight. By the time (forty minutes)
we reached Fuentes Georginas at the road's end, clouds had enveloped us,
and in the dusk we spotted with some difficulty the emerald-green waters in
a cliffside basin. Getting *into* that 110° bath is more difficult than finding it.
Anyone foolhardy enough to dive would probably die of shock. We let
ourselves in ever so gingerly and then lay on our backs, floating, gasping
for breath.

Suddenly from the road ten feet above, a harsh voice broke the stillness,
"Out! . . . Out! . . . Out!" and from the murk of clouds appeared a
witch, complete with broom, shaking it. "It is absolutely forbidden," she
croaked in Spanish, "to swim here without your underwear shorts!"

"Si, señora!" we said, smiling up at her, and much too enervated to move a muscle. Bill in his idiomatic Spanish added: "See you in a little while up there where the calla lilies grow."

This was the witch's hut that we had already seen and thought deserted at the end of the road, where separate streams of clear water, yellow, pink, black and green converge. Climbing out and dressing, we knocked on her door and were admitted to the single circular room, a fire in the middle, and the eaves black with a thousand stalactites of soot. She was all smiles now, and offered us bits of goat cheese on black bread. She also conducted us to a crumbling two-story shack that serves as "hotel" for those interested in "taking the cure." Two remarkable signs dangle from the porch. "Be patriotic!" says one; "Pay for your bath!" Says the other: "This pool was flagstoned by General Ubico, but the Chivos [citizens of Quezaltenango] didn't think much of it."

CHICHICASTENANGO

The Inter-American Highway east from San Cristóbal Totonicapán passes close to Nahualá on its way to another north-south fork—north to Chichicastenango, south to Sololá and Lake Atitlán. Nahualá is not to be missed, for although gone are the days when liquor could not be sold and *ladinos* (who sell it to the Indians in order to exploit them) were chased out, Nahualá is far enough off the Highway to have escaped the main flow of tourism, and sufficiently lacking in such obvious attractions as big fiestas and imposing works of art to have preserved its costumes and character intact. Like Zunil, Nahualá is still unspoiled, and like Zunil, it will probably be *ladino*-ized in a decade.

Tourism has actually *saved* the marvels of Chichicastenango, at least a great many of them. Chichi is the most famous of Guatemala's all-Indian towns, and deservedly. But so much has already been written about it, and so few are likely to pass it up, that I shall not describe it in detail here.

One reason Chichi has been saved is that fifty years ago an enlightened and courageous priest, Padre Ildefonso Rossbach, befriended the Indians, won their confidence, and instilled in them a conscious pride in their customs and artistry. In consequence, when leaders of the *cofradías* (the religious brotherhood that governs an Indian town's ceremonial pagan-Christian rites) visited the capital to protest against *ladino* trespassing, General Ubico heeded them. But the Mayan Inn has been another savior of Chichi's barbaric charm. Furnished tastefully from a monumental private collection of Guatemalan antiques, and insisting that its staff of servants dress in their own authentic town-costumes, this unique luxury hotel has contributed to the general pride in keeping things as they are—at least outwardly.

The ideal time to visit Chichi is for the pre-Christmas festival of Santo Tomás, the town's patron saint. At 10:30 A.M. on the 21st, the red-canopied images of St. Thomas, St. Joseph and St. Sebastian cross the jammed square between the two high, white churches, on the steps of which *chimans* continuously chant as they swing their smoke-wreathed censers. Mirrors attached to the velvet canopies, as in pre-Columbian times, reflect the sun. Rockets, some but not all in metal mortars, explode. And as the procession approaches the larger church, dancers, masked to represent Alvarado with blond curls and sweeping mustachios, give way, and acrobats at the end of ropes swinging around a pole, come down, and the resplendent twenty-foot-high images are borne aloft to the three portals. Now on a long wire from the belfry descends *Tsijolaj*, a tiny figure of a man on a horse, riding up and down, up and down, never quite reaching earth or heaven. Mysterious symbol! . . . perhaps a counter to the humiliating Dance of the Conquest, in which Alvarado always triumphs and Tecúm Umán is always slain?

For those who do not like to see Christianity and paganism thus happily mixed, it might be said that it is easier to see an all-pagan ceremony at

Chichi than an all-Catholic one, and the place to see it is across the *barranca* behind town and past the mask-makers' workshops. Here on a high hill stands the *ídolo*, called Pascuál Abáj, and here—to a consumption of *aguardiente* that surpasses even the phenomenal intake in the town proper— chickens are sacrificed and the *brujos* ply their magical trade.

There is a swimming pool in a very deep gorge to the right of the Quiché road, very hard to get to, and this too is worth the walking time.

Crossing the main Highway again at Los Encuentros, and continuing south, the good dirt road passes through Sololá. This is an important market center with distinctive costumes including the famous braided bat-wing jackets and black and white knitted bags; and a very beautiful nearby waterfall, the Cascada de San Buenaventura. But already glimpses of the great lake far below usurp the senses, and one hurries through lesser wonders to get to it. . . .

THE MOST BEAUTIFUL LAKE IN THE WORLD

Stephens was an obsessive volcano-climber, and he had his blind spots— nowhere in those two volumes of acute observations of the Middle America of 1839–41 is there a single mention of the extraordinary *clothes* the Indians wear—but though he found no ruins in the central highlands to make him stop anywhere more than a day or two, Atitlán did give him pause. "There were no associations connected with this lake," he wrote, "and until lately we did not even know it by name; but we both agreed that it was the most magnificent spectacle we ever saw."

Stephens passed along the legends that the lake—surrounded by volcanos and itself occupying an ancient crater—is bottomless and has no outlet; but he was too much of a pragmatic outdoorsman to accept the local notion that the waters were too cold to swim in. After having a swim himself, he sat and watched "Mr. Catherwood supported by his life preserver without taking any exercise."

"Mr. Negron," I said one morning at sunrise to my latter-day Catherwood, as we stood by the Hotel Monterrey's dock, "would you mind lying out there in your life-preserver for a few hours so that I may observe your symptoms?" But this latter-day artist was looking inward rather than out-ward, and put one finger over his lips.

"If *you* think this lake is necessarily nature's most magnificent spectacle," he whispered, "just step behind this hedge with me a moment and watch what's coming out of the Monterrey."

I could imagine what was coming. We had already christened the buxom blond sixteen-year-old German girl who was our fellow-guest "Brunhilda," but as I joined the sneaky artist in his blind I suggested that "Susannah" might be a more appropriate nickname.

"Watch it!" he said. "Here she comes."

We held our breaths as down the garden path, barely contained in her bikini, sped "Brunhilda," hit the water in a perfectly flat dive, leaving a boiling wake behind her as she headed for Volcanos Atitlán and San Pedro across the lake. I was speechless but Negron, perhaps recalling his Navy service, finally closed his mouth and said:

"It's like—it's like the launching of the carrier *Forrestal!*"

By this time "Brunhilda" had executed a sweeping turn and was climbing ashore.

"Was it cold?" we asked her weakly.

She gave us a Wagnerian contralto laugh, snapping her bath towel: "Eets coo-king!"

Of all the hotels at Panajachel, the resort village on the huge lake's northern shore, the Monterrey is the cheapest; but it is also, along with the luxury Tzanjuyú, the closest to the water. When Stephens and Catherwood came to Panajachel they camped "at some hot springs, so near the edge that the waves ran over the spring." Presumably these are the springs at the base of the cliffside home the American photographer, George Holton, has built; and we had already bathed in them. Panajachel's art colony is dominated, depending on which of them happens to be there, by Holton and the architect-water colorist Pat Crocker, who helps run the "Casa del Carmen" gift shop in Antigua. Holton took us in his outboard to nearby Santa Catarina, one of the dozen Cakchiquel and Tzutuhil villages that border the lake, and later on to the most famous of them, Santiago Atitlán, directly across.

Every one of the villages has its distinctive costume, but that of Santiago is the most spectacular. The women, almost always to be found at their hand looms, wear long red skirts, white-and-purple striped *huipils* with intricate embroidery, a fringed red and blue *rebozo*, and a headband of embroidered silk in six different colors wound in the hair to resemble a halo. Climbing the walled "streets" of black volcanic rock with brown water jugs on their heads, or bargaining daily in fierce whispers at the marketplace, these women are an unforgettable sight, tall, beautiful and of

majestic carriage. The strange, lumplike mound (Cerro de Oro) across the
bay is thought to contain the treasure of the Tzutujil capital that Alvarado
destroyed, and the Indians have been known to shovel back at night what
archaeologists have hazarded to dig out by day. Coffee *fincas* far up the
slopes of the volcanos provide seasonal labor when the weaving, duck
hunting, fishing, and crabbing fail to feed hungry mouths.

I came back to Santiago in April, with my friend Jorge Ibarra, Guatemala's leading naturalist who heads the Museum of Natural History, and a
Dutch cameraman for BBC, Nils Halbertsma, to see the strange ceremony
of the *Maximón*. Every year during Holy Week only, the image of this
Judas (who is somewhat confused with Saint Jude—and with Alvarado) is
brought out of the house of the *cofrade* assigned to his service. The glass
coffin under a very African crucifixion with grinning skull is illuminated
by candlelight. Aromatic yellow-flowering herbs (*Oja de Santa Apolinaria*)
hang from the smoky eaves, interspersed with red gourds, huge balls of
paper trash, and sausages. Amid the yellow tapers, pine needles cover the
black stone floor.

Dressed like every other male in Santiago in mauve-striped pants, but
sporting a shiny new pair of *ladino* shoes, three felt hats, and a foot-long
cigar, the *Maximón* emerges from the *cofrade*'s house at 1 P.M. Promptly,
too! As he was about to be carried across the threshold on his keeper's
shoulders, there was a quick checking of wrist watches. No . . . only 12:57,
and back he went. When he finally did cross into the sunlit world, his
carrier, who had been lying near him on the floor, perhaps drunk with
aguardiente, banged him so many times against the thatched overhang that
he lost all three hats. There was a tittering in the crowd waiting to see him
emerge, and then they fell behind him. "What does he signify?" Nils asked
the *cofrade* at this point. "Alvarado," was the answer. "He's a bad spirit—
but he can do good if you treat him right." He pointed to the dark area
above the ridgepoles in the sacred chamber. "That's where all the old
Maximóns go." No one, we heard later, except the *chiman* who puts them
together, is permitted to know what's inside a *Maximón*.

Amid the funereal wails of sax and trumpet, and a steady roll of drums,
the *Maximón* proceeded rapidly through the streets now, his bearers almost
charging. Why was he going to the Municipal Building, we asked. "To
cover up (whitewash) our difficulties with the government," was the answer.
First he was set up facing the church, while the thirty bearers who accom-

panied him decorated the altar with flowers and fruit. Then he was placed in a small outside Moorish-style chapel—built for him some years ago when a *padre* refused him the church, and was almost killed for refusing. There he was tied with strangling ropes by his neck to a straight square pole—aggressively tied, we thought—where he would stay until Good Friday's parade when he is returned to the *cofrade*'s, and his "grave" in the attic.

At one point, and on account of the wind apparently, two Indians came up with an old Turkish towel and two safety pins and thoughtfully bound up the *Maximón*'s exposed neck. "*Now* I've seen everything," said the phlegmatic Dutchman as we headed back to the capital via San Lucas Tolimán and Patzún.

COBAN, AND THE ADVENTURE OF THE DISPLACED PAINTER'S MOTHER
There are four ways of getting to Cobán, the Germanic capital of the Alta Verapaz, and all but one of them are interesting. To fly there, weather permitting—which it almost never does—is dull. Cobán is in the clouds, and so is the plane. The most interesting route is the longest, continuing north from Chichicastenango as far as Sacapulas and Cuñén, and then striking east 130 kilometers by way of Uspantán and San Cristóbal Verapaz. This is a dirt road but not a bad one, and though it takes all day from Chichi, passes through many places of unspoiled beauty and interest. The ruins of Utatlán, for example, are just outside of Santa Cruz del Quiché, and here it is easy to appreciate the thoroughness with which Alvarado razed the Quichés' stronghold.[1] Half an hour's driving time farther north, San Pedro Jocopilas is a lovely town with a commanding view of a broad valley, and two hours beyond that lies Sacapulas on the Chixoy River, a tributary of the great Usumacinta flowing past the Petén and on into Mexico. Sacapulas specializes in salt and candy—we watched our own purchase of the latter being stretched between trees and then patterned on woven *petates*—and has one of the most interesting churches in Guatemala. A few miles north of Sacapulas, a branch road leads to Nebáj, Cotzál, and Chajul, villages as primitive as Todos Santos and as surrounded by untouched ruins. The main road continues east for another four hours past Cuñén and through Uspantán to San Cristóbal, where a small, deliciously

[1] Among the desolate accumulation of overgrown tumuli and fire-blackened walls surrounded by deep gorges is a pathetic little sign saying "This is the ballcourt where the victorious Quichés celebrated their great victories."

cold lake provides just what the dusty traveler needs to ride into Cobán, half an hour further, refreshed and alert.

Cobán may also be reached by road from Lake Izabal,[2] but it was by the third route (which I do not recommend), driving east from the capital and then branching north at El Rancho through Salamá and Tactíc, that I came to it first. The circumstances were unusual. An Italian journalist, Tarcisio Tomasini, and a photographer from *El Imparcial*, Raúl Gonzales, wanted to round out the story of a celebrated modern painter living in Germany, Nan Cuz Schaefer, who had been born in this region and taken to Germany as a child by her German father; she was expected to return in triumph next summer, as a guest of the government, to the country she paints "out of her racial subconscious." The idea was to track down her peasant mother and find out whether mother and daughter had kept in touch. A four-wheel drive Jeep was the contribution of Jorge Ibarra and his wife, Amparito; and I was taken along as a fifth passenger for the ride, though it soon became apparent that only I knew how to handle this vehicle—a skill I was soon to regret possessing.

It was a rough but pleasant trip of six hours until we reached Tucurú (Cakchiquel for "owl") where Nan Cuz' mother was supposed to live. The drive along the Polochíc River from Tamahú had been especially exciting. High mountains, wreathed in mist, loomed over both sides of the narrow valley, their flanks glistening with the myriad greens of banana and castor bean, pine and giant fern. Clusters of orchids hung from *ceibas*, brandishing their red daggers. Yellow-flowering *chacté* and red-flowering *chiltoté* seemed but earthly extensions of the birds that flew between them, *montezumas* and gold-black Guatemalan orioles. And the native Kekchi women in their blue skirts and wine-dark *huipils* were carrying bundles of daisies and calla lilies on their heads, their necks supporting "breastplates" of Peruvian silver coin. Through chasms hung with lianas rushed the turquoise river, now filling deep pools, now crashing into boulders and sending white spray as high as the road. The stones of the crumbling churches were covered with an orange lichen so brilliant that the walls seemed to tremble in the sun. And on the verandas of the thatched huts with their high pitched roofs from which smoke rose to mingle with the clouds, hung pyramids of yellow tapers suspended by their wicks. Only the men, with their long machetes in leathern scabbards, bent over under the immense packs hung from the

2 See Chapter 5.

tumplines across their foreheads, seemed out of key with this efflorescence, reminders of the centuries of subjugation. But in Tucurú no one remembered Filomena Cuz.

No one until an old man came forward and offered to guide us into the high mountains behind the town where, he said cheerfully, "she should still be living." She was—but I never thought we'd make it alive. Our guide squeezed in, directed us through a cut in the wall, and then we began to climb on a rutted cow-track in the cliffside, never wider than the Jeep. I was driving in low-low now. At every hairpin turn—and there were dozens— I had to go backward and forward four to six times, pitched at such an angle I could never see the hood, and knowing that a matter of inches separated us at each switch from a drop of a thousand feet into the chasm below. To make it worse, we were soon enveloped in clouds with visibility less than ten feet, and the footing turned into slippery red mud.

By the time we reached the *finca* on the mountaintop I was in a cold sweat—aud so were my frightened passengers, who had been kind enough to offer me no advice during our ordeal. Filomena, a portly Indian woman in Kekchi dress, came to the gate to greet us, and showed us recent photographs of her beautiful daughter, with whom she had been in close touch for twenty years. But what really made us forget our ascent were two pretty little orphaned Indian girls Filomena had been caring for, one with a shepherd's crook. I gave this one a fifty-cent silver piece and told her to share it with her sister. The rest of the time we were there I caught glimpses of the two in the garden, passing the coin back and forth between them, and smiling every time they could catch my eye. The trip down the mountain was a breeze.

Cobán is a city of many attractions—most of them out of town. The church on the central plaza isn't much, and directly in front of it is a hideously ugly bandstand with off-center circular platforms connected by spidery staircases. Don Coleman, the Peace Corps operative here, calls it "The Tortilla Smasher." There are two good little hostelries, the Monja Blanca and the Posada, the latter enriched by a fine patio with a *jacaranda* in which sits a *guacamayo* with two feet of red tail-feathers and a gorgeous blue and yellow breast. The Calvario church on a hill overlooking the city is the place to go for a stunning view of the rich valley. A giant stone stairway leads up to it. Pagan altars with smoking copal are in the balustrade posts all the way up. I was lucky to find a leaden sky building up over the mountains, for this gave me a photograph of Cobán that somewhat resembled El Greco's mystical "View of Toledo."

Coleman, who accompanied us to the Calvario, is supposed to be teaching the Indians how to build co-ops, but says this makes little sense since they think in terms of family rather than group activity. Instead he's teaching them to grow cauliflower and asparagus rather than the traditional corn and beans. "At least they can sell these for cash. As soon as the Americans leave them with their complicated co-ops, the co-ops will fall apart." I asked him why he was learning Kekchi. "Because I'm coming back to Guatemala to work in education when my term here is up. Kekchi is the third most widely spoken *lengua* in the country.[3] 260,000 still speak it. Eighty per cent of the people in the Alta Verapaz speak nothing else." I asked him about Indian-*ladino* relations and he laughed. "The *ladinos* over there in San Pedro Carchá—which has the second largest *municipio* in the country— tried to stop a religious procession recently. The Indians went back to their villages in the hills and returned with their machetes. The procession went on as scheduled!" As with most of the Peace Corps boys who are idealistic and in love with the Indian, the Director's recent decision to re-orient in the direction of the Pacific-slope *ladinos* is distasteful. The argument is that the Indian doesn't want change, that the "rising middle class" holds the key to needed social reform. "Of course they don't want change!" said Coleman. "They have something good and they know it. Why not build the future on that? After all, they *are* the majority. *Ladinos?* You start with nothing and you'll end up with nothing."

GUATEMALA CITY AND ANTIGUA

I left the paved Inter-American Highway, diverging for Cobán, back at the Chichicastenango-Atitlán cutoff. Continuing east along the highway toward the capital, the next stop—not to be missed, because it is one of the few roadside restaurants in Middle America, and probably the only good one— is the restaurant Katók (Cakchiquel for "welcome"). Built in Swiss-chalet style, founded, operated, and stocked from his own nearby farm by Paulino Jarquín, Oregon-educated Nicaraguan of great enterprise, Katók is at Kilometer Marker 87 about halfway between Quezaltenango and the capital. Besides the excellent food, it has two attractions. It employs a family combo unique in the world, the "Arco-Irish Infantíl," a marimba, bull fiddle, accordion and trumpet played by father, mother and growing boys. Katók

[3] After Quiché and Cakchiquel.

is the gateway to Tecpán and Iximché. Tecpán, off the road just south of the restaurant, has a colorful Thursday market, and was the site of Alvarado's first capital. Iximché, a few kilometers beyond, is the ruins of the Cakchiquel capital Alvarado destroyed in 1527. Because it has not been "restored," Iximché is a more interesting ruin than Zaculeu, and with the volcano Fuego fuming in the background, it is more spectacular.

A few kilometers beyond Katók, a dirt road off to the left leads to Comalapa, an Indian hill town in which reside two of Guatemala's three "primitive" painters [4] and where the church of San Juan Bautista, one of the richest and most beautiful in Guatemala, is not to be missed; the life-size sculptures of saints on its façade are repainted in brilliant colors every few years. When I visited. Comalapa, the town was in an uproar because a sensationalist newspaper in the capital had just accused the Peace Corps of trying to steal a large pre-Columbian *idolo* from the cornfield of a peasant. What actually happened was that the peasant, distracted by the curious, had asked the Peace Corpsman to help him sell the sculpture— or just have it removed. *Ladinos* in the town, furious with the Peace Corps because it had brought in a tractor and given the Indians free use of it— the *ladinos* had been charging exorbitant rates for the use of their tractor for years—tipped off the newspaper. There is no law in Guatemala prohibiting the sale of artifacts within the country, but the buyer was arrested (temporarily) anyway, with flashbulbs popping; and that was that.

Chimaltenango, Santiago Sacatepéquez and San Lucas Sacatepéquez, all a short distance off the Highway between here and the capital, are worth visiting, but not if one is in a hurry to get to the latter.

Guatemala City is a modern metropolis, clean, cool, sunny, and surrounded by mountains. It was built from scratch in 1775 when the worst of a succession of natural disasters wrecked the ancient capital, Antigua, twenty-five miles to the south. It was rebuilt in 1918 after a succession of earthquakes of its own. It is the focus of all the roads, railroads, commerce, industry, politics and art in Guatemala, and its 572,000 population may be divided four ways. Two classes, the so-called "cosmopolites" (aristocracy, businessmen, politicians) and resident foreigners, control most of the nation's wealth—at least the movable and negotiable part.

---

[4] Andrés Curuchích, an old man whose art has already succumbed to the demands of tourism, and Santiago Tuctúc, a young man with potentialities. The third painter, Juan Sisáy, lives in Santiago Atitlán.

Some Indians live in the outskirts, serve as domestics, or drift in and out with their merchandise. The *ladinos,* who form the bulk of the population, are middle-class or declassed citizens of mixed blood, engaged in industry or marginal trade, and tens of thousands of them are chronically unemployed.

The climate of Guatemala City is wonderful. Mexico City is too high. Sea-level capitals like Managua and Panama are too low. At five thousand feet Guatemala City is cool at night, never unbearably hot by day, and in the winter, at least, sunny all day long. It has one comparatively small but superbly appointed luxury hotel, the Guatemala Biltmore, and dozens of lesser hotels and pensions to suit every taste and pocketbook. Its Archaeological Museum has the finest collection of pre-Columbian sculpture in the world outside of Mexico, but it is poorly organized. Jorge Ibarra's Museum of Natural History collection next door also operates on a shoestring but is brilliantly displayed. Halfway between these museums and the shopping center of the city dominated by the bizarre National Palace, Moorish and olive-green, a new complex of modern banks and administration buildings is rising. Carlos Mérida, the veteran Guatemalan artist who has always lived in Mexico, has decorated several of these structures with his gay semi-abstract mosaics. But the most spectacular item in the complex, and probably the most impressive monumental contemporary sculpture in Latin America, is the series of six-story reliefs forming the façade of the Bank of Guatemala. Efraín Recinos, the young sculptor-painter who conceived and executed this brilliant *tour de force,* is also an engineer-architect, and was currently superintending the erection of a fantastic outdoor theater, with modernistic turrets in poured concrete, to cap the old fort that lies behind these other buildings. I asked this friend of earlier visits why the government was spending millions for a theater when Guatemala has no stage tradition or professional actors at all. It seems that two years ago Costa Rica's theater received a lot of publicity on the radio; at once people began saying "Guatemala has no theater! We must have one at once— bigger and better than little Costa Rica could ever afford!" So plans for this outdoor theater, indoor theater, theater-arts building eight stories high, with actors' studios, a stage museum, revolving stages, restaurant and bar were drawn up, at a cost of eight million dollars.

Recinos lives on the road to Antigua, and after having a hilarious visit with him one morning, Negron and I continued on to Antigua, which both of us had visited several times before. We drove first to Ciudad Vieja (Old City) which had followed Iximché and Xepau in Alvarado's capital-building merry-go-round, but this was no day for serious sight-seeing. As we stood in front of the great sculptural façade, an hour of our time was taken by an English eccentric on a motorscooter who insisted on showing us a book he was writing in minuscule script on the blue parts of six Shell maps. We picked up another author, hitchhiking into Antigua. This one was a blond German lad *walking* from Alaska to Tierra del Fuego, as first stage in a project to write a peripatetic travelogue of the world in two hundred volumes. He was mailing his opus home volume by volume and talked about it well, but since he was traveling light, and carried only one shirt, we were not sorry to get him out of our Volkswagen in the Plaza de Armas.

One can take just so many ruins. And Antigua is as full of ruins as a supermarket of tin cans. Many are beautiful—like the University of San Carlos' patio, Santa Clara's cloister, La Merced's intricately appliquéd façade and great fountain, and especially the cathedral's shattered vault and open crossing where the cup of blue sky with its dazzling, puffy clouds provides a more exciting dome-interior than Brunelleschi or Michelangelo ever imagined. But after a while the views of Agua through a cracked ogive or Fuego in a fractured finial pall. And in place of crumbling golden stone, O so mellow with age, artfully wreathed in bougainvillea, one longs for a Cape Cod cottage or even a good honest gas pump.

Antigua, there is only one thing you have more of than ruins, and that is fakes! It begins in the museums. Portrait after portrait of Don Pedro de Alvarado, all of them based on an "original" in Guatemala City which is itself no more than a "heroic" pose dreamed up by some hack a century after the big bully's horse rolled over him near Acapulco. Rooms full of rusty pistols, fountain sculpture (which is fine for fountains), moldering pseudo-Murillos, pages from classical tomes without passion or poetry, relics of reliquaries, vestments worn by authoritarian fanatics under whose bureaucracy the native race still lags in feudal somnolence. And when

you're not looking at fakes, you're having them thrust at you by a legion of tattered gamins ("guides") who insist that their *monolitos* or *idolos*— "Mayan" heads, torsos, potsherds, whistles and whatnots—are genuine ones. And for the more sophisticated dupe, there are the Gift Shoppes serving up more artfully antiqued pre-Columbiana and assorted painted crockery at prices high enough to tempt the most taste-hungry Texan.

These in their ten-gallon hats and silver-clip string ties roam the *ruinas*, guidebook in hand, several steps behind their wives (poodles attached), spurring them on in search of color and authenticity at any cost.

Antigua's foremost citizen, and one of the great men of Central America, is Wilson Popenoe. Thirty years ago, the house he and his wife Dorothy restored and furnished with a treasury of period pieces, was the subject of a bestseller, Louis Adamic's *The House of Antigua*. I had known Adamic and I wanted to talk with his old friend about the mysterious circumstances surrounding the writer's death in my native New Jersey. But all of that was far and gone, and instead we talked about Guatemala. I think Louis would have preferred it that way.

At seventy-three, Popenoe, or "Pop" as he was called then and now, is bronzed, athletic, alert, an omnivorous reader, and when he talks his blue eyes snap with acerbic humor. He is of course much more than a restorer of old mansions. A specialist in agronomy attached to the staff of United Fruit, here, in Honduras and in Ecuador, he is one of the world's authorities on tropical fruit and has developed the avocado as we know it today. "That *fuerte*," he said, pointing to a modest tree in the corner of the magnificent patio, "is the granddaddy of all avocados." His view of his adopted country is conservative, paternalistic and, within those terms, highly intelligent.

"At almost any cost," he said to us, "the Indian should be left alone. He has his own way of life, his own culture, and in most respects his ways are better than ours. Left alone, his life is a rich one, and relatively happy. Uproot him and give him *ladino* clothes, and what have you? You men-

tioned the scrambling ugliness and filth of Escuintla. There you have it. Escuintla is a Communist town, a town full of brawling, discontented wage slaves grubbing for a larger slice of the *ladino* pie—jukeboxes, radio sets, store-bought clothes, prostitutes, Coca Cola and plastic throwaways.

"The good presidents of Guatemala," he continued, "were inevitably conservatives—Barrios, Ubico, Castillo Armas, Peralta—concentrating their efforts neither on getting inordinately rich nor on forcing 'improvement' or 'land reform' on the Indians. They created an atmosphere of peace and stability. Dictators, yes; tyrants, no. You name me an effective Latin-American president who *hasn't* been a dictator!"

He denied scornfully that Arévalo and Arbenz, with their leftist revolution of the early 'fifties, had done anything to improve the lot of the Indians. "They expropriated a little land or took some of the state's land and gave it to their political yes-men—soldiers, policemen, taxi drivers, unemployed, declassed drifters, and the like. They did little or nothing to help the Indians (most of whom have quite enough land) to grow more corn per acre, or more diversified vegetables and fruit on what they have. That is the only kind of aid that really matters—that and rudimentary health and sanitary services. Education? Does it make sense to teach an Indian languages or political philosophy or solid geometry? These things may make *us* happier—though that's an open question! But they only fill the Indian's head—and it's a good head—with confusion, discontent, and rebellious disarray."

Dorothy Popenoe's cypress, the one she found growing out of rubble before the house was restored, still dominates the patio; and some of the more verdant smaller courts, with their old plates on the wall, are lovelier still; and the dining room with its adjoining kitchen, and the sunken bath, and the little frame "office" so improbably England in that jungle of orange and pepper trees, still breathe the spirit of two lives well lived. But the principal chambers are too much museums of antiquities, and the rigor of their Spanish furnishing is forbidding—to our tastes. "How much more *warmth* in one native Indian textile!" my wife Carole put it, on an earlier visit. "Yet there isn't a one in that house." Perhaps appropriately so, for Antigua is Spain, not Guatemala. Alvarado, the blond destroyer, and Doña Beatríz, his fanatical widow in her black shroud, are still King and Queen in Antigua; and it will take more than earthquakes and waterspouts, restorers and agronomists, to gave Mayaland back to the Mayas.

5 GUATEMALA II: THE LOWLANDS

I SUGGESTED at the beginning of the last chapter that Guatemala's Pacific "lowlands" are to its "highlands" as a rusty carburetor is to a poet's wings. If you add to the first part of the equation a broken fan belt, a clogged distributor, some greasy, disgruntled mechanics and a lot of black sand, the comparison is not unapt. Fortunately, however, Guatemala has *two* sets of lowlands, and the Atlantic set is just about as idyllic as the Pacific set is noisome.

The frightening thing, though, is that thirty years ago the Pacific slope was just as idyllic as the Caribbean one. Thirty years ago the Pacific *tierra caliente* was jungle most of the way from Mexico to the El Salvador border. A German coffee *finquero*, displaced by the war, wrote a memoir of life in the area between Zunil and the port of Champerico; in it he described virgin forests alive with exotic birds;

battles between anacondas and crocodiles; pythons and jaguars. A guide-book to Guatemala written during the war describes the Chiquimulilla Canal, running from Iztapa to the Salvador border as "vivid with jungle vegetation, red and white herons, egrets, macaws, monkeys, pumas, and alligators. The surface of the water is almost covered with the balón, a kind of lotus with immaculate white blossoms." When I visited Champerico in 1965 there was no jungle, much less wild animals; cotton plantations covered everything. When I traversed the Chiquimulilla in the same year there were no water lilies, the only bird life I encountered was two flycatchers and a grebe, and trolling all day I didn't come up with so much as a strike.

What happened? Man happened. Businessmen in the capital saw an opportunity for a quick killing. Coffee prices had been falling, and coffee takes years of cultivation and hard work. Cotton can grow anywhere if the land is rich and hot; it requires no shade, and very little labor. In came the bulldozers and removed the trees—all of them. In came the tractors and cotton-pickers and out went the Indians; the few that stayed became *ladinos* perforce—defrocked, uprooted, without land, at the mercy of ab-sentee proprietors—for a cotton planter, unlike a coffee planter, rarely if ever visits his fields. And then came the planes to spray the fields with DDT and insecticides more lethal; and that was the end of whatever animals survived the stripping of the trees, *and* the end of the birds, which live on insects, *and* the end of the fish. Civilization had triumphed again.

How long will it be before the same thing happens to the jungle-covered Petén and the rich Caribbean littoral to its east? It is only ten years since Puerto Barrios has been connected to the capital by a road. The signs are already there. As for the Petén, roads are being pushed in as fast as they can be built and the climax forests are already beginning to fall. An ecologist told me that if the tree-cover is stripped there, the topsoil will leach into the porous limestone and within twenty-five years the Petén will be a desert like northern Mexico.

Will the government of Guatemala wake up before it is too late? Judging by what had already happened to one 90° slope we saw near Zunil—the whole jungle-cover leveled and set afire to make way for one miserable, almost untillable *milpa*—it may be too late already.

There is little to say about the Pacific slope except to tell where the roads go. Leaving Mexico, the driving time between Tehuantepec and the Guatemala border at Tapachula (258 miles) takes about six hours—half the time it takes to come by way of San Cristóbal las Casas, El Tapón, and

Huehuetenango. Once across the Talisman Bridge at the border, the motorist has the option of taking the dirt road east (100 kilometers) to Quezaltenango and the highlands, or the paved road south and then east to Coatepeque. From there to Retalhuleu (42 kilometers) the road is being paved; but from Retalhuleu to Escuintla the road is first-rate again—as it is thereafter from Escuintla north to the capital, or from Escuintla (see Chapter 6) to San Salvador.

A paved road only 39 kilometers long runs south from Retalhuleu to Champerico, and here is the best accessible ocean bathing between Acapulco and El Salvador. The drive is through cotton fields all the way. The town itself was once a busy coffee port. A long wharf for lighters and fishing smacks leads out into the Pacific. Cleaned up and provided with a modern hotel, Champerico could become a great resort. There is less undertow than at any other of Guatemala's Pacific beaches and the black sand is unmarred by debris. There are also lifeguards, though the three in attendance the day Negron and I went swimming had their eyes riveted (as were ours) on fifty nubile high-school girls who had just been bussed in from the capital (four hours away) and were lying prone in their smocks in the foot-deep trough of the breakers. We picked up a lunch of fried bananas wrapped around beans—a white, caterpillar-like, pitted flesh that comes out of long, green pods—washed down by coconut milk. The crone who chopped the nuts open for us at her surfside stand told us that *aguardiente* is often added to the milk in this province.

"In your country," she added, "it would be whiskey?"

"Good heavens," said Bill, looking at her unblinkingly, "we never drink whiskey in our country!"

"What are you," she said, failing to catch his tone, "Evangelists?"

We drove back through Retalhuleu, a town of defrocked peasants where most Indian palm-leaf raincapes are still made, and turned east for Mazatenango. This is a more colorful provincial capital, its buses fire-engine-red and canary-yellow, its bandstand earth-red and viridian, its town hall white and hunter-green, and its common buildings whitewashed or Tamayo-blue. Near the fairgrounds we noted a sign reading "SCHOOL OF HELIOSOPHIC MAGNETICS. *Consult every Monday and Friday at 7. If you come any later your trip will be worthless.*" Our trip was worthless, and we continued on toward Escuintla through pineapple, sugar and rubber plantations and more cotton fields.

The less said about Escuintla the better. We fought our way through its steamy slums and crowded, ripped-up streets as rapidly as we could. The road north climbs past active Pacaya Volcano and through Amatitlán to the capital. Amatitlán is a nondescript town beside a nondescript gray lake; why it is the favored resort of the capital's medium-wealthy, no one was ever able to explain to us. "They just go there because they've always gone there, and it's less than an hour's drive" was the usual answer. A more attractive swimming hole, fifty kilometers from the capital and five short of Escuintla, is the waterfall of San Pedro Martyr; but, unfortunately, to get in to this one requires a pass from the Empresa Electrica de Guatemala, the hated American company that supplies the capital's power. An ugly turbine-shed has been built in such a way that it is visible from every part of the jungle grotto. With a minimum exercise of good taste, an open-door policy, a dredge and a couple of truckloads of white sand, the Empresa could make San Pedro Martyr a counter-irritant in the face of the pervasive Communist propaganda about "American imperialism."

At least a few of the Amatitlán die-hards are getting wise and moving further south to Puerto San José. Likín and Chulamár are American-type "developments" flanking Guatemala's principal Pacific port. Likín is de luxe with ultramodern homes going up around an elaborate four-part swimming pool that had no water in it when we were there. The houses sell at from eight thousand to thirty thousand dollars and are built on a treeless sandflat out of sight of the nearby ocean. Chulamár is the more modest brainchild of Don Manuel Uruela and already contains fifty-seven units, a few with pools, renting for fifty dollars a week and up. Some of the houses are overlooking the beach and all are within walking distance of it—and of the Chiquimulilla Canal which parallels the ocean almost all the way to the El Salvador border.

Surf bathing at San José is exciting but dangerous. The undertow is very strong. Those who like black sand point out that it doesn't reflect the sun's rays like white sand; those who don't like it point out that it retains the heat and is twice as hot to walk on. There's no question at all that once you get far enough from the grubby town, a sort of poor man's Coney Island, the San José beach is a magnificent visual spectacle.

LAKE IZABAL TO LIVINGSTON BY BARGE

Since Negron had to fly back to New York to be with his family briefly, I made the trip to Cobán into the Caribbean lowlands, and back to the capital along the new highway from Puerto Barrios, in the company of another friend. Daniel Schafer, who had just opened Guatemala's first gallery of modern art, is a young American artist and poet who loves his adopted country so much that he has given up his American citizenship lest his loyalties be divided. He was born in Bananera, the United Fruit Company town near Barrios, and to visit its fading respectability with him later on, and hear him recall the days of its glory (and ill-repute) was a fascinating experience.

We drove south and then east from Cobán along the route through Tactíc, Tamahú and Tucurú already described. There's a curious railroad that parallels both the road and the Polochíc River between Pancajché and Panzós—curious in that it never reaches either Cobán's coffee plantations at one end, or the lake port of El Estór through which the coffee reaches the Atlantic, at the other. But there it is, the *Ferrocaril Verapaz*, and though the Germans have gone and most of the lucrative coffee business with them, and though what coffee remains is now trucked out by road, the little locomotive still chugs up the incredible grade from La Tinta to Pancajché once a week. Why? we asked the engineer, who smiled and said: *"Costumbre!"* [habit] If we didn't keep operating, we might forget how."

The road to El Estór is serviceable all the way, and by the time we reached the shore of Lake Izabal, Wednesday, it was dusk. The barge that would be towing our Volkswagen through the lake to Livingston is supposed to leave Estór every Thursday morning at five o'clock. A friend who has a *finca* nearby advised us to stay at the tiny hotel operated by Felipe Bautista because his own ranch house might be "unsafe." Last week, it seems, one of his tractor drivers was killed by the Communist *guerrilleros* whose stronghold is in the mountains around the lake. This evening a small television set had been set up in the village square and on it a crowd of several dozen was watching silently as a shaky image of Colonel Peralta harangued the nation about his new "state of siege" which is supposed to keep the dissident movement in these mountains under control. Dan had an interesting conversation with a young *ladino* on the veranda before we turned in. "There are two forms of nocturnal recreation here at Estór," he was told. "If there are women, we have women. If not, men. No women tonight. Interested . . . ?"

Don Felipe, whose seventy-five-cent pension serves good food and is as clean as a Maya whistle, trundled into our room at 4:15 in his knee-length nightshirt and shined a torch in our faces. He might as well have saved his sleep and ours. For although we'd lashed our car aboard the iron barge the night before, and been told not to be a minute late, it was almost two hours before the crew of our towing vessel, the *Liberación,* could be roused. At 6:30 we cast loose, and a good thing, because the fifty-mile run to Livingston through the gourd-shaped brackish lake and its celebrated narrow outlet to the ocean (Rio Dulce) takes a good twelve hours . . . the way we did it, anyway. Twice we were cast adrift in the center of the lake while the *Liberación* sped ashore to pick up passengers. Once the launch forgot us while we were taking a swim off the San Felipe Castle dock and had to come back. Once we were caught in a storm so violent the waves broke over the barge, forcing us to eat our sandwiches in the Volks with our windshield wipers on. And once we circled completely around Paloma Island in a vain effort to see whether its reputed owner, an American beach-comber named Bill Taft, was at home.

We found blond, blue-eyed Bill Taft (pronounced locally Beel Tahft) on the streets of Livingston after dinner. Livingston, though it's supposed to be Carib Indian, is, like all ports along the Atlantic coast of Central America, predominantly Negro. In his blue T-shirt and battered Stetson, the one-time California pilot and present jack of all fisherman's trades, was slapping Livingston's black immigration inspector on the back and sug-gesting that the two of them lead an expedition to Punta Gorda and the Sarstoon River "and bring back some contraband." It was clear that the leathernecked Taft, with his easy winning smile, was on joking relations with the good-natured Livingstonites. And it was clear five minutes later that he had no intention of returning this night to his native wife and child at Cayo Paloma. He and Ludwig Anker, the proprietor of the excellent little local hotel, the Del Mar, had every intention of settling down in the bar for a night of serious drinking and less serious yarn-spinning, and they would be pleased if we'd join them. We were more than pleased.

Taft came to Guatemala a few years ago to take, as he put it, "fifty thousand photographs of the Maya ruins for *Life* magazine—they used eight." He then went into partnership with a California businessman to operate a de luxe hunting and fishing camp for the big game of the Lake Izabal area, and this affair, since he's lost contact with his partner, has left him a little embittered too. "I'm a professional hunter," he said. "I've hunted from Africa to Ecuador, from Brazil to Alaska—beast and man."

"Man?"

"In two wars, ETO and Korea, and I thought it was going to be a third when they mobilized forty of us old air force men down here during the Cuban missile crisis. Now I may have to hunt man again—in San Francisco. Here I hunt deer, *tigre* and *tepesquintle* [1] by the 'still' method, scouting spoors by day on the Indian trails that crisscross the deepest jungles, waiting patiently with a torch at their feeding places by night."

"How about manatees?" I said—Dan and I having watched in vain all day for any sign of the gigantic prehistoric mammals that haunt the lake's shallow waters.

"It's against the law to kill manatees," Taft said. "But I've observed scores of them feeding by moonlight on the beach of Paloma. They stare motionless into the beam of my torch."

We'd been told that Taft was writing a treatise on snake bites, so we asked him about the local varieties. "I killed hundreds on my island—all there were, including *fer-de-lances* and corals. My book describes eight hundred poisonous species, as against Dr. Dittmar's three hundred, and there may be twelve hundred in all. All that stands in the way of publication is good color photographs." Was it true, I asked him, that there is no remedy for the coral snake's bite?

"Not true," he said. "There's an antivenom for even the worst bite, the rhinoceros viper's. Provided the victim doesn't panic and start running so that the poisoned blood moves rapidly to the heart. If you're bitten, lie perfectly still."

We laughed and he laughed too. "But I mean it. Actually it's not easy to be bitten by a coral snake. His fangs are not retractable, like a rattlesnake's. The 'pit' in pit vipers is a sensing device, just as the snake's forked tongue is his 'ears.' If you stand still, a snake won't strike. You'll be like a tree to him and your body heat won't be much more than the tree's. By the way, did you know that St. Patrick was sainted for bringing vipers to Europe? That arrested the Black Plague, which was carried by rats. Another fallacy is that death by snakebite is necessarily painful. I saw a Cajun girl die at a snake farm in Louisiana twelve hours after being scratched by one fang of an Egyptian Cobra. There was none of the proper antivenom closer than Florida and by the time the Army jet got it there

---

[1] A small hybrid piglike creature prized for its sweet, tender meat which brings twenty-five cents a pound in Livingston. The *tigre* is the North American jaguar.

she was dead. But meanwhile her first symptom was elation: she danced and danced! Then slowly, as a little blood began to ooze from her ears, nose and eyes, she became paralyzed; but there was no suffering."

Dan asked Taft what his chances were of making a go of it with the splendidly constructed fishing lodge he'd built on Paloma.

He shook his head and opened another bottle of beer. "Sometimes Ludwig and I get together and admit frankly that we'll never make it. We're born failures. We just don't care that much about a buck. Take the case of the two desperate *gringos* I saw one night, *paddling* past Paloma in the motor launch they'd rented. Their situation was hopeless. They didn't see me. I went out in my launch, towed them in to my pier, fed them, put them up for two nights, gave them five gallons of gas, and conducted them to this hotel where they spent two more nights, fishing with my equipment and on my boat. Then they left, not offering to pay, but both of us assuming that they would when they got home. The following Christmas I received a card from Minnesota, and three months later another from the Petén, saying they'd bought a hunting lodge there, and wasn't that great news! It was—for them. That was the last we ever heard of them."

I asked Taft if it was true that the Indians were honest. "Absolutely. They're the only part of this population that will never steal, though the others don't call it stealing. Civilization brings *ladrones* (robbers) and worse, *envidia* (envy), the most vicious phenomenon in this country. I was respected when I came to Livingston because I was loaded—with that $19,500, my share of that one-way partnership. When it was gone, they didn't know me. Except Ludwig, here; and those who are as poor or poorer than I am."

"Are the *guerrilleros* around the lake any problem?" I asked.

"They were. But not any more. Politics doesn't affect this province at all. They may have a state of siege in the rest of the country. We don't even know it here."

How was it, I then asked, that our friend's tractor-driver was beaten and killed last week? As always, Bill Taft's answer was definite, unqualified:

"He wasn't. He died of loss of blood from a vampire bat that sucked at him while he was asleep or drunk. This happens. Before I screened my house, it happened to me once. I woke up to find my big toe bleeding. If

I'd slept another six hours, who knows? I might have bled to death. The bat anesthetizes the wound. You feel nothing."

True or untrue? Who knows. Bill Taft asserted just as positively that the Maya used the wheel in their vast building complexes, though all the archaeologists say no. "They used it in their toys, didn't they? Besides, I have *proof*. But you'll have to wait for my second book, the one on the Mayas, for that one."

Taft and Anker knocked themselves out next morning, when the *Liberación* threatened to stall for days over a load of coffee, to find us another barge. With the help of Señor Zacapa, of *Ferrocarril Verapaz*, they prevailed on a tug to pull us across Amatique Bay to Puerto Barrios for twenty-five dollars, and four hours later we were driving up some improvised timbers and onto the concrete pier.

THE TIRED OCTOPUS OF BANANALAND

Puerto Barrios is a brawling, ramshackle banana port, with plenty of attractions for sailors and stevedores but none for tourists. Two bearded Dutchmen who had just helped load a freighter told us that with the exception of Puerto Cortés, a few miles down the coast in Honduras, this was the sleaziest port of call on the whole Atlantic seaboard. In their company we visited Puerto Matias de Galvéz, a smaller port across the harbor that the Guatemalan government is developing as a modern replacement for Barrios, and had a swim in a delightful public pool while our friends netted tropical fish for their aquarium on the freighter. We spent the night at the immaculate Texaco Guest House outside Barrios, though Dan looked dubiously at the mammoth tanks outside our window and said, "If there's an uprising these will go first, and we'll go with them." Actually the United Fruit Company headquarters just off Barrios' main square would probably be the first target of any such hypothetical coup—just on the basis of the American company's ancient and largely undeserved reputation as the Octopus of the Americas—though revolutionaries would have to know their way around to ever identify a yellow, paint-blistered, rotting 100-foot-long shack without signs of any kind, that looks like a house of ill repute in a Somerset Maugham story, as the administrative headquarters of the most prosperous fruit company in the world.

Dan and I had already visited United Fruit's similarly unmarked offices in the capital and asked why this was. The manager had pointed to a pile of rocks in his fireplace. "There's your answer. These have all come through this window. What would they throw, I wonder, if we advertised our presence." The fact that United Fruit, at least since Sam Zemurray took over in 1933, has been a socially progressive company paying the highest wages ever paid rural workers in the tropics, that it pioneered in giving social benefits, free housing, hospitals, and schools, that it made thousands of acres of dismal swampland and jungle healthy and economically productive, that it built the port facilities and railroads of Guatemala from scratch, and that it has left within the production areas seven dollars for every one dollar it has taken out, are apparently as nothing to the fact that its public relations have been inept. One failure was the inability to establish any communication between workers and management. Another was to think that sprucing up ruins like Zaculeu and Quiriguá would somehow counter the leftists' propaganda that *"El Pulpo"* was bleeding the country white. But worst of all (and perhaps this one was inevitable) was housing the workers in segregated "company" barracks right next to the management's American-style homes complete with sprinkled lawns, swimming pools, golf links and movie theaters.

Bananera, which the Guatemalans resent so deeply they don't even include it on their maps, is a case in point. It lies on a spur of the main coastal highway 50 kilometers from Barrios and 220 from the capital, a peeling, dilapidated shell of its days of glory (1934-54). It has never recovered from the Arbenz revolution which collapsed in that last year, when, according to the Communists, United Fruit called for help and the CIA stepped in to back Castillo Armas and his "National Liberation" army bogged down near here on the Honduras frontier. Either United Fruit lost heart after this final blow to its image, or it decided deliberately to leave its installations looking seedy. The lawns and hedges and flower gardens that Dan remembered from his boyhood had gone to pot. The houses were unpainted. The theater was abandoned. The pool (still with its telltale sign reading *"Tanque de Natación Exclusivo para los Socios y Familiares"*) was half filled with black water. "It used to be turquoise blue," said Dan nostalgically, "and I remember how my first impulse to be an artist was publicly frustrated here. They'd just put up that iron fence so the guards could check on whether interlopers—like the Negroes from Livingston whom all the kids loved—were swimming. I proposed planting a hedge to conceal the visual and moral ugliness of that fence, and of course my silly idea was promptly vetoed." Only Bananera's golf course appeared to be still kept up, though no one was playing on it.

WALKING THE TIES TO QUIRIGUA

Fifty kilometers further along the highway to the capital is the entrance to the ruins of Quiriguá—if you can find it. Without Dan I never would have been able to. A big Coca Cola sign on a high bluff to the left of the road contains the famous name in unreadably small type. And once you do drive in to the town on the banana railway you have to hope that a *gringo*-hater won't point the wrong way up the tracks. For it's a fifty-minute walk along the crooked ties in the blazing sun, and (seemingly) much more coming back. The ruins are actually only a few hundred yards from the highway but neither United Fruit, which "owns" them, nor the government of Guatemala, which might be expected to cash in on the only major archaeological site in the country accessible by road, has ever bothered to bulldoze a path through the bush.

Quiriguá was discovered in 1840 by Stephens and Catherwood, following an extensive survey of Copán fifty kilometers south of here across the Honduras border. Copán's existence had been vaguely known for a century or so, and the two enterprising travelers had bought it for fifty dollars. Maudslay, who visited Quiriguá in 1881, used his ivorybacks so fiercely to prepare the deeply carved *stelae* for photography that his valet back in England, looking at the ruined brushes, thought the master's head must have turned to stone. Maudslay was impressed by Quiriguá's setting. "What a marvellous place it was! What a fearful restless struggle for existence was going on in the vegetable world before one's very eyes. Everything was fighting its way upward toward the air and sunlight." Half a century later still came Sylvanus Morley and Eric Thompson, the latter speculating that the wheel-less Maya must have obtained the leverage to move the sixty-five-ton, thirty-foot-high central *stela* "as today Indians do . . . by pulling ropes over polished logs." Thompson noted on another occasion that the computation on one *stela* "sweeps back accurately over ninety million years" and that "on another stela at the same site the date reached is some four hundred million years ago. These are actual computations stating correctly day and month positions."

In the deathlike stillness of that close-cropped jungle park, the enigmatic brown stones are still an awesome sight. As sculpture there is probably nothing in all Maya art to compare with the intricately carved "Zoomorph P," a monolith shaped like a hunchbacked turtle with its scriptural glyphs in sockets like lidded eyes.

There are many lovely churches, inviting rivers and cozy inns along the highway after Quiriguá, but the haven that pleased us most that hot day was the Posada Doña María on the river of the same name twenty kilometers beyond the ruins. Steak sandwiches at twenty-five cents and a swim in clear, cold green water are an irresistible combination after walking railroad tracks.

ESQUIPULAS, MECCA OF PILGRIMS AND PIMPS

Fifty kilometers further, at Rio Hondo, is the left turn onto an unpaved road that leads to Zacapa, Chiquimula and Esquipulas. To those Guatemalans who regard Castillo Armas not as a puppet but as a national hero—and they are many, perhaps a majority—this is hallowed ground. For it was here that the exiled little colonel dared to invade Guatemala in 1954, at first against great odds.

Hallowed ground to the faithful for centuries has been the shrine of the Black Christ at Esquipulas. The massive, four-towered cathedral stands not far from the junction of the three countries (Guatemala, Honduras, El Salvador) and a day's muleback ride from the great Maya ceremonial shrine of Copán, with which pre-Columbian Esquipulas is presumed to have been associated. The cathedral was erected in the eighteenth century by a bishop grateful to the Black Christ for his cure from a contagious disease. The image, carved from balsam wood two centuries earlier by Quirio Cataño and blackened by candle smoke, was "shining like jet" even when Thomas Gage visited here in 1632. Now it is the focus of an annual pilgrimage from all over Central America, exceeded in numbers only by that to the shrine of the Virgin of Guadalupe at Mexican Tepeyac. If one is not unduly disturbed by religious ardor, commercialism and crowds, the time to visit Esquipulas is during the *Dia de Esquipulas*, January 15, or later during Lent and Holy Week. Remembering having been almost crushed to death and asphyxiated at Tepeyac, I visited Esquipulas a little in the wake of these two festivals.

What impressed me on my first visit was the extraordinary *scale* and noble proportions of the sanctuary, white and golden-domed against the intense blue sky. I was impressed too by the five American Benedictine monks who administer (if that is the right word) the shrine, and live in it in style. And by the brazen effrontery with which a team of Indian *chirimia* players hammered out their savage rhythms on drum and flageolot inside the portal while the congregation was responding to High Mass right in front of them.

It was the unbridled commercialism that has been permitted to dominate Esquipulas that surprised me most the second time. The one-hundred-thousand peasants and lower-middle-class penitents who journey here devoutly, some on their bleeding knees, are exploited in every conceivable way. The trucks and buses that bring them, the fleabag pensions that hold them, the innumerable booths selling everything from spoiled meat to plastic kewpie dolls take their money. Even whorehouses are provided. At the *Calvario* church across town, which has a Black Christ of its own, hundreds of these simple people were standing in line for hours to kiss the feet of this image. In front of it sat two characters who can only be described as gangsters. Without credentials of any kind, they were holding out their hats and collecting a small fortune in nickels and dimes from the credulous poor. Overhead, loudspeakers brayed devotional invocations, and on all sides hawkers peddled the pink straw *leys* which decorate even the spokes of the bicycles we saw returning by the hundreds all along the dirt road, and then along the highway itself, to the capital.

TIKAL: CLIMAX FOREST, CLIMAX RUIN

There are three good reasons for taking one of the complicated, expensive air-excursions into the Petén. First, this is the nearest and largest tropical climax forest on the North American continent; its jungles and lakes contain an abundance of game; and unless one comes by canoe out of Mexico or drops by parachute, there is no other way of getting here. Second, this is the western gateway to the continent's least-known country, Belize. And third, there is Tikal.

The first time I flew to Tikal, I was traveling with a student from Mexico City College, Bill Dwyer. He was as anxious as I was to push on into Belize, so we saw very little of the famous ruin. Especially since the first thing we did was to get stranded in Flores. Flores, capital of the Petén, is a village on an island in a big lake at the Petén's geographical center. Flores was also the focal point of whatever history the Petén had after the Mayas abandoned Tikal and their lesser ceremonial centers in the seventh or eighth century A.D. Cortés came to Flores (missing Tikal, fifty kilometers north) on his incredible march to Honduras in 1524; and it was at Flores that the Itzá tribesmen held out against the Spaniards for almost two centuries after the Indians had capitulated everywhere else. Cortés had left a sick horse on the island, and when this last aboriginal citadel fell in 1697, the Itzás were found to have added the exotic animal to their pantheon of deities. Dwyer and I thought we'd have just time to take a quick look for the horse's image, reputed to have been thrown in the lake from Tayasál, the Itzás' capital. After all, hadn't the *Aviateca* pilot assured us that he would be loading cargo for forty-five minutes before continuing on to Tikal? And hadn't the enterprising local boatman assured us that he could circumnavigate the island in half an hour? The tourists watched us embark with pity, and one of them said: "We may never see you again." How right she was! For our undoing was the heat of the sun, and my whim to do a little skindiving on the opposite side of Flores. There was a roar of motors. We

raced for the dock. And just as we made it, our plane took off, skimmed
the jungle giants, and became a speck on the horizon. For days the only
other aircraft scheduled to touch down at Tikal (whither our suitcases,
passports and money were now landing) was a freighter leaving late that
afternoon. Fortunately we were able to persuade the pilot to take us
along. We had a couple of delicious shaddocks with him, and a bottle of

barrilito in the village bar, and then he lashed us to the sixteen five-hundred-pound drums of gasoline that filled the entire hold, and we were off. "They're gonna see our flames at Cape Canaveral," said Dwyer, as the whole cargo jerked tailward with a fearful shriek of ropes on the takeoff; but we made it, and soon we were skimming the Maya pyramids that poke above the two-hundred-foot *ceibas* at Tikal, and were being greeted on the dusky strip by Toño Ortíz, carrying our precious bags.

Toño is a native of Flores. Those who envy his unusual enterprise call him a monopolist who has cornered the market in ruins, has the airline and the only hotel in his pocket, charges what the market will bear (thirty dollars for the round-trip flight, eleven dollars a day with meals, and a quarter for a six-cent Coke) and is in cahoots with a rainmaker. Since his guesthouses were full this night and he put us up on cots in the bar for free, and we missed his strenuous tour of the ruins, and it didn't rain, *we* liked him fine. Shrewd business isn't Toño's only talent either. The sylvan lodge, dining hall and cottages are in perfect taste—thatched roofs, beams tied with sisal, Mayan glyphs painted in black (by Toño himself) on the yellow adobe walls. His wife makes exquisite rubbings of the *stelae*, and sells them at good prices. And Toño picks up five dollars a head more for those guests who want the full treatment, climbing the steep pyramids, crawling into the dank ceremonial chambers, and receiving a really professional lecture in perfect English on the history of Tikal and what the current team of archaeologists from the University of Pennsylvania is now doing to uncover more of its vast acreage of still-buried treasures.

Tikal is much the most extensive of all the pre-Columbian ceremonial cities, and its setting in the deep jungle, alive with parrots and monkeys by day, and the screams of the big cats at night, is incomparable. But in some ways (unless, of course, you're an archaeologist) a study of the tourist—his plumage, feeding habits, mating calls and camera antics—is more entertaining. Bill Negron, for instance, took Toño's big safari with an outfit called Through-the-Lens Tours. As he described it to me, the Group Leader, when he wasn't picking up old ladies in tight skirts who had fallen over tree roots, or reassuring the young that the monkeys weren't really on strings, would step forward and say: "All right, girls, anybody want a reading? . . . I have F.3.5 at 1/15!" Gasps of dismay: "I might tremble!" Careful, now. Elbows in. Squeeze gently!"—and simultaneously twenty-seven shutters would click. After dark in the lodge, not a word was spoken about

the ruins. For hours the talk was of built-in gyroscopes to eliminate the need for tripods; film speeds; flash attachments; batteries to control photoelectric cells; etc. One lady complained because the showerhead in her cabin had only one hole. "Well," said her husband, "it might have been worse." Other tours were on the way: Happy Holiday Tours, Bachelor Tours, Lepidopterists United. "There's probably even a tour for study of the hibernation of the coral snake," Bill said. "Venom-kits optional."

BELIZE: WHOSE COUNTRY?

Dwyer and I were off early the next morning on another cargo plane that promised to drop us at Melchor de Mencos. This is a strip due east of Flores on the Belize border. If we could hitchhike our way across the frontier to Benque Viejo we could catch a bus, we were told, to Belize City. It all worked out exactly as planned, except that a Negro woman on the bus gave birth to a child between Roaring Creek and Butcher Burns just as a torrential rain hit the windowless vehicle, and by the time an ambulance arrived from the capital, the bus, which had thoughtfully stopped on a treeless knoll, had to be bailed out. Belizeans, with little to be happy about, are the world's happiest people. Once the poor mother had left us, the two guitars aboard struck up a jig and by the time we rolled into Belize everybody in the drenched bus was singing. But I'm getting ahead of my story.

At the Belizean customs in Benque Viejo, Dwyer and I had had an encounter that set the stage very well for a review of the peculiar Belize problem. The problem, briefly, is: to whom shall Belize belong? Under an agreement of 1859 with Guatemala, Great Britain made the coastal strip (which its loggers and traders had occupied *de facto* for centuries) its colony, calling it British Honduras. Guatemala, going back to Spanish claims, and pointing out that Britain welched on its promise to build a road opening the Petén up to the Atlantic (part of the 1859 agreement), considers 'Nuestra Belice' part of Guatemala. Mexico, with covetous eyes on the northern part of Belize, doesn't recognize either claim. And the Negro inhabitants, who in 1963 elected George Price their first executive, say: A plague on all your houses!

When Bill and I entered the frontier customhouse, two handsome young Negroes in uniform were cleaning house, one with a broom, the other with a bottle of water out of which he shook bursts from time to time. They saw us waiting but paid no attention. Finally one moved to the inner office and motioned me in. When he had taken our passports and established that we were not Guatemalans he relaxed, handed me a long blue form to fill out, and asked where we'd be staying. We threw up our hands.

"What? You don't know?"

"How could we know? We've never been here before."

"You know anyone?"

"I have a letter to your governor."

He took his time writing that down, and then said: "You'll have to fill out another blue form." The wind had blown the first one face down into one of his puddles of water. When I had completed the second, the two of them began inspecting our bags, item by item, even opening tobacco pouches and probing into pockets. "Hmm," said one of them, leafing through a paperback, "J-U-S-T-I-N-E. . . . Very interesting writer, De Sadé [sic]. But what's this? (finding a paper bag with two sandwiches and a banana) You can't take that!"

I groaned appealingly. "We'll starve on the bus."

"All right. Take the sandwiches."

"Enjoy the banana," I said.

"Wouldn't touch it," he said, tossing it out the door and looking across the border at Guatemala, "Dirty country. . . ."

We started out, but I couldn't resist turning around and saying, "You've forgotten to search our coats and pants."

Both of them laughed. The ice was broken. "This," said Bill, "is probably the most thorough search ever conducted on earth since this silly custom was invented." They were in stitches.

It was at this very customhouse that General Miguel Ydígoras Fuentes made his grandiloquent bid to take over the little country in April of 1958. Ydígoras was the President of Guatemala between Castillo Armas and Peralta, a corrupt but likable ruler who had once swung Indian clubs on

TV to counter a newspaper story that he was too old and infirm to rule. When Ydígoras had crossed the border with an armed retinue, a corporal had been on duty here and had told the General he'd have to wait while he telephoned the governor general for instructions. After a very brief conversation he turned to the Guatemalans and said: "I'm sorry. But I have instructions to conduct you back across the frontier at once." Which he did.

I asked our friends what had happened to the corporal. "He was promoted to sergeant," they said. They showed us also one of the Guatemalan leaflets, scattered along the border at that time, exhorting the Belizeans in very bad Creole to join Guatemala. It read:

FREEDOM!

Just across de boundary-line is 'Guatemala.' Dem called dem 'Panier.' Dem is a nashun good people, an how dem is enjoying life togedder. It is quite a contrast between Belize and Guatemala, all de time de build house, an do all sorts of ting for dem people to feel good. De President Ydigoras Fuentes de order day sent surveyors an mark out 200,000 acres of lan to gib de peple an each one of dem will get 200 acres free wid all kine of help. . . .

COMMITTEE RECUPERASHUN OF BELIZE

"Any Belizeans put in for acreage?" I asked. They were in stitches again.

The capital city is a shanty-town in the wake of Hurricane Hattie which leveled it in October of 1961. But it is a shanty-town with indomitable spirit. I don't think I have ever been in a place where people, going about their business, don't give an obvious foreigner a second look, and yet if you speak to them will give you their house and children to make you feel at home. And there's more night life in one block of Belize—dancing, singing, whooping it up, and drinking—than in all the rest of Central America as far down as Panama. Two very good hotels (the Fort George, with pool; and the Bellevue, with Miss Jean Dinger, one of those kindly, efficient Britishers who make you wonder why the Empire ever foundered) take care of the thin trickle of tourism. It's too bad, too, because the little country has mountains, Maya ruins, and colorful Indians of its own; beaches and skin-diving at the thousands of off-shore Cayes; fishing as good as any in the world; and infinite charm.

After a chat with Sir Peter Stallard at Government House ("When there is any trouble, which there rarely is, I call for Mr. Price, who is a reasonable chap, and we settle things amicably") we visited the Premier. Belize had had self-government for exactly 365 days the morning we went to see

George Price. He is a self-assured, clear-eyed young man, his face unlined and his temperament optimistic. His critics call him fanatical—and about Belize's ability to conduct its own affairs and solve its many desperate problems, he is. We had already heard his morning invocation on the radio: "Belizeans! Wake up and work! . . . If we project our Belizean identity throughout the world, the world will be ours." Belizeans, he told us, must become conscious of their identity—"Our superior literacy, 95%, the highest in Central America, isn't enough—if we are to achieve true independence. The problem is that Belize's $15,000,000 budget can only be met with a $6,000,000 subsidy from Great Britain—in other words, the tiny nation's 105,000 people import $6,000,000 worth of goods more than they export."

"When you do correct the imbalance," I said, "with your stepped-up citrus fruit production, sawmills, fishing, and so on will you cut loose from London completely?"

"That is at least five years away, that economic independence," said George Price, "and even then we would have to be a self-governing nation within a true Central American federation."

"As part of Guatemala or Mexico?"

"Never. Should either of them be mad enough to try to force us into such an arragement, we'd defend ourselves; in the case of a major invasion effort, we'd have the help of British land, sea and air support. *You* wouldn't take kindly to such an aggression, either. So they'll not try it, I suspect."

Sir Peter had already told us that Belize offers everything that Guatemala legitimately needs in the way of a Caribbean outlet for the resources of Petén—"but they accept nothing. Obviously they prefer the intangible of an emotional issue, something to shout about whenever things go badly over there." Premier Price made the same point. "We give them fish for Lent and take a few spoonfuls of their good coffee in return. What else do we have that they could possibly want? Bananas?"

We laughed, but George Price didn't laugh. A Peace Corpsman told us later that Price takes his mission so seriously that when he sees him in a blue-and-white seersucker suit he invariably compliments him on wearing the new national colors. "And he *means* it!" The Premier takes loyalty to his party (the P.U.P.) so seriously that his *Belize Times* this week was making a point of not mentioning the law degree just conferred in London on Mrs. Goldson, wife of his rival, the leader of the N.I.P. It is hardly surprising that Price takes little interest in such frivolous pursuits as hunting and fishing;

or that he regards tourism as less important to Belize's future than a project he had now embarked upon to abandon the present capital and build a new one from scratch near Roaring Creek in the center of the country. I ventured to mention the billions sunk by Brazil into their white elephant capital, Brasilia, a project that had almost bankrupted one of the world's richest nations, but George Price's answer was both unanswerable and the measure of his visionary nerve. "Belize," he said, "is not Brazil."

Actually Mr. Price was kind enough to ask his information chief to take us hunting and fishing, despite his distaste for these pursuits. Bill and I were sitting in the bar of the Fort George that afternoon, waiting for the fulfillment of this promise, when I happened to glance at a nearby table and pointed out a grizzled, bearded, outdoor type with blue eyes that seemed to be scanning distant horizons.

"What about him?" Bill said.

"He looks like Hemingway. And I'll bet *he's* a fisherman."

We asked him to join us for a drink, and as it turned out he was a professional who had operated fishing lodges in Michigan, Key West, and the Isle of Pines, and had several times gone fishing with the writer. Escaping from Cuba by night with his boats just as Castro's police were about to seize the latest of his lucrative sportsmen's camps, he had made it to Belize in a hurricane, with all his superstructures blown away, and one member of his defected Cuban crews lost at sea. "For fishing, Belize beats all of them," he said. "I have one camp in the Cayes for deep sea parties, and another on the river for snook, tarpon and bone. But unfortunately I can't take you to either—I'm tied up for the rest of the day. Too bad you're leaving tomorrow. But if you ever come back ask for Vic Barothy. Your names—?"

"Selden Rodman and—"

"Oh no, oh no!" he doubled over with laughter. "You know why I'm waiting in this bar? Rudy Castillo, Price's information boss, asked me to come here and take you two fishing!"

It was the first of two fishless fishing expeditions I was to go on within a month, both of them delightful. By the time Dwyer and I arrived at Vic Barothy's camp, a torrential rain had been falling for hours. Not only was the Belize River in flood; it was so brown with the runoff of the Maya Mountains and the eastern Petén that the tarpon would have had to have radar to find our lures. Vic told us it was a waste of time, but we donned his slickers and trolled anyway, getting a good look at the romantic river, with its drooping coconut palms and mangrove jungles, that for years was the only outlet for the chicle and mahogany of the Petén—flatboats guided by ropes negotiating the treacherous cataracts upstream. And then we settled down in the spacious trophy room and listened to hours of fabulous fishing stories. Vic charges American enthusiasts $25 a day—$64 for deep-sea excursions; and for ten days of jaguar hunting $1500—"at least one *tigre* guaranteed or their money back."

"Any refunds?" we asked.

"None. If worst comes to worst, we have our dogs tree the cat and then spotlight him for an easy shot."

Emmett Gowan of Tennessee runs a less posh pair of camps, here and in the Cayes. And from all accounts both pioneers have more customers from the States than they can handle—without any advertising at all.

GUATEMALA ENVOI

My second fishless fishing trip took place in Guatemala many weeks later, and in that part of the Petén which is still so untouched, so rich with unexplored Maya temples, and so indescribably beautiful that even to mention it seems faintly criminal. I speak of those square miles of wilderness lying 100 kilometers southwest of Tikal, 100 kilometers north of Cobán, and 100 kilometers southeast of Yaxchilán and Bonampak. At Altar de Sacrificios the Usumacinta is formed by the confluence of two noble rivers the Salinas, which is called the Chixoy in the Cobán area, and the Pasión which rises in the mountains north of Lake Izabal. Between these rivers lies the wonderland. Sayaxché, on the south bank of the Pasión, is the airstrip by which one enters, the terminus of a new road south from Flores, the place to take on supplies, the depot for dugout canoes—with or without outboard motors. It lies midway between El Ceibál, the gorgeous riverside ruin presently being excavated by a team of Harvard archaeologists, and the entrance to a constellation of lakes dominated by the lordly Petexbatún.

I was lucky to be one of a party making a dry run of this territory in anticipation of intensive (and expensive) game expeditions to come. Whether "Sakbé Safaris" [1] will ever solve its logistic problems, develop a regular schedule and become big-time, I don't know. But there is no doubt that, whoever becomes the Toño Ortíz of Sayaxché (and Toño is already moving in with a lodge of his own), many will be the debtors of the two adventurous girls who were our hosts.

[1] Sakbé is the Maya word for "safe trails."

Joya Hairs, born in Honduras of Jamaican parents, is one of Guatemala's outstanding photographers. Sue Miles, brought up in Illinois and educated at Chicago and Harvard, is an anthropologist-archaeologist presently teaching at the University of San Carlos and quite possibly the youngest full professor of her sex anywhere. The two friends, however, conceived Sakbé Safaris less from their professional enthusiasms—though these, of course, receive full satisfaction in the area—than from a mutual passion for hunting, fishing, and camping. The camps they had already set up in the jungle were marvels of ingenuity and rustic comfort. Both girls are experts with gun and tackle, but both are so much in love with the beauty of this wilderness that bagging game becomes incidental. With one cast of a harpoon, a native pilot supplied us with tarpon enough for three days. We hunted the *tigre* by night, but only to test a new "mating call" consisting of a rawhide thong suspended from a hollow gourd—to which several males responded awesomely.

There was a magical moment one day at sundown when the jungletops were etched dark green against the peach-colored sky: a coppery iridescent bittern stepped gingerly out of a tangle of tree roots on the riverbank, and four macaws in formation with long, black tails and beaks accenting their red bellies floated overhead. But the climactic lyrical moment (and fitting coda to any Guatemala symphony) would have to be our voyage to the source of the X----- River. This stream, which shall be nameless, appears on no map, and I couldn't describe how we found it, if I wanted to—which I don't. Following its many bends over shallow ledges of intricately fluted yellow limestone, with water lilies choking the margins and even seeming to flower underwater, we came finally to a circular pool perhaps fifty feet in diameter and thirty deep. The bottom is sandy in patches, with here and there clusters of pulverized mollusk shells of the deepest blue flecked with tiny spots of scarlet. Around these sand patches, and the big central one through which the spring bubbles, are underwater plants, their yellow-green leaves undulating rhythmically as thousands of tiny, almost translucent fish with yellow eyes swim in and out.

We dove into this enchanted garden, being careful not to disturb the great painting which is its floor; and then we caught some of the fish on tiny spinners, and threw them back. By that time there was an unspoken feeling among us all, I think, that if we didn't leave the wilderness of Petén as we found it, we might come back some day and find an Escuintla here—and die with *that* on our consciences.

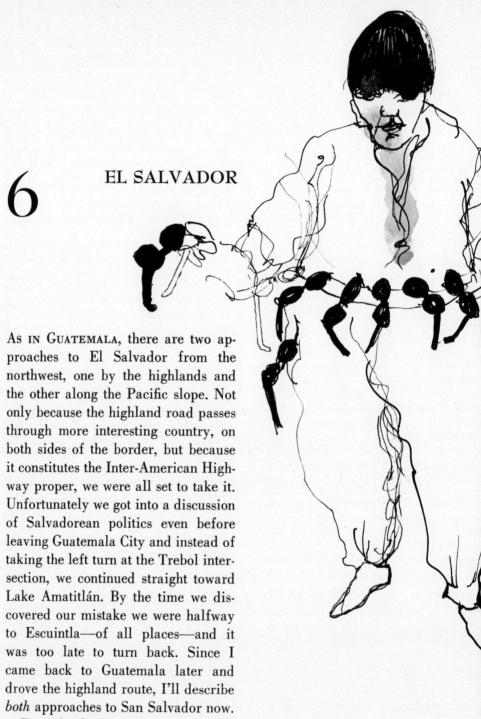

6 EL SALVADOR

As in Guatemala, there are two approaches to El Salvador from the northwest, one by the highlands and the other along the Pacific slope. Not only because the highland road passes through more interesting country, on both sides of the border, but because it constitutes the Inter-American Highway proper, we were all set to take it. Unfortunately we got into a discussion of Salvadorean politics even before leaving Guatemala City and instead of taking the left turn at the Trebol intersection, we continued straight toward Lake Amatitlán. By the time we discovered our mistake we were halfway to Escuintla—of all places—and it was too late to turn back. Since I came back to Guatemala later and drove the highland route, I'll describe *both* approaches to San Salvador now.

First the lowland way. The drive from Guatemala's capital through Escuintla and on to the frontier village (called, appropriately enough, Frontera) took two and a half hours. All roads macadam and first-rate. Customs absorbed another half hour, most of it converting *quetzales* into *colóns*, with a few dollar bills, good in all countries, to complicate matters. An hour later we were in the tree-shaded square of Sonsonate.

Capital of Salvador's southwest, and the little country's fifth city with a population of about twenty-five thousand, Sonsonate's principal attraction is not the cathedral. This building was once famous for its seventeen shining porcelain cupolas, but the largest are now sheathed in tin and the smallest are no more than ventilators; and the interior, with flyspecked walls and the usual saints in glass caskets, is drab. If I haven't mentioned the countryside along the way, it is because it is drab too: an extension of the drabness to and from Escuintla. The colonial ruling class avoided the lowlands, leaving no fine homes or magnificent churches to soften the impact of their centuries' domination. Only the bright yellow blossoms of the leafless *cortes blanco* and the fiery orange of the *fuego* enliven the dust of the dry season.

The peasants on both sides of the border—and this applies to the whole of El Salvador—have discarded their costumes along with every other aspect of their Indian culture. This makes even the moderately well-off minority look poor, and the majority beggarly. And as if to dot the 'i,' every Salvadorean peasant woman carries on her head a cheap tin pitcher, exact replica of the handsome earthenware jug it replaced. Driving into town, we had seen one peasant on a hillock tossing wheat into the wind to remove the chaff; but agriculture in this part of Central America seems well on the way to mechanization. More characteristic is the small plane in its shed for spraying insecticide on the cotton fields.

There are two adequate hotels in Sonsonate. The Eden is in town and has a small air-conditioned restaurant. The more attractive Cabañas, with a nice pool and rustic dancing pavilion, is on the road to Izalco. We noticed the sign of Roberto Rodriguez, possibly the only surgeon in the world with swinging doors ("He doubles as bartender in the off season," said Bill), and a funeral parlor optimistically entitled *Fenix* (Phoenix) which reminded us of one in Cuernavaca called more pessimistically *Quo Vadis?*

It must be said that Sonsonate is a little bit redeemed by the pebbly brook that rushes through a deep gorge in midtown. But to find its real aquatic redemption one must drive four and one-half miles out of town, just beyond Izalca, to a spot called Atecozól. This is an enchanting complex of pools, canals, waterfalls and shallow cataracts, shaded by a dense park of *amates*, almonds, avocados and *ceibas*. Some of the latter, filled with orchids, are a hundred feet high. The central pool, perhaps 150 yards long by 75 wide, is deep enough to dive in at one end and shallow enough for wading at the other. The water is very clear and green. Platforms, steps and benches, carved out of the black volcanic rock, surround the pool and its tributaries, and are shaded with masses of hibiscus and bougainvillea. One brook, in a shady chasm, was filled with peasant women, most of them stripped to the waist, washing themselves or beating their laundry on the sudsy rocks. Only a sound truck at the entrance, advertising Café Listo (Instant Coffee) shattered the illusion of paradise.

The fifty additional miles into San Salvador reveal nothing memorable.

It takes longer to drive the highland route between the two capitals, but it's still only a day's journey. We drove the 140 kilometers to Asunción Mita, twenty-one kilometers shy of the frontier, in two and a half hours though only about half the highway had then been paved, and at Culiapa there was a ten-kilometer detour. The Maya ruins at Asunción Mita mark (along with Copán, across the Honduras border eighty kilometers northeast, see p. 160) the easternmost penetration of this great civilization. But two grassy mounds, on either side of the road, are all there is to be seen of this lesser site.

A little beyond the town, where a suspension bridge crosses the Ostua River, the lovely arches of a colonial bridge may be seen to the left, still serving those who prefer what's left of the ancient post road linking the capitals.

A beautiful lake, Atescatempo, reflecting a distant volcano, lies just off the road, in a valley four kilometers short of the border. I went for a swim in it, though one has to wade through a lot of mud and water plants to reach deep water. Many fishermen in *cayucos* with double-bladed paddles were bringing in net-loads of *cilapas, tigrillos, mojarras*, all resembling sunfish. Glimpses of a much larger lake, Güija, may be seen far to the left of the highway. Most of this lake lies in El Salvador but a small part is in Guatemala—a circumstance that is still causing trouble between the two countries, for this is a source of El Salvador's principal river, the Lempa, and of much of its vital hydroelectric power. Constructing the necessary dams, here and farther south at Guajoyo, backed the lake up so much that fields along the Guatemalan bank were flooded. In compensation Guatemala claimed a third of the power from these turbines, and presumably is getting it.

From Asunción Mita the road descends 121 kilometers, through Santa Ana and Santa Tecla, to San Salvador. It is an easy three hours' drive and the scenery is spectacular. In the shadow of the two great volcanoes,

Izalco and Santa Ana, lies Lake Coatepeque, filling what must have been the deep, round crater of an ancient third. As clear and blue as Atitlán, it resembles that most beautiful of lakes in other respects. It has no known outlet, and its excellent fishing, swimming and boating make it a favorite resort for the capital—in this case only fifty kilometers distant. The source of its water, we were told, is Atecozól, Sonsonate's memorable swimming hole.

While we were waiting for lunch under the shade of a fantastically cork-screwed 100-year-old *amate* (nature's original jungle-gym) at the rustic Hotel del Lago, a local resident filled us in on the folklore of iguanas, earthquakes and volcanoes. We had asked for iguana eggs, but had to settle for a lesser delicacy, soup made from Coatepeque's fresh-water crabs. We were already familiar, from Cuernavaca, with the peasant method of securing iguana eggs—slitting the belly of the female, removing the sac, and sewing her up. The Salvadorean twist—practised only by very unscrupulous peasants, we were assured—is to pack dozens of nuts in the empty egg-sac, sew it up, sell the iguana to *another* egg-dealer, and take flight.

It was about this time that we felt the first of many Salvadorean earth-tremors. "When the real bad ones come and you don't know what to do," our friend told us, "it's best to do nothing." The 'quakes, he added, are not directly connected with the volcanoes—"Remember that you had one of the worst at San Francisco, which lies on the same oceanic fault-line; but there have been so many of these little ones lately that the hospitals in the capital are getting ready for a major catastrophe. . . ." We looked, nonetheless, at Izalco's cone a bit apprehensively. He laughed. "Nothing doing there! See that neighboring peak? They built a big resort hotel there a few years ago, so the tourists could enjoy the fireworks. But no sooner was it built than it was out of business. Izalco quit."

In the steep slopes around Coatepeque, and closer to the capital, behind the lava fields surrounding San Salvador Volcano, we saw plenty of evidence of a deadlier pyromaniac—man. Entire mountains covered with ash. The forests gone. Smoking cornfields. Were it not that El Salvador's rich volcanic soil is highly permeable to rain, most of the country, in the opinion of an expert, would already be a desert. Some of it already is. The big coffee and sugar patrons cherish their estates. But cotton, the big new cash crop for export, that is rapidly taking over the best lowlands, threatens to "cotton the soil to death" as in our Deep South. And the remaining seven-eighths of the arable land that must support 2,600,000 people (Latin America's densest population) in an area the size of Massachusetts, is tilled by peasants who have neither the resources to fertilize the soil nor the education to terrace it. The storage reservoirs are filling up with detritus. The little topsoil left on the hills is running into the Pacific. The soil conservation budget is only half a million dollars, and salaries at the Agricultural School are so low that the usual stay of a faculty member is two years.

Two movements, and two alone, seem to offer any hope that El Salvador can escape being crushed between its narrow confines and its exploding population. One is an organization known as *Amigos de la Tierra* (Friends of the Land) which campaigns intensely in the press and on the air for soil conservation. The other is the Central American Common Market, gaining strength throughout the isthmus, but concentrated here. The leading figure in both movements is Francisco (Chico) de Sola. Since we were lucky enough to have an introduction, we decided to call him as soon as we'd checked into our rooms in San Salvador.

ONE OUT OF FOURTEEN

On our way out to the de Solas' home—for we were not only invited to come for the evening, but a chauffeur was dispatched to our hotel lest we get lost in the maze of hills overlooking the city—we reviewed what we already knew of El Salvador's history. The de Solas, we knew, were one of the *Catorce Grande* (The Fourteen Families) reputed to rule the little country's economy but not necessarily its politics. The Fourteen are not old aristocrats but new ones, self-made men or the sons and grandsons of self-made men, merchants and landowners as famous for their progressive enterprise and liberalism as for their fabulous riches and their *noblesse oblige*. Apparently this has been a tradition in El Salvador. Gage in the Colonial period described San Salvador as "a poor city," but by the time Stephens came here in 1840 it was already the richest city in the isthmus and its surrounding plantations were yielding fine tobacco and "the best indigo and the richest balsam in the world." Here came the great reformer, Morazán, "the best man in Central America," after the Indians of Guatemala had been persuaded to take up arms in defense of their traditional exploiters, the *patrones* and the Church, and drive him out.

El Salvador, Stephens wrote, "exhibits throughout an appearance of improvement, a freedom from bigotry and fanaticism, and a development of physical and moral energy not found in any other [country]. The Salvadorans are the only men who speak of sustaining the integrity of the republic as a point of national honor." Later on, as the big landowners shifted from indigo and tobacco to coffee, sorghum and cotton, this tradition sustained itself. The progressive Fourteen, importing the latest in fertilizers and machines, investing their profits for the most part *at home*, gave their little country the dominant position in the coffee trade, and a yield per acre in cotton second only to California's. Only in the matter of permitting social change to keep pace with the booming economy—cutting labor and the peasants in on a fair share of the wealth, developing consumer industries *and native consumers*, providing social security, education, and democracy—were the Fourteen Families backward. It took the army—a middle-class army which resented the exclusive country clubs of the aristocrats, and the polo fields and sports cars of their Ivy League sons; an army which had already fought the Communists for two decades and knew that it would be a losing battle as long as three-fifths of the people had a family income of less than $240 a year—to force through minimum social reforms. But even in this sphere the de Solas were said to be pioneering beyond their class. The Fourteen were said to have been shocked when the military decreed a seventy-cent minimum wage and nationalized "their" privately owned bank in 1960—but not, reputedly, the de Solas.

Even by the standards of second- and third-generation American wealth, the de Solas' town house is awesome. The living quarters, library and banquet hall, faced with walls of plate glass on the inside, surround an immense patio shaded by superb trees. A huge *ceiba*, its trunk encased in philodendron forty feet high and illuminated by spotlights, provides the focus for the lawn-terrace. Under this tree, white painted metal chairs had been arranged around a glass table. Servants had already brought the silver coffee service, decanters of Armagnac and Napoleon brandy, and snifters.

Leonora de Sola, an ebullient American, introduced us to her husband, and to their guests, the Roberto Parkers, all of whom speak excellent English. Mrs. de Sola designed the house, perhaps with an assist from her friend Edward Stone, designer of New York's Museum of Modern Art, and chose the Marinis, Tamayos and choice pre-Columbian pieces which adorn its walls and gardens. She is an enthusiast of the arts and promised to show us El Salvador's best tomorrow. Mrs. Parker, who has one of the finest collections of sculpture from the local digs, graciously offered to take us to her bathing lodge on the Pacific. Not to be outdone in hospitality, her husband, a former cabinet minister, said he would drive us home. But here, as probably in most gatherings, Francisco de Sola was the dominant figure. He is tall and very commanding. His aristocratic Sephardic features, sad-fierce eyes under beetling iron-gray brows that contrast with a reserved voice and gently smiling mouth, gave me a twinge of guilt— an uneasy sense that my superficial knowledge of his country might not quite qualify me to be talking to him. ("Did you notice," I said to Bill later, "the way he asked whether we'd made any engagements, and that when I said that we had a date two nights from now to play tennis with two Salvadorean champions, he told me peremptorily that we didn't have time for tennis, that his driver might not be getting us back in time from the *fincas* and hydroelectric projects he insists we must see. Do you think," I added jokingly, "that we're in Chico's power-orbit?" "I think," said Bill, "that he's a direct descendant of one of Alvarado's muscle-men—with the muscle converted into brains.")

There had been reports in the papers that Washington, after the imbroglio in Panama, was thinking again about the old proposed canal-route through Lake Nicaragua, and I asked Francisco de Sola what he thought about that. He answered that it would be the best solution possible, not only for Nicaragua and Costa Rica, but for the whole region. Central Americans, he added, should pay for it entirely without American aid—for the sake of their own self-respect and as a symbol of their resolve to better their condition. "Unfortunately," he continued, "very few Central Americans see it this way; they're too concerned with feathering their national or personal nests." This was especially true of the Guatemalan ruling class, I gathered; and, for different reasons, of the Costa Ricans, whose progressive and decentralized government comes of a long tradition of living off import-taxes in splendid isolation from their unstable neighbors. Much to my surprise, he praised Nicaraguans as the most cultured and politically sophisticated of Central Americans. "They alone have a tradition of two parties, Conservatives and Liberals, and there has generally been a fruitful dialogue between the two. The Somoza family dictatorship is only a passing phenomenon, and is indeed in process of being phased out. Their money, for example, no longer leaves the country; it is being invested in new industries at home."

More surprising, perhaps, was Chico's comment on his old friend Wilson Popenoe. I'd told him of our conversation yesterday, and of Popenoe's admiration for Ubico.

"Of course," he said, "of course. I dearly love Pop. But he's been an employee of United Fruit for so long that he inevitably sees things in their paternalistic frame of reference. *Ideas*—even disorderly ideas—are more important than order. In the long run it would have been better for Guatemala had Arévalo come back. They must learn to fight out these problems in the political arena, with give and take. Our military establishment here is unlike theirs."

"Why?"

"Because ours genuinely represents the middle class, and is interested in developing the country rather than squeezing it for quick profit." He admitted that this was true of Guatemala's Colonel Peralta to some extent, though Peralta's regime had been imposed from above to stifle the circulation of "dangerous thoughts."

In the period when the Communists threatened to take over El Salvador (1932–34), he himself had been among the young men armed by the Hernández Martínez regime to patrol the capital day and night and suppress the insurrection that for a time ruled Sonsonate. "But even Martínez, though ruthless in suppressing the insurrectionaries, was more liberal than Ubico. He had to be. Because here we have never had the tradition of each local politician being a *jefe* or *caudillo* supreme in his own bailiwick, and the *jefe* in the capital being supreme over all of them."

Assaulted by such waves of intelligence and hospitality, the fumes of the Armagnac, and the sight of the moon mingling with the stars in the jasmine-scented night, it was hard to be critical. What disposition I had had to question the wisdom of San Salvador's opulent few ordaining the snail's rate at which El Salvador's masses are permitted to emerge from their faceless, tin-helmeted existence, was vanishing. Suddenly there was another of those earth-tremors, slight but unmistakable. "Think nothing of it," said Roberto Parker, "there are four hundred recorded shocks here every day. In 1919 the city was destroyed. And once, several years later, a shock lasted twelve hours and was so strong we all had to sit on the floor and hold hands. But we don't live in fear. We don't think of what might happen. We can't. We have to go on living."

Roberto Parker drove us home, casually taking a pistol from his pocket and flipping it into the glove compartment before starting the car. Could there be a psychological connection, I wondered, between the *sang-froid* which masks the suppressed fear of imminent natural catastrophe, and the liberalism which overlays the fear if not the guilt of the *Catorce Grande*, never knowing when another peasant revolt or Communist conspiracy will threaten their peace.

There was never any question in our minds that Francisco de Sola is a great gentleman, and that within the framework of El Salvador's unstable social system he had achieved the universal esteem in which he is held by dint of superior intellect, integrity, and hard work. This conviction was reinforced when a mutual friend told us a little about the making of the family fortune. Chico's ancestors were among the Jews forced out of Spain during the Inquisition. They migrated to the Virgin Islands and to Curaçao. Chico's father, Don Herbert, died only a couple of years ago, aged ninety-eight. The son of a merchant, it had been his marriage to an heiress from Panama that really solidified the family fortune. Hard work, withal, had been the mortar. "In this country," as our friend put it, "most men work two hours, by which one *eats* well. Those that work four hours, *live* well. But those who work eight hours, as in your country, become almost automatically millionaires. The De Solas work sixteen hours." He had been present once when the old man, then ninety, arrived as usual for work at his office at 8 A.M. In that year, however, he had already turned over management of the vast family holdings in coffee, cotton, linseed oil, insurance and banking, to his sons. That morning he had come in with a new kind of beehive, suggesting that the house import or manufacture it. Chico took a good look at it and rejected the idea. His father insisted. Finally Chico said to him: "All right. Go ahead. But you'll have to finance it entirely out of your monthly allowance." At which the canny old man looked sidewise at our friend and winked, as if to say, "My son is now a worthy successor."

Chico's son was not only overprotected as an infant, but was put on a time schedule. Not surprisingly he rebelled, refusing to eat. This was obviously giving him a bad start toward St. Mark's and Harvard, so he was taken to New York to be checked. The doctors recommended that he be permitted to play with other children, and the de Solas' response typifies both their open-mindedness to new ideas and their civic-minded patriotism. They solved their personal problem by establishing a public kindergarten, El Salvador's first.

THE COFFEE COMPLEX

Considering that only Brazil and Colombia in this hemisphere export more coffee than little El Salvador, it's amazing how little of it one actually sees, driving along the country roads. One explanation is that a great deal of it is grown across the poorly defined northern border in more fertile Honduras, whence it is "smuggled" in for processing in El Salvador's up-to-date mills. We saw several of these in the company of Edouardo Craik, manager for the Central Coffee District of H. de Sola & Hijos. Contrary to popular belief, coffee doesn't grow on trees, nor does it leap, fully armed for wakefulness, from its native habitat to the grinder and the pot. It grows on bushes *under* trees—shade brings slow ripening; and then it is subjected to so many necessary "processings" that the wonder is it proves profitable to grow at all. To begin with, all picking is by hand. Then it must be 1) sorted in water, where the sound berries sink; 2) siphoned out to the dispulpers which remove the red-skinned outer pulp; 3) divested by fermenting of the sweetish outer slime; 4) sluiced through washing canals so the light beans will float off; 5) spread to dry in the sun on cement platforms; 6) have its flavor "set" by artificial dryers; 7) turned with wooden rakes and bedded away at night lest the rain rot it; 8) separated from its parchment covering and inner membrane by hullers; 9) polished to light blue under pressure—to impress buyers; 10) shorn of its remaining light component by fans; 11) separated and graded by machine; 12) bagged. This does not include a special going-over of the low-grade beans by hand, to remove the "elephants" and "peaberries." Nor, of course, does it include the roasting, grinding and boiling that must take place after the coffee is shipped. In Guatemala (and quite possibly here too) only eighty pounds of cleaned coffee are salvaged from every 500 pounds of ripe berries dumped into the initial receiving-vat.

The first mill we visited (Tecla No. 3) is a dry-processing plant which sorts and packs the higher grades for shipping. The coffee is bought from 23,000 producers. The sorting is done by fully automatic machines with photoelectric "eyes" and "fingers." The 150-pound hemp bags are made by H. de Sola & Hijos on the family's own hennequin plantations.

The second stop was at the "Curaçao" mill where the raw bean is processed straight through its cycle. We saw the beans lying in water, being raked and reraked in beautifully symmetrical furrows, stacked in twenty-foot-high mounds under patched canvas (these look like armies of faceless giant sentinels), and sorted by hand. The quick-fingered Indian women who do this sorting of the inferior grades draw $1 (US) a day plus social services and extras for overtime, as against 70¢ daily for labor in the fields, though most of the field labor is paid by piecework. "The fieldworker, if he wanted to, could make $3 a day," Craik remarked. "He

gets room and board and some medical care and insurance for free. He is not unionized. And he works as little as he can, living on corn and beans, still this country's staples." Coffee's chief enemy, Craik told us, is the Leaf-Miner, a new leaf-worm encouraged by the latest insecticides. It wiped out half of Guatemala's crop last year and now threatens El Salvador's.

Coffee is indeed the tenuous pivot on which El Salvador's great wealth and teeming poverty balance precariously. And in the next few days we heard a great variety of opinions regarding the identity of the villain who could any day upset this balance. The most interesting came from Roberto Aguilár, a self-made man of the enterprising new middle class, and from Raúl Castro, an Arizonian of Mexican parentage, who is our Ambassador.

Suppressing the guilt which Chico de Sola had momentarily instilled in us, we had played tennis not once but three times with Aguilár and his friends under the lights, and after one of these exciting encounters (in which Bill and I asked to be split up lest the United States be overwhelmed by Salvadorean power) Aguilár had taken us to his club for pink rum punches and the most superb dinner we were to have on all our travels. Aguilár, in the time-honored Latin-American tradition, never did get around to introducing us to his wife and nine children, though we saw a lot of him during our stay in San Salvador. He is a Guatemalan by birth, educated in the States, who came to El Salvador after the war to make a living by painting portraits. For a while he led an adventurous, Bohemian life. (An amusing incident from this period was a visit he had had from an American artist who had refused to take orders from the military during an abortive Communist uprising ten years ago and was shot in the back. His friend, after believing that he was dead, got up unharmed. The bullet turned out to be made entirely of *wood*.) But soon Aguilár began to be involved in a variety of businesses, and today he is not only a textile and soap manufacturer but runs one of the country's leading advertising agencies.

Aguilár recognizes the dangers inherent in a one-crop, or even two-

crop, economy, with El Salvador's precarious stability depending upon the vagaries of the international market. He recognizes the value of De Sola's Central American Common Market crusade; but, unlike Chico, Roberto is no crusader. To turn away from export crops, to turn the peasant into a farmer capable of growing the whole country's food, or into a *consumer* with sufficient buying power to purchase the manufactures of home industries, seems Utopian in a country belatedly experiencing the first "golden opportunities" of capitalism. The possibility that *time* is running out, that the masses can be persuaded *not* to wait several generations for the fruits of free enterprise to sift to their level, is not generally recognized south of Mexico. "The United States criticizes us for not paying higher wages," Aguilár complains with some justice, "for not dividing the wealth more equably, for not providing more and better education. How can we?—when the prices of coffee and cotton rise and fall entirely as a result of factors in *your* 'international market' over which we have no control? We're Central America's biggest importers, and close to its biggest manufacturers, but we must pay for all this with our exports of coffee and cotton. When you turn to Africa to buy coffee, where six-cents-a-day wages are paid as against one dollar here, thus causing our coffee prices to toboggan, how can you blame us for not doing better? Is the fact that you claim to be turning to Africa in order to prevent Communism from spreading there, our affair?"

The Salvadorean business community is wonderfully diversified among Lebanese, Swiss, Turks, Germans, Syrians and Chinese. It was refreshing to see a "foreigner" like Roberto Aguilár identify himself so completely with his adopted country; and it was equally refreshing to see an Indian of Mexican extraction holding down the American Embassy and genuinely concerned about the welfare of El Salvador's *mestizo* underdogs. We asked Raúl Castro if his name got him into any trouble, and whether he'd be here if fellow-Arizonian Barry Goldwater had been elected last November. He laughed. "When I went to the White House, the Secret Service turned me upside down and shook me before letting me in. As for Barry, he and

I have always been friends. I think I'd be here still." Was there anything in the rumor we'd heard, we asked him, that his predecessor in the Embassy had been asked to leave because he'd been friendly to Communist sympathizers seeking to penetrate the Rivera government? "No truth in it at all," he said. "They say that about anyone here who'd like to see the people share a little in the fortunes being made."

"Some of the *finca* owners," I said, "claim that a drop in the price of coffee prevented them from raising wages."

"When did those people ever *raise* wages when the price of coffee went *up*? As it did," he continued, "for years and years after the war. That's the trouble here. With the exception of a very few farsighted people like the de Solas, the Salvadorean businessman has never made any effort to cut the *campesinos* in on the exceptional wealth this progressive little country produces. The rich get richer and richer while the working people go right on receiving the same one dollar a day wage as always. Result: no consumers."

What about the military government, we asked him; was there any meeting of minds with Colonel Julio Adalberto Rivera? ("Liberal" military men, we knew, had been governing El Salvador off and on since the overthrow the dictator, Hernández Martínez, in 1944—some with an assist from the radical labor unions and the Communists, but most, like the present one, with a rather astonishing awareness that they must steal the Communists' thunder and make at least the beginnings of a social revolution themselves in order to survive.)

"I get along very well with the Colonel," said Raúl Castro, "and he likes Americans, but he knows—and he is right—that if he is even seen talking to me at a reception beyond the minimum required by courtesy, all the people who think that we call the turn for every move made in this part of the world will manage to brand him as a puppet of 'American Imperialism.'" We wanted to ask him whether it was true, as one Salvadorean had told us, that the president here always has a five-million-dollar "secret fund" on which to draw, for which no accounting is required, but forgot to.

Probably no good ambassador would admit to such knowledge, even if he had it. Happily the Latin American tradition of making a killing while in office, and banking it abroad pending a quick exit, runs against the grain in El Salvador.

ARTSCAPES AND SEASCAPES

One of the best-known Salvadorean poets, Alberto Masferrér, wrote a book entitled *La Doctrina del mínimum vitál*, the point of which was that the rich should not live off the blood of the poor, and that the poor, once they have achieved *their* "vital minimum" should be self-reliant and not charges of the state. If El Salvador's artists take any such interest in their country and its welfare, such work was well hidden during our stay in the capital. Mrs. Castro was sponsoring a big show of the local painters at the Embassy Residence and Leonora de Sola took us to San Salvador's only art gallery, the Forma, on Avenida Rubén Darío. Julia Díaz, who runs the gallery, makes a halfhearted resistance to the fashionable modes in her own work, but almost all the artists she exhibits work unconvincingly in the tired cubist or abstract expressionist traditions. The artist currently being shown constructs huge surfaces of grey sludge and faintly enlivens them with wobbly "canals" in black or acid green.

San Salvador's modern architecture—and it's almost all modern, earthquakes having levelled the old buildings—is at least colorful and full of variety. Eastern mosques, Chinese pagodas and Italian campaniles mingle gaily with all-glass office buildings and the stainless-steel San Salvador Intercontinental which dominates one hillside overlooking the city. An enormous new cathedral, the Don Rua, with massive dome and freestanding bell tower, was a-building. But the standout structure in the whole country is probably the new Jesuit church of Santa Ignacia, designed by Nolterius-Choussy, with its nave-length roof-comb of gleaming chromium "wings."

Our last day in San Salvador we drove to the Roberto Parkers' charming country house in Santa Tecla, where Señora Parker showed us her unrivaled collection of pre-Columbian sculpture from the El Salvador area. One of the reasons why there is almost no indigenous folk art to be seen in this country is that the Pipíl Indians who inhabited the area at the time of the Conquest had degenerated, losing even the memory of the fine arts their ancestors cultivated in Maya times and earlier. Remains of their civilization, showing influence of the Toltecs from Mexico, and of a much earlier culture called Usulután, have been excavated from tombs all over the country in this century. These were modest arts, judging from Señora Parker's collection, almost miniature, with an admirable refinement of detail in the intricate forms engraved on black stone and polished jadeite.

Señora Parker had hoped to take us to her beach cabaña, Cecimár, on the Pacific coast west of La Libertad. Unable to go herself, she graciously gave us a note to her beachkeeper, who probably has nothing to do six days out of the week, for he was so happy to introduce us to his family and help us up and down the steep slopes that we thought we'd never get into the water. The coast is very dramatic here, bristling with black volcanic rocks against which the waves break thunderously. The Parkers have had concrete basins built into the cliffside, but even in these one is in some danger of being swept out to sea. We preferred to take our chances on a stretch of black sand in a somewhat protected cove to the east. The swimming was as exciting as the scenery.

There is a fine public beach at La Libertad itself, with no rocks and many miles of almost-white sand, but unfortunately the land is being bought up so rapidly by developers that soon it may be hard to find a way through from the highway to the beach.

We sampled El Salvador's other favorite bathing site, Lake Ilopango, on the way out of the country. It lies just off to the right of the Inter-American Highway going east, half an hour's drive from the capital. The wealthy have their private docks and cabañas, well guarded by gatekeepers. We joined the boisterous middle class at Apulo. The bathing isn't much, but the antics of the bathers, the wide variety of food and drinks, and the friendliness of these carefree people, made it a memorable experience. We almost had another on the way out. "Watch out!" Bill cried as we rounded a curve. I swerved the Volkswagen and narrowly missed a family of six, with picnic baskets spread out—seated in the middle of the road. "What are they doing?" I gasped. "I don't know what they're *doing*, but they're going to be *having* a Kamikaze Sandwich if they stay in that spot much longer."

We crossed the Lempa on Central America's biggest suspension bridge, Puente Cuscatlán, and soon saw the massive and still mildly active San Miguel volcano off to our right, with fertile fields crowding its slopes. Three hours of driving after leaving the capital we were at the Honduras border.

7   HONDURAS

WE WERE PERFECTLY CERTAIN, crossing the border and heading for the checkpoint, that there was going to be nothing tame about Honduras. Everything we had heard about it spelled adventure. Other Central American countries have had periods of relative calm, even a blank decade or two when nothing at all seemed to happen, but not Honduras. Even the names of its historical personages—Tibúrcio Carías Andino, Policarpo Bonilla, Nepomucena Zelaya, Teréncio Sierra, Froylán Túrcios—have a fierce, predatory ring. The very name Honduras comes from the Spanish word for depths, and the land itself is so crisscrossed with rugged mountain chains, rushing streams, rain forests and jungles that very few roads have ever been built—or survived for long if they were. As a matter of fact, there is only *one* road of any consequence in Honduras, the one we were about to

take. It cuts north from the Inter-American Highway at Jícaro Galán, is paved as far as Tegucigalpa, and then lazes to ancient Comayagua, degenerates to San Pedro Sula (deliberately, say the citizens of that progressive city) and finally picks up confidence enough along its final sixty-six kilometers to reach Puerto Cortés and the Caribbean. Alone of all the Central American states, Honduras has no railway connecting its capital to the rest of the world.

We were not disappointed. Adventure began right at the customs. Entering cars are lined up in a long shed, off which offices open on both sides. In each office sits a bureaucrat at a rolltop desk. An assistant or two manipulate the rubber stamps, the piles of forms, and the cash box. We never did find out exactly what was being done to us in each office, but the end result was always the same: one *lempira*, a bedraggled, brown piece of paper currency worth fifty cents. The explanation at our first port of call was interesting. The official was enjoying his siesta. For one *lempira*, we were politely told, he would be happy to wake up. Could we come back later, after siesta-time? we asked. We could, but unfortunately, señors, without the forms from this office, none of the other offices would be able to refer on *their* forms to the serial numbers on *this* office's forms. . . . We paid our first *lempira* and were on our way.

By the time we had gotten to the sixth or seventh cubicle, an hour had passed and my own papers—passport, entry permit, exit permit, registration, driver's license, Hertz rental card, vaccination forms, etc.—were in a more disorganized state than any of the officials' desks. My Otomi bag in which I kept most of these documents as well as my money, my reading glasses, my sunglasses, my camera, several rolls of film, three filters, three tennis balls, two pipes, tobacco, pipe-cleaners, a lighter, a pair of pliers, and the obsolete coinage of half a dozen countries, had been emptied and restuffed so many times I was dizzy. Suddenly I froze in front of the seventh desk.

"Bill!"

"What's wrong?"

"I've lost my passport-case—and *all* my travelers' checks!"

"Might I suggest that you look under your left armpit?"

"Bill—this is no time for joking—I'm serious—"

"Your—left—armpit."

There it was.

In front of the eighth cubicle some kind of an altercation was in progress. A truckdriver and two mechanics who had been working under the hood were shouting at each other and they were soon joined by an officer and a half-dozen of the Honduranean soldiers in their baggy uniforms and high boots, hand grenades dangling from their belts and pockets. Not only did it look like a potentially explosive situation but we had no way of getting into the office; and if we didn't leave soon we'd never make Tegucigalpa before dark. I looked around in desperation and noticed an election poster on one of the walls. The name of the present dictator was legible. I stepped up to the officer, cleared my throat, and said calmly but firmly: "Lieutenant, perhaps you can help us. We are reporters. We have an appointment to see your chief"—(with another quick glance at the poster)—"Colonel Don Osvaldo López Arellano. . . ."

"Watch out!" said Bill, "the grenades may go off automatically!"

In a non-flash the crowd dissolved. The door to Cubicle No. 8 snapped open. The official at his desk rose to greet us with a warm handshake, his other hand juggling every rubber stamp in sight. Would we overlook the inconveniences? And would we take a soldier along with us in the car? We would, gladly—though uncertain whether we would be carrying a private bodyguard, a hostage, a spy, or a time bomb. We held our breaths while the soldier wedged himself into the back seat.

"Are we captives?" I asked Bill as we drove off and he handed our passenger a chicken sandwich and a cup of coffee.

"I don't think we're exactly captives," he replied, "but if you go over another bump with the speed with which you just hit that last one, there may only be a brief flash in the sky to mark the spot where *The Road to Panama* came to a dazzling but premature end."

TEGUCIGALPA

The road northward from Jícaro Galán ascends through arid mountains, outcroppings of black rock alternating with precariously tilted cornfields. Pines on the higher slopes have turned brown in patches: a blight, we were later to discover, that aerial sprays, in the hands of the American A.I.D. mission have done little to arrest. But the most noticeable and welcome difference from the man-made desolation of the Salvadorean settlements is the Honduranean peasant's home. It has a well-proportioned veranda running right around the low house. The tiled roof has a handsome overhang supported by chocolate-brown beams. The walls are painted dazzling white. And the fences that surround the yard are generally made of intricately fitted stones or wooden palings alternating orange and blue. These homes, by the look of it, are here to stay. Pride, thought, and a sense of design, went into their construction.

Tegucigalpa is dramatically nestled on the hillsides at the far end of a broad valley split by the Choluteca River. Comayagüela, as the part on the western bank is known, was once a separate village. After passing the airport, the road crosses an arched bridge flanked by some pretty slummy houses, a primitive scene enlivend by women washing their clothes in the shallow stream-bed; and then—wham! directly in front is the capital's steep hill with a complex of ultramodern stainless-steel-and-glass administrative "skyscrapers" on one side of the climbing street, and the fantastically turreted Moorish-style National Palace on the other. (Since it wasn't night yet, we failed to notice a giant "Pilsner Beer" bottle outlined in green, red and yellow neon which caps the entire scene.)

It was four o'clock of a Friday afternoon, so we had an hour to establish residence in a hotel and make arrangements to be flown to Copán and the Bay Islands before everything shut down tight for the weekend—and the holiday election contest between Colonel Osvaldo López Arellano and Ramón Villeda Morales on Monday. Our already shrinking resources made it incumbent upon us to solicit a maximum of Honduranean hospitality.

First we drove to the Gran Hotel Lincoln. The Guatemalan tourist office had already wired ahead, explaining that our ultimate objective was to make tourists aware of the opportunities for travel in Central America. Honduras, alone in the isthmus, has no tourist office; but the Gran Hotel Lincoln wasn't taking up the slack. It even disclaimed receiving the telegram. Bill and I were discussing a move to the nearby Prado when an American mining prospector stepped up to us and said loudly: "Save your time. Those kikes at the Prado never give away anything. I'd never be seen in the place, myself." It seemed like a good introduction, so we drove to the Prado at once, and were not disappointed. The hotel was jammed with reporters and V.I.P. election-watchers, but the two proprietors, without even asking for our credentials, gave us one of their own rooms, gratis. Later that evening, as we were waiting for dinner, who should walk in and sit down at the next table but our informant of the Lincoln, the choleric American mining engineer. I walked over to his table and asked him if he was ordering *gefüllte fish*.

Two hours earlier, however, we had gone to our room overlooking the patio only to discover that all government offices would close in ten minutes. We consulted the proprietors and they told us that the Foreign Ministry across the street was the only office we could get to in ten minutes. Without changing our clothes or even unpacking a coat and tie, we rushed across the street, flew up the marble steps, and asked the appointments secretary whether we might have an emergency interview with the Minister. She ushered us into the antechamber, and as we sat there panting and contemplating some aluminum-painted statuettes of Mars, Venus and La Libertad, we asked ourselves how crazy we could be.

Jorge Fidel Durón, Secretario de Relaciones Exteriores, is one of those great gentlemen to be found in all Central American governments, no matter what the character or political coloration of the reigning *jefe* may be. He ushered us into his office ahead of a delegation of impeccably dressed American businessmen, asked us to be seated beside his desk, and when he had heard what we wanted to do, called in his secretary and dictated letters of introduction to the three top officers in the Air Corps. It was a good thing he *had* dictated three, too, because the first two colonels we called on were nowhere to be found. It took us the better part of two days to locate Colonel Chinchilla, the third, but he did fly us eventually to the Bay Islands. Meanwhile our problem was: how to get to Copán?

The problem was solved after twenty-four hours of frantic negotiation. It began when we left the Foreign Ministry and returned to the lobby of the Prado. Out of nowhere, three friends materialized. We'd never laid eyes on any of them until we started telephoning the colonels from the lobby phone. They saw we needed help and before long the five of us were having dinner together and drawing up plans.

Aldo Bacuzzi works for Esso. He has a plane of his own but he said it would be tied up tomorrow with previous commitments. He is a great-grandson of Francisco Bertránd, an old-time dictator (1911–19) who got tossed out by revolutionaries after two remunerative terms. Educated at Louisiana State, Aldo talks in a Deep South drawl and is as cynical as any character in Faulkner. "At least under this lil' ole Blue Party that is rerunning Colonel López on Monday, there is order and some industrialization. If Villeda wasn't a Commie, he was the next thing to it, giving Fidel plenty of room to fool around along our north coast. The 'ins' always do well financially speaking. With million-dollar expense accounts and everything else they want for free, why should they steal? Both parties sweep whatever gains their predecessor made out the window. Villeda's Red Party set fire to a fine park that *his* predecessor had made, just out of spite."

An acquaintance of Aldo's, who had come up to the table at this point, expressed similar views. He was an air force colonel with 12,000 hours flying time, who had flown with our 105th Observation Squadron out of Langley Field during World War II. His name is Luis Alonso Fiallos. In 1933 he had founded Honduras' military air arm, and two years earlier still he had organized Central America's principal airline, TACA, with Lowell Yerex.[1] He is now retired and has a *finca* outside the capital in which

[1] TACA is called "The airline that started from an eye" here because Yerex started it in 1933 with money given him in gratitude by the dictator Tibúrcio Carías Andino for his bombing of the revolutionaries, in which engagement Yerex had lost an eye.

he has invested $150,000. He swears that if Villeda Morales wins on Monday, he and all other men of substance will leave the country. "Villeda may not be a Communist, but he will turn the country over to them just as he was beginning to when we overthrew him last year. You helped him almost until the end—I say 'almost' because López Arellano's *golpe* could never have succeeded without you. You helped Villeda because some of you still think countries like ours can be run like democracies. They can't. Only the military can provide stability and progress. The liberals make only chaos. Villeda's labor reforms, under which we still suffer, have ruined business. Not so much the minimum wage as the clause that makes it impossible to fire inefficient or disloyal help. But I don't believe Villeda has the popularity he once had. Have you seen any posters? Or meetings? No, Villeda won't win."

The talk veered to Castro, and Ramón Osuna, our second new friend, who is here surveying the arts in Central America for the Pan-American Union, contributed his memories of Castro's visit to Montreal in 1959. Ramón is a Cuban by birth and his father had then been Ambassador to Canada, with the job of keeping the unpredictable Fidel and his enormous entourage of 149 joyriders out of trouble. "Raúl was on the phone from Havana day and night," Ramón said, "telling his brother that the Cuban papers were saying he'd already sold out to Wall Street and the State Department. That did it. By the time Fidel got to Dallas, where Raúl flew to meet him, he was in the Communist bag."

Our third friend, Harold Fonseca, by-passed politics with the suggestion that we visit some of the artists. He is a painter himself, a Costa Rican who works here for both the OAS and the Pan American Union—with a little moonlighting for the McCann Erickson corporation thrown in to keep him solvent. First we visited the home of Arturo López Rodezno who does exciting glazed-enamel work on copper—*his* moonlighting being the direction of the Bellas Artes museum. Then we looked at some of the wonderful primitive paintings of Antonio Velasquez, an old Indian from San Antonio Oriente who paints only one scene, the plaza of his native village, but does it with such loving care than no two views are the same.

It was now long past midnight but Aldo insisted that we take a scenic tour "of this li'l ole city." For an hour he drove us up and down every hill —so fast that we couldn't have seen anything even if the street lamps had been lighted—recounting in Faulknerian tones the glorious sins of *caudillos* past and present. Sunday he would take us fishing in the Gulf of Fonseca, and tomorrow he would fly us over the Guayambre River where there are "lost cities bigger than Tikal" buried in jungles so dense "you-all could drop a toothpick and it would never reach the ground." But tomorrow, we kept reminding Aldo, was Copán day, and if his plane was tied up, couldn't he find us another?

COPAN BY ESSO MAP

Aldo could, and did. But it took a lot of traveling. To and from the airport three times; side trips to the homes of air force majors, lieutenant colonels and colonels; and finally success in the most improbable of locations, the loft of a downtown grocery store. Aldo shouted up through an open trap door, and down the ladder came Jesús Ricardo Flefíl, a tall, thin, handsome young man with Arabic features, whose moonlighting from the grocery business turned out to be a Piper agency. Yes, he'd be glad to fly us to Copán this afternoon, though he'd never been there, if we'd pay for the gas. (As it turned out, he never let us pay for even that, insisting that he'd had too good a time.)

Departure was set for four o'clock, so after a big spaghetti lunch at the excellent Roma restaurant with Harold Fonseca, we decided to take a siesta and make up for last night's loss of sleep. Our eyes had been shut about five minutes when the political experts moved into the patio and started holding a full-dress rehearsal of the coming election. The walls shook. Bill snapped upright from his pillow like a hinge with a spring.

"Jesus! This place is noisy. I'm going to ask for my money back."

"What money?"

"Tomorrow I'm moving into the closet. The top shelf looks inviting."

"I'll join you, if they supply seat belts."

"You want everything?"

We stopped in the lobby to talk to an American girl who is here trying to reteach the natives to weave textiles, make straw hats (even these are now imported) and carve the great native woods instead of exporting them for bars and roulette wheels. It's all part of the A.I.D. program which the cynical Aldo calls "The Gravy Train." At the desk, where Ramón had joined us, an American lady leaned over and asked the clerk hopefully: "What is there to *see* here in Honduras?"

The clerk looked up from her typing and said: "Nothing."

"But don't you have—maybe—a museum?"

"They burnt it down five years ago," said the clerk without changing tone or expression, "in a revolution."

The tourist would not be detoured. "Any—ruins?"

The clerk gave her a chilling glance. "There's ruins everywhere in this country, Ma'am. Americans blasted the tops off some new ones out by the lake last week—with dynamite."

Ramón, who is an amateur archaeologist, blanched. A professional one probably would have dropped dead. But the ruins had been blasted, as we were to learn from Ambassador Burrow on Sunday. Perhaps it's just as well that Copán is hard to get to. . . .

By car, it's an all day trip one way, over bad roads. By plane (three time a week) the round trip from Tegucigalpa costs $36. From Guatemala (the ruins are only 14 kilometers from the border) the round trip takes three days via Zacapa and Chiquimula, involves a 40-kilometer Jeep ride from Jocotán, which can only be made in the dry season, and requires a passport with a Honduras visa. We were glad we'd met Flefíl.

At 2:30 we were ready to take off, Flefíl and Ramón in the front seats of the Piper Apache 219, Bill and I in the back. Flefíl revved up, then cut the motor, turning around. "What's the matter?"

"Where is Copán? I have no map!"

I reached into my sack and handed him our Esso road map. "Perfect!" We were off.

After crossing a succession of mountain ranges, some barren and some covered with jungle, we set down on the pasturelike runway of Copán. It was 3:40. Tobacco plantations were on both sides of us, and directly in front a pair of mating horses eyed our intrusion suspiciously. Through a grove of trees, less than five minutes walk away, lay the famous ruins: the oblong high-relief stelae standing like timeless sentinels in the parklike plaza; the acropolis with its various pyramids, ballcourt and stairways; and farther back the Copán River—once threatening to undermine the whole site, now diverted by the archaeologists from its original channel and flowing shallowly over smooth boulders.

Having little more than an hour before the fading light would require us to take off, we took as many photos as possible in the hope of studying at leisure what we couldn't possibly observe carefully on the run. But the black-and-white film would not show what surprised us most—and what was not commented on by any observer, from Stephens to Huxley to Morley, to our knowledge. The incredibly beautiful color of the stones! Stela "C," for example, is weathered in several shades of delicate pink. The very deeply cut Stela "B," in which birds and butterflies were roosting, is in various tones of pale green and yellow. Stela "M," at the bottom of the steep Hieroglyphic Stairway, is grey, its particular lichen blending almost to camouflage with the stones of the noble monument behind it and the bark of the huge *ceibas* and other trees that grip its steps in their tentacle-roots.

I had seen pictures of "The Young Corn-God" and of the similar figure with breastplate and raised hand that are in the little museum here. But I was unprepared for such wonders as the big head at the northeast corner of Temple 11, or the magnificent "Ik" god with negroid features, brandishing a massive scepter and holding a serpent in his month. I was not prepared either for the *extent* (though hardly comparable with Tikál) of the ruins, or for the immense variety and quantity of the sculptures, unrivalled by any Maya ruin. I was a little shocked, too, by the obvious deterioration which the weather is causing to the soft stone, but I'm not sure that placing these great monoliths in a museum would be the answer. Half of the beauty of Copán is in the setting. Covers would be murderous. Perhaps periodic sprayings with some preservative plastic might arrest the slow decay.

For anyone who has the time—and how we wished we had!—there is a very good little hotel, the Maya (three dollars a day with meals), fifteen minutes walk from the ruins. A turn in the road is marked, appropriately, with a stela.

NORTH TO THE BAY ISLANDS

San Pedro Sula, capital of Honduras' rich northwest, applied to Tegucigalpa for a jetport recently, though knowing full well that the politicos who roost in the arid capital's rookery would turn it down. They did. Undaunted, the enterprising local merchants raised three million dollars and built one without federal help. The fact that the politicos have managed to keep the big airlines from landing there yet, doesn't discourage the San Pedro Sulans. Everything, they believe, is bound to come their way sooner or later. And they are probably right. For here, only two-and-a-half hours from Miami by jet, is a modern city built by a new breed, and the gateway to the richest of agricultural lands, and the best beaches on the Caribbean coast, and the Elysium of the Bay Islands.

So fearful are the politicos of Teguc, however, of yielding hegemony to those who would know what to do with it, that they've managed to keep even the automobile road in poor repair. Along its 200 kilometers are preliminary attractions. Comayagua, about a third of the way, was the first capital of Honduras, and contains most of the fine architecture in the republic. The cathedral and five other churches date from the 1500s, and some of the sculpture on the cathedral's massive façade shows Indian influence. But Comayagua, with its mummified bishops, its ingrown "Castilian" society, and its pride in having lost precedence to Teguc for snubbing a *caudillo's* mistress, is almost a ghost town.

Lake Yojoa, fifty-three kilometers farther north, is a livelier attraction. In size between Atitlán and Coatepeque, and almost as beautiful, Honduras' only lake provides the best fresh water fishing in Central America. There are good breeding grounds in the reeds along the shore, and bass up to fifteen pounds may be taken with plugs. Until recently, at least, the condor, world's largest of birds, could be seen soaring overhead; and the nearby forests have deer aplenty, and puma.

Vast banana plantations stretch along the coast in an almost unbroken line from Puerto Barrios in Guatemala as far as Trujillo three hundred kilometers to the east. They are served on the Honduras side by a network of railways running from south of San Pedro Sula, through that capital, and north to the United Fruit ports of Puerto Cortés and Tela; a third line runs eastward along the coast of La Ceiba, the Standard Fruit port, and then halfway to Trujillo, where Columbus made his first continental landfall in 1502 and William Walker met his timely end in 1860. There is argument whether the white sand beach at Tela or the one just east of La Ceiba (La Cocita) is the best of the Caribbean coast, but there can be little doubt that both will support big resort hotels once this area is opened up by San Pedro Sula's ghostly jetport.

Unless, that is, the Bay Islands steal the whole show. As well they may.

Colonel Chinchilla's pilot, Lt. Carlos Aguirre, flew us over from La Ceiba in his single-engine Cessna 180. The first of the chain, Utila, lies some thirty-five kilometers due north. Roatán, largest of the group and quite mountainous, has the loveliest south shore, deeply indented at several points with many-fingered inlets, on several of which nestle attractive red-roofed towns. There is a great arc-shaped white sand beach with coconut palms north of the western tip. Coral reefs, ranging in hue from sapphire to lemon yellow, lie off most of Roatán's coast, and off the eastern tip of Barbaretta, third and smallest of the four. This comparatively forbidding, heavily wooded island already has a beach-side airstrip to match those of the bigger three, and is said to be the prospective site of a big hotel. Why, we couldn't find out. Easternmost of the Bays, and most spectacular, is Guanaja, whose capital (also called Guanaja) covers the whole of one of the many "satellite cayes" along its protected eastern shore. The airstrip for small planes is on the main island, a ten-minute boat ride from the town, but the larger strip for regular SAHSA flights is on the northwest shore, almost an hour's walk from the ferry. The man to contact in Guanaja is Jack Coffey, whose launch, *Lady Cynthia*, is available at the small plane strip, and who is agent for the purchase of satellite cayes—complete with cocoa palms, beaches and the best skindiving anywhere—for as little as three thousand dollars. Guanaja is the highest (fifteen hundred feet), the most populous, and the richest in virgin pre-Columbian burial mounds, of the Bay Islands, which "belonged" to the British until 1859 and whose inhabitants, descendants of liberated African slaves from the colony of Grand Cayman, still speak English and much prefer their seafaring cousins in Belize and the Caymans to their tax-collecting godfathers in Honduras proper.

DICTATORS AND DEMOCRATS

Ephraim George Squier was one of those remarkable nineteenth-century antiquarians and practical dreamers, like Stephens and Maudslay, who left an account of Central America that has not been surpassed. This New York businessman's "beat" was Honduras and Nicaragua, and his long-out-of-print study of Honduras begins with a description of the "great transverse valley" through Comayagua uniquely linking the two oceans, and an assertion that Honduras will never come into its own until spanned along this natural ditch by a "great Inter-Oceanic Highway." As a child of progressive nineteenth-century mercantilism, Squier naturally saw this highway in terms of the Iron Horse; and as a true Anglo-Saxon liberal of that era, he saw only one solution to Honduras' endemic political turmoil. "It is only by a judicious system of colonization," he wrote, "which shall ultimately secure the predominance of white blood, at the same time that it shall introduce intelligence, industry and skill, that the country can hope to achieve peace, prosperity and greatness."

Honduraneans, just as naturally, wanted no part of the solution, though its native strong men, in the hundred years that followed, played off one group of enterprising white intruders against another, partly in the hope of getting Honduras "developed," but more often as a means of securing their own grip on the floundering economy for a quick killing before the inevitable counter-insurrection. Monday's election, which we were about to witness, represented the latest phase in the confrontation between that old order and the first effective native reform movement in Honduras' history. The result, it was already quite clear, was foreordained. The current dictator, Colonel López Arellano, had the guns, and the backing of effective American power. The reformer, ex-President Ramón Villeda Morales, whom López had overthrown in the 136th *coup d'état* of the 142 years of Honduras' independence from Spain, had none of the guns, and only the moral blessings of the American liberals from the Ambassador on down.

We talked with the Ambassador, with Adolph Berle, who was here on some kind of unofficial face-saving mission from the Department of State to see that the election was "fair," and with Villeda Morales himself; and there was general agreement that the dictatorship would win.

At Sunday lunch in the Embassy Residence, Ambassador Charles Burrow spoke to us with genuine nostalgia of the Villeda Morales presidency, when "most of Honduras' progress toward modernization and enfranchisement took place"—so much so, in fact, that at one point Mrs. Burrow said nervously, "Chuck, don't you think we've strayed a long way from Copán?"

Mr. Berle, in his room at the Prado, expressed great alarm over reports that *Liberalista* election-cards were being seized by the military "guarding" the polls, and that troops from the Somoza dictatorship across the border in Nicaragua were crossing over at El Paraíso in mufti to help López Arellano's soldiers "maintain order." There had been violence in the countryside already, Berle added, and one liberal party organizer had already been driven into the capital with a broken head. Mrs. Berle said sadly: "I wish so much we were doing what you're doing—looking for artists and works of art. . . ." I asked the former Assistant Secretary of State what he was going to do when he returned home. "Write a book on the sources of *power*," he said with a wry smile.

We found Villeda Morales in his spacious home overlooking Teguc, not far from the Embassy Residence. Why had he been permitted to return from exile to contest the election? Presumably at the "suggestion" of our State Department, irked by criticism that we had not only acquiesced in his overthrow on the eve of the 1963 election—which his prospective successor, Modesto Rodas Alvarado, would surely have won—but also that we had clandestinely aided the army coup. Villeda had been a celebrated pediatrician and author before he entered the political bullring. Balding and mild-mannered, he talks like a liberal college professor; and without bitterness or a trace of the anti-Americanism his enemies accuse him of having.

If anything, he seemed a little bewildered over the Administration's two-faced solicitude—he himself having been the *only* Honduranean invited to President Johnson's "Christian Breakfast-Lunch" in Washington two weeks ago. He made no allusion to the belated action which had presumably "forced" the military to oust him two years ago, his organizing of a 2,500-man civil guard to prevent the army from counting his successor out at the polls—the army in Honduras being an institution over which the president has no control and which always sides with the big landowners in a showdown.

I asked Villeda whether he considered himself a socialist.

"Perhaps," he said, "but of the right wing."

"To the right of Norman Thomas?"

"Yes. You might say that my politics is of the Roosevelt or Kennedy or Adolph Berle persuasion. President Kennedy promised me, in fact, that he would never permit my government to be overthrown by the military, but there was not enough time after the *golpe,* and before his assassination, for action. He would never, I feel certain, have recognized López, and therefore López would not have survived."

I pointed out that the Dominican military clique that had overthrown Juan Bosch had been recognized, and so had Peralta; but Villeda claimed that Honduras' situation was quite different. "Military regimes," he added, "are the *antesalas* (waiting rooms) for Communism. *Coups de'état* are the negation of the Alliance for Progress. Capitalists will always—shortsightedly, for their own health—back military governments."

I told him of the complaints we'd been hearing in Teguc that Communists had infiltrated his government. He threw up his hands. "The proof that they *didn't* was in fact that the military regime ousted *none* of my appointees —except, of course, my cabinet. Even some of those were offered posts."

Why had he been allowed to return and campaign? I asked the scholarly leader. "Because your government only recognized López on condition that these elections tomorrow be held."

"Can you win?"

"Our party will receive a big majority, as always; but outside of the capital and San Pedro Sula, the army's intimidation will be too great to allow us to win."

ON TO NICARAGUA

We watched Villeda's gloomy forecast being fulfilled Monday, the peaceable voters at the polling places oddly segregated by sexes following the passage

of a universal suffrage law seven years ago. But before we left the capital, we visited one of the most unorthodoxly decorated but beautiful churches I had ever seen. We had already stopped at the cathedral, with its chiruguer-esque altar, gold-leafed and busy. There Bill had photographed a priest investing in lottery tickets, and a leper, hooded and begging alms. "Shake hands, Ramón!" he greeted our friend outside the portal, and after Ramón had let go of his hand, "I just shook hands with a leper!" The really interest-ing church into which Ramón guided us is Nuestra Señora de los Dolores, a few blocks away. The façade has some fine primitive saints of a greenish cast framed in bone-white niches. But inside everything is as fancy and gay as a Greek wedding in Chinatown. "Naïve baroque," I christened it; but Ramón pointed out rightly that the surrealistic overtones—three swans for the Holy Trinity, varicolored light bulbs framing saints, and above all the red neon halo of the Virgin emerging from the golden forestry behind the altar—qualify Magritte for an assist.

Though he never saw it, the Belgian painter would surely have been enchanted by this symphony of the unexpected. Blue vaulting, very low, with rosettes and elaborately carved medallions, from which swing circlets of little lights. Faked marble in the apse and transepts. Columns and pilasters of orange and blue, decorated here and there with old gold. Everything against the rules of good taste; everything working perfectly.

8 NICARAGUA

WE CAME SO CLOSE to missing the earthly paradise—and the choicest little hotel in Central America—that it still gives us chills when we think of it. We had crossed the border at El Espiño with all the dispatch to be expected from a benevolent dictatorship that still prides itself—after thirty-one years of family rule—on its efficiency. No baggage inspection, no waiting, no fees. We duly admired that masterpiece of American nonobjective art, the white stripe down the middle of the road. We followed "Nic 1" sixty-five kilometers to Estelí and forty-six more to Sébaco. Cattle in neatly fenced ranches, tobacco under cheesecloth, cotton being mechanically picked; not much else. Then we elected to swing twenty-eight kilometers east on "Nic 3" for a quick look at Matagalpa before pushing on to Managua. If we'd continued east we'd have come to the end of the line (or almost) at Muy

Muy, but that would have been too much, too much. Matagalpa is a pretty, provincial capital but no earthly paradise. There is a handsome gray-white cathedral surrounded by cypresses like exclamation points and I was photographing it from the top of a bus, when Bill came up and said, "Let's take a look at this hotel and shove off." The hotel he referred to was listed in our abbreviated road-guide as *"Santa María de Ostuma. Relaxing atmosphere. American Plan. No hot water. Pets allowed."* Our first two inquiries drew blanks. A pride of schoolboys in black suits, white shirts, string ties, and the faces of hungry ferrets gave us a variety of answers. But they all pointed north. Five kilometers out of town, ten kilometers . . . no sign of any hotel. Twilight was not far off. "We've missed it," Bill said, "if it exists at all. Let's turn and head for Managua." I agreed with him, but I hate to be proved wrong. "So you don't want to relax? We've gone this far, let's ask one more peasant." We did, and to our astonishment he said "Five kilometers farther." Luckily for us.

SANTA MARIA DE OSTUMA

We saw the sign, finally, and turned up a winding drive into the hills, the way somewhat ominously marked with stakes sharpened to points and covered with fresh, red paint like blood. One approaches the rustic chalet from the back, and there is nothing to prepare one for what lies in front. —Except for the proprietor in leathern jacket, who in this instance happened to be doing some gardening and greeted us. Don Leopoldo Salazar is a jolly, round-faced man with a ruddy complexion and white hair. When we told him in Spanish that we intended to take a quick look at his establishment and then press on to Managua, he smiled tolerantly and said in perfect English: "Come in, gentlemen, come in and look around."

That was all Don Leo needed to say, and he knew it. We stepped inside the hotel, stepped out through the wall of glass at the "front," took one look, and rushed back to the Volkswagen to unload our cameras and suitcases. There is a lawn in front of the hotel, and then a six-foot hedge that gives off an overpowering perfume—a masculine perfume of mountains and freedom. Behind the hedge are seven magnificent ornamental trees, fifty feet high or more, each different, and cunningly spaced. There is a narrow opening in the hedge, after which the lawn, now only twenty feet wide, continues for another fifty feet. Then it vanishes!

Hundreds of feet below this "tee," and as far as the eye can see, lies a "driving range" of the gods, the fertile valley of the Rio Viejo, laid out in thousands of fields, their varied shades of blue-green depending on the crop. Far on the western rim, but not visible, lies the town of Estelí, through which we had passed three hours ago. *Back* of this lookout, over the top of Don Leo's flat chalet, is the westernmost extremity of a cloud-forest, the Cordillera Isabelia, extending hundreds of miles northeast through the valleys of the Tuma and Bocay rivers, and finally into the unexplored jungles of eastern Honduras. Scores of tributary rivers water this noble forest. Jaguar, puma, wild boar, tapir, sloths, howler and spider monkeys, and of course deer, roam a veritable unexploited game preserve, while every kind of parrot and the almost extinct *quetzal*[1] flash through the upper reaches of the *ceibas*.

After a sumptuous dinner of boar-steak, avocados, saffron rice and bread-fruit, we walked back to the "tee" to watch the moon drift out of the low-hanging clouds. Then we settled down with Scotches-and-sodas to hear Don Leo's stories of life in the Nicaraguan hinterland.

A question about how he prepared his wild boar for the table (ours had been cooked in wine, but sometimes he uses beer) reminded Don Leo of the time his son had been treed by a pack of forty of the ferocious creatures, and had had to shoot five of them with his rifle before they retreated. On another hunting expedition, alone, Don Leo had been attacked by swarms of bees, which the peasants call *quitacalzones* for a good reason. "They go up the legs of one's pants. I jumped off my mule, took off my pants, then my shirt, then my underdrawers, throwing all three over the saddle. But then the mule took one look at *me* and bolted. He didn't recognize me without my clothes! For two hours I ran after him, trying to get my clothes. Suddenly I ran into a group of Indian women. They screamed 'El diablo!' and ran away from me faster than the mule."

On another occasion, Don Leo's dog had been asleep on the veranda roof. "He must have had a bad dream because he rolled off—and landed on a peasant woman taking laundry off the line. The dog lay on the ground, stunned. The laundress fainted. A Negro servant ran out to see what all

[1] Worshiped among the pre-Columbian Indians, and prized for its emerald-green tail feathers, this ruby-breasted trogon of the Central American cloud forests was rare then and is almost extinct today. In Guatemala, where it is the national emblem, a very few may survive in the Alta Vera Paz. There may still be some in Costa Rica (see p. 184). But here, and in the forests of the Jicaques in Honduras, the male quetzal is still king. Sixty visitors from the Audubon Society would be visiting his hotel shortly, Don Leo told us, to observe the royal bird, dozens of which he has observed on both sides of the Continental Divide without leaving his 4,800 acres. The last word on the mating habits and domestication of the quetzal is contained in *Jungle in the Clouds*, a beguiling Honduranean adventure by Victor Wolfgang Von Hagen, the archaeologist whose *Ancient Sun Kingdoms of the Americas* for the first time brings the Mayas to life.

the barking and screaming was about and when she saw the laundress under a sheet, *she* fainted. I had to revive all three of them."

Don Leo wanted us to write in his guest book and he pointed out proudly the signatures of various "celebrities." King Leopold of the Belgians had been enchanted more than once. Frank Sinatra seemed to have enjoyed the seclusion, Peter Townsend had spent a week digging in Don Leo's private ruins to escape the wolf pack of reporters in the wake of his hectic affair with Princess Margaret. What about "Tacho" Somoza, we asked Don Leo, had the old Nicaraguan strong man slept here? Perhaps because we had already expressed regret when the news of Villeda Morales' defeat came in over the radio, Don Leo answered obliquely.

"We Nicaraguans have little respect for the people of Honduras," he said. "They hate us, and we couldn't care less. Villeda was a two-faced ruler, weak. Castro's guerrillas, trying to overthrow Tachito [Tacho Somoza's son, now army chief-of-staff] infiltrated Honduras' northeast corner, and Villeda *pretended* to send expeditions after them, but took care always to warn them first. That is why he was overthrown. He fooled you, but he didn't fool Honduras' army."

But what did he think of Tachito, and Tachito's brother Luis, and their puppet, the present President, René Schick? we asked Don Leo.

"Well," he answered with a grin, "maybe we're a little tired of the Somozas after thirty years, but they *are* good rulers. Look at our prosperity. The fantastic money being made in cotton these days. Do you know that the alluvial thirty-foot loam between León and Commandero and between Tipitapa and Lake Nicaragua yields 7,300 pounds for every two acres, and that pickers get up to two dollars and a half per hundred-pound bag? Consider also that our good relations with *you*, because of our implacable anti-Communism, we owe to the Somozas. I lived here and saw my personal property stolen and destroyed by Sandino's [2] bandits in the early 'thirties. Under the Communists it would be the same. We have learned that the only way to handle them is to shoot them."

We were glad to be wearing our sweaters when we turned in about ten

---

[2] Augusto Cesár Sandino won enduring fame in Latin America by defying the second Marine intervention in Nicaragua and successfully eluding capture. In 1934, after the Marines had left, Sandino was invited to dine with President Sacasa, and as he left the National Palace was murdered by members of the National Guard. The Guard was commanded by "Tacho" Somoza, who ran for the presidency with Liberal Party backing two years later, and won. The Somoza family has operated government and business in Nicaragua ever since.

o'clock and we were still wearing them when the valley filled with sunlight at six the following morning. At this altitude of 4,500 feet, it is never *hot* in Santa María de Ostuma except when one is in direct sunlight. The air, washed by the scudding clouds over the jungle, is always exhilarating.

"Breakfast is waiting for you," said Bill from his bed, "a half boar on toast."

"I'll have mine with fried quetzal eggs," I said.

"*Male* quetzal eggs, naturally," he said.

We breakfasted more modestly on scrambled eggs and bacon, black bean paste and sour cream—local products of Don Leo's productive acres, like everything else in this "Switzerland of Nicaragua." While Don Leo was showing us his pet baby sloth, hanging upside-down by its three-toed feet from his walking stick, we asked him for our bill. "No bill," he said, "you're my guests. You're writing a book, aren't you? Well, when it's finished, send it to me and I'll *sell* it for you."

RUBEN DARIO AND WILLIAM WALKER

Far and away the most celebrated names in Nicaragua's history are those of Rubén Darío and William Walker, and although Latin America's most famous poet and its most infamous symbol of foreign piracy are about as unlike as any two men could be in motives and accomplishment, they do share qualities of courage and detachment.

Among his other bounties to us, Don Leo had given us from memory an unpublished poem by Darío, quite possibly the poet's first. Don Leo's father had been president of the Nicaraguan Senate, and as a child in 1875 he had gone to school near Matagalpa, and never forgotten the extemporaneous quatrain that the eight-year-old Rubén had recited when asked to stand up and comment on Central American unity:

> Brindo por el primer clarín
>> Que toque la primera diana,
>> Por la union centroamericana
> Del uno al otro confín.[3]

By the time he was twenty-one Rubén Darío was already abroad, publishing his first book in Chile, drifting from there to New York, to Paris, where he led a dissolute life, to the Argentine, to Spain, to New York again, with fleeting visits to Central America now and then, and death of cirrhosis of the liver here in León at the age of forty-nine.

---

[3] Roughly translated: 'Toast to the first bugle/ That plays the first reveille/ For the union of Central America/ From one end to the other.'

For most of his unhappy life, Rubén Darío expended his genius introducing the "modernism" of the French Parnassians and Symbolists to the Spanish-speaking world. His first book's title, *Azúl,* he explained as an attempt to capture "the color of dreams, of art, Hellenic, Homeric." A tone of deliberate frivolity, elegant and hedonistic, characterized his efforts to carry further Verlaine's pale burden of "Music above all else, and after music, shade." But in 1903 Darío was shaken by Theodore Roosevelt's seizure of the Panama Canal, and he fell under the influence of the Cuban poet-patriot José Martí who had said that "the poet must cut off his Zorillan locks and hang his red vest on the tree of liberty," that Latin American countries "must be saved by their Indians," and that the ruling classes were "men who do not want to do the work of men." In one of his late volumes Darío included a poem on TR, apologizing for its inclusion in these words: "If in these songs there is politics, it is because it seems universal, and if you should find reference to a president, it is because there is a continental clamor. Tomorrow we may be Yankees (and this is most probable); anyway my protest stands written on the wings of the immaculate swans, as illustrious as Jupiter." Like almost all Latin American intellectuals, Darío liked to think that materialism is a monopoly of *Norteamericanos;* art and spiritual values of Latins. The poem is interesting, for its ambivalent beginning, its sentimental center, and its conservative conclusion:

You are only to be reached, hunter,
with the voice of the Bible or a verse by Walt Whitman!
Primitive and modern, simple and complex,
with something of Washington and four of Nimrod!
You are the future invader
of the ingenuous America which has Indian blood,
which still prays to Jesus and which still speaks Spanish.

Mighty and strong, you typify your race;
you are cultured; you are resourceful; you oppose Tolstoy.
And taming horses or murdering tigers,
you are an Alexander-Nebuchadnezzar
(a professor of energy
as the madmen of today say).

You believe life to be a flame,
that progress is eruption;
that where you place the bullet
you place the future.
　　　　　No.

The United States are powerful and grand.
When they move there is a deep tremor
that runs through the vertebrae of the Andes.
If you clamor, the sound is as the lion's roar.
Hugo has already told Grant: "The stars are yours."
(The Argentine sun, rising, hardly shines
and the Chilean star awakes . . .) You are rich.
You join the cult of Hercules to that of Mammon;
and lighting the way to easy conquest,
Liberty lifts her torch in New York.
And what's more, our America that had poets
since the ancient times of Netzahualcoyotl,
that has guarded the footprints of great Bacchus;
that consulted the stars, that knew Atlantis,
whose name we hear resounding in Plato;
that lives from light, from fire, from perfume,
from love,
from the remotest moments of its life;
the America of the great Moctezuma, of the Inca,
the fragrant America of Christopher Columbus,
the Catholic America, the Spanish America,
the America in which noble Cuauthémoc said:
'I am not lying on a bed of roses'; that America
that trembles from hurricanes and that lives from love . . .

Men of Saxon eyes and barbarous soul . . .
Take care. Spanish America lives!
There are thousands of the Spanish lion's whelps loose.
You, Roosevelt, would need to be . . .
a terrible rifleman and mighty hunter
to keep us in your claws.

And, even if you have everything, one thing is lacking: God!

Rubén Darío's lyric poems still give pleasure, wherever Spanish is spoken. William Walker's life work, pursued with as much singlemindedness and ardor, bedevils relations between North Americans and Latin Americans to this day. And who is to say that idealism, closely knit with a yearning for power over the souls of other men, didn't provide the motive power in both cases? Hedonism, however, only destroys the compleat hedonist; missionary zeal can destroy whole nations and races. William Walker was a puritan; wine, women and song played no part in his life—unhappily for him and for everyone who got in his way. For this ascetic, humorless teetotaler with cold grey eyes, who loved only his mother, and began life in Nashville, Tennessee, as a fundamentalist disciple, somewhere along the line conceived the idea that he had a mission to bring moral rectitude and American know-how to the benighted "half-breeds" south of the Rio Grande; and once he had embarked upon his mission *nothing*, not Protestantism itself (for he eventually embraced Roman Catholicism), and least of all human life, was permitted to stand in his way.

Had William Walker been a different kind of man, ready to compromise, capable of making friends, he might have accomplished all he set out to do. Nicaragua, and indeed Central America, was ready to be "saved" in 1855. Since 1521 when Gonzáles Dávilla found a people "happy, well-fed, and comfortably housed," and the Spanish conquistadors who followed him had depopulated the land, fed the youth to the dogs and sold girls for the price of salt meat, Nicaragua had been in bondage. Three centuries passed. The "liberation" of 1821 did not change matters much. Slavery continued under another name, and the habit of dictatorship persisted. There had been 15 "presidents," alternating between the "Legitimists" of Granada and the "Liberals" of León, in the six years preceding Walker's arrival. Little wonder that the soft-spoken clean-living little filibuster, with his fifty-eight swashbuckling "Immortals" at first carried all before him, opening the prisons, cleaning the streets, disarming the tax-collectors, and promising Central American unity. He was received by the back-country Indians as the reincarnation of Quetzalcoatl, by the liberals as far away as El Salvador as a counterweight to the clerical reaction then being re-imposed on most of the isthmus, by the American press and public as the biggest sensation between the Gold Rush and the impending Civil War, and by Commodore Cornelius Vanderbilt as a heaven-sent means of securing his lucrative Accessory Transit across Nicaragua.

Walker, stubborn, conceited, self-righteous, managed to offend everybody —except, oddly, the Indians he would have re-enslaved, who went on fighting for him even after he was licked. He began by turning the Salvadorians against him and adding them to the ranks of the Guatemalans, the Honduraneans and the Costa Ricans who had their own reasons (not all of them noble) for wanting to get rid of him. When he made himself president and began augmenting his "Immortals" with all the riffraff of the docks and dives of San Francisco and New Orleans, he forced his original hosts, the Nicaraguan "Liberals," to make common cause with the "Legitimists" whose magnificent city, Granada, he senselessly burnt to the ground. To the American public, he was a romantic hero for a year or two, and street ballads, like this cynical one in New York didn't interfere with his recruiting:

> Have you heard the way
> That's out today,
> To better your condition O?
> Those who delight in
> Blood and fightin'
> Join Walker's Expedition O.
> There you can have all you can steal
> Without the chance of getting a meal;
> Your names will live in books of story,
> And you will live on martial glory.

But when this one-time Abolitionist promised the Southern states to make Central America safe for slavery, and when Secretary of State Marcy— for fear of England and the Northern vote—refused to recognize him, there was only one man on earth who could have saved William Walker, and that man, though he swallowed his pride and offered the little filibuster a fortune in bribes, William Walker refused to deal with.

Until Cornelius Vanderbilt, who had already built a fortune out of the ferries and steamship lines in New York, organized his Nicaraguan Steamship Line and Accessory Transit Company, there were only two ways for a prospector to get to the gold fields of California. One way was overland by covered wagon, and the other was across Panama, and both ways were fraught with peril and disease; in addition they consumed money and time. Vanderbilt personally piloted a riverboat through the San Juan River to Lake Nicaragua to show it could be done, and he then built a macadam road (the only one in Central America) over which a fleet of skyblue carriages rolled from the lake port at Virgin Bay to the Pacific where his steamers for California were waiting. In one year he took a two-million dollar profit. True, he had made a contract with the Nicaraguan government agreeing to pay it ten percent of his profits, but for some reason the Commodore's books always showed losses. . . . Opposed by his own government, Vanderbilt turned to the British and got the naval support he needed. He had been carrying Walker's recruits to him free of charge, when the spiteful Walker, not fancying a power superior to his own, accused the Accessory Transit of cheating, seized its properties and forced Nicaragua to give the concessions to Vanderbilt's New York rivals.

It was Walker's biggest blunder and a fatal one. Vanderbilt at once encouraged Central America to unite against him, in particular luring Costa Rica's General Mora to attack him from the south in the hope of supplanting Nicaragua in the future "canal" profits. The allies of the other three countries, who had been about to give up, now forced Walker out of Granada and into Rivas, the scene of his brave opening engagement two years before. On May 27, 1857, William Walker was ignominiously evacuated by a company of American Marines. But the Central Americans, taking no advantage of such a symbol to put their house in order, promptly fell apart and resumed the political in-fighting that would soon set the stage for interventions that meant business.

> *MANAGUA, NICARAGUA, WHAT A BEAUTIFUL SPOT. . . .*
> *There's coffee and bananas*
> *And the temperature hot . . .*

So goes the old popular song, and we sang it with our appetites suitably quickened, as we drove down Don Leo's drive of noble *ceibas*, their fluted trunks red with lichen, Spanish moss hanging from them in tatters like skeins of dust from a vacuum cleaner's bag. The landscape unfolded, came down to earth gradually. Soon there was cotton again, and wheat—trios of threshers on tiny elevated platforms, enclosed on three sides, beating the grain with long poles, contrapuntally.

We encountered our first big road-sign on the outskirts of the capital. It was in English:

STRICTLY STATE-SIDE

GOOD AMERICAN FOOD. *El Colonial*

AIR CONDITIONED

Then came the industrial plants exhaling their foul vapors. "We're entering by the Ole Factory Route," I said to Bill. But the pollution had only begun. It came from doors. It was running in the streets. It crawled out of drains. It farted from crowded buses. It steamed from the slate-gray lake. It hung from poles and dead trees. It squatted in the sky. It ringed the sun. The sun stank like sulphur. The declassed peasants, white cloths covering their mouths, noses and ears, slank along the street like zombies. The dust-covered trees were as motionless as mummies. And there, suddenly, as we rounded a corner, was a wall, bone-white, with the accusing scrawl in black flung at us nakedly:

VIVA SANDINO! VIVA PANAMA!

There are two hotels in Managua, both, to put it mildly, run down. The

Gran was full, but a friend of ours who was making a survey of accommodations throughout Central America, and who goes into ecstasies about the humblest pension in the smallest village (so long as it is clean and has a spray of bougainvillea by the window) described the Gran succinctly as "wall-to-wall cockroaches." The pool is emptied every Thursday, so for two days there is no water at all, "and by the following Tuesday it is thick as *flan*, with discs of chlorine spinning around on the surface, effervescing like mustard gas. There are air conditioners in every room," he added, "each one louder than a cement mixer."

We holed up finally in the Gran's rival and twin sister, the Lido. It was also full, but after explaining our predicament, we were finally permitted to bed down after curfew in the bar. I pointed out to Bill that we were within diving distance of the pool, but he shook his head, muttering something about my being on my own if I hit a submerged body.

Nikifors (Old Nick), the obsequious manager of the unmanageable Lido, is an aging Lebanese Rudolf Valentino with a personality part Jeremiah and part Volpone, and the expression of an anguished Byzantine *zopilote*. He would have liked, if he could, to avoid having us describe the Lido as it is—the flyspecked rooms with swinging doors, the boy who spends all day hosing down the tattered palms around the pool but never turns the nozzle on the row of cabanas, each with a rivulet of sludge running out from under the door—but he didn't want to spend a cent more for our presumptive good will than he had to. His way of letting me know the first night that our room (the bar) was on the house, but *not* our food, was to come up to my rocker on the veranda and present me with a small pre-Columbian figurine which he had already told me was "probably a fake." The gift disarmed me, so that instead of presenting him with a list of complaints, I swallowed hard, shook his outstretched hand, and said ". . . *con mucho gusto.*"

We spent the evening with Alejandro Aróstegui, a young artist who expresses Managua relentlessly in his dark, gritty, brilliantly textured pictures, and who is quite possibly the most original painter in Central America. Here, and at nearby Lake Nicaragua, infested with sharks, there is an evil glint to the light reflected from the slate-gray choppy waters, and this light Aróstegui captures to give an eerie illumination to his scenes of isolation and alienation. I was particularly struck by a large painting in which a circle of shoreline tilts abruptly in the moonlight, hanging like the curve of earth itself against outer space, while on its edge perch those scavengers of the tropics, *zopilotes*, sole beneficiaries of the man-made desolation.

ASPECTS OF SOMOZALAND

Early next morning a colonel in sweaty shirt under rotating blades that threatened to come loose and decapitate us all was explaining that there was only one man in this country who could fly us to Bluefields or the Corn Islands, and that was the Señor Don Generál himself.

"In Honduras, mi coronel . . ."

"Ah, but gentlemen, this is not Honduras. In this country there is only one man . . ."

He stopped, picked up a can of insecticide, and sprayed madly at a fly that was buzzing around his head. "What was I saying—?"

I looked out the window at Lake Managua, sultry in the gray heat, its dirty waves flapping against the fetid shore like feathers of lead. Paint was peeling from the buildings on every side, gray buildings, olive drab, shit color, more gray. Why gray—of all colors for a hot country?

We drove to the president's palace, which is not gray, and which sits on a hill overlooking a small, clear, clean volcanic lake that is so well guarded no one can even look into it except from the president's palace. The palace looks something like two cylinder heads shoved into a Kleenex box and covered with caramel. We got as far as the General's secretary, a Mr. Kelly, who said the General was in the barber's chair. We thought of barging in, but remembered a story told us by a friend who had been at a reception given at the opening of the Panama Hilton some years ago, attended by Tachito's father Tacho. There had been a power failure and when the lights came on in the grand ballroom Tacho had been found at the bottom of a pyramid of bodies—his loyal guards. We didn't want to find ourselves in a pyramid with open razors flying around. So instead we spent a pleasant hour talking to the government's chief information officer, Hernán Aróstegui, who turned out to be Alejandro's brother. On the waiting-room table was a booklet entitled "Nicaragua Land of Lakes and Volcanoes" with the following interesting piece of prose:

> His excellency, the President of Nicaragua, who on November celebrated his birthday among the rejoice of all nicaraguans, who appreciate his constant worry toward a better understanding among nicaraguans, and who is surely leading the country toward an authentic democracy. . . .

Hernán Aróstegui is intelligent and well aware of the problems keeping the tourists away in droves—lack of a road to Bluefields on the Caribbean with its fine beach and nearby Corn Islands,[4] the pollution of Lake Managua and the unsightly waterfront, the lack of a first-class hotel. The government has nine million dollars appropriated for the latter, which an American hotel combine is preparing to build at El Socorro fifteen hundred feet above the city.

Ambassador Aaron Brown thinks that the wealth is being distributed among more and more families and that the Somoza family is now reinvesting most of its vast profits at home. On the theory that revolutions are endemic here, people with only a few dollars buy a *finca* as a hedge. "Only a Communist revolution," he added, "takes the *land* away." Thus land reform, after a fashion, is being effected by the prudent middle class. The two political parties, like ours, have little ideological difference. The Conservatives boycotted the election of René Schick, charging the Somozas

---

4 Bluefields, long an English stronghold on Nicaragua's Miskito Coast, has no road connecting it with the interior at all. Nor is there any way of getting to the Caribbean beach outside the harbor, except by boat. Big and Little Corn Islands lie seventy-five and one hundred kilometers out to sea, and have good beaches and landing strips. The English-speaking inhabitants (many, like the Morgans, descendants of pirates) are prosperous lobster-fishermen, sometimes "banking" as many as one thousand of these crayfish-without-claws in the three-month season and selling them for a *córdoba* or two apiece. The Nicaraguan unit of currency is worth thirteen to fifteen cents U.S.

with puppetry; but they won't again: they're too anxious to get their own fingers in the till. Marxists, Ambassador Brown told us, undoubtedly write the Sandino slogans we've been seeing. "If caught, they are seized, but not held. There is no specific anti-subversive law. Five bank robbers were recently *released* from prison when they pleaded that they had committed the larceny for *political* reasons."

The luxurious cities of León and Granada are not what they used to be in the heyday of their political (and clerical) rivalry. They are not exactly ghost towns, but they are close to it; all over Latin America the magnetic pull of politics, jobs and cultural opportunity in the capitals is draining everything but the stones out of the provincial cities. León, one-and-a-half hours of fast driving on a good road northwest of Managua, is especially ghostly. A measure of its fading glory is that the best restaurant in town is Chinese—and a poor one. The cathedral (largest in Central America) is a fortress of mouldering yellow stone, its bellports over the main portal "supported" by straining giant male caryatids. A stone lion crouches on the steps, and another over Rubén Darío's tomb inside. The oldest of León's sixteen churches is that of Sutiaba, dating from 1560. It was being repaired when we visited it, and the roof over the crossing was open to the sky. The gaily painted square wooden piers had rotted away and were being replaced by exact duplicates, carved and painted on the spot by skilled craftsmen. The female saints, their faces and bodies covered with white cellophane and blue tissue paper, their outstretched hands filled with dust, were a sight to have made Cartier-Bresson's mouth water. We didn't wait for him, one of us shooting the ghostly sisters from every angle while the other restrained the helpful carpenters who insisted they must uncover the saints for us.

Granada is a different kettle of fish—mostly sharks. The most voracious and destructive, of course, was William Walker, who left nothing but a charred stick with the legend *Aqui fué Granada* sticking out of the smoking ruins in 1857. Las Isletas, the 533 bite-size volcanic islands clustered in a crook of the 3,228 square-mile lake beyond Granada, are surrounded not only by man-eating sharks (Lake Nicaragua is the only fresh-water lake in the world to have them) but by five-foot tarpon and swordfish. Most of the islands belong to the rich, and are understandably equipped with swimming pools. To get to them from Granada is neither easy nor cheap. Here lived Asilia Guillén, Nicaragua's incomparable "primitive" painter, and this was her subject. Ten years ago a local connoisseur, "Kiki" Fernández, showed her needlework to the painter Rodrigo Peñalba at the Escuela Bellas Artes in Managua, and Peñalba persuaded her to switch to paints. In the decade that ensued before her death last year, the great artist would spend a month or more "reducing" an island, with all its trees, flowers, bathers and babies, to minuscule scale, every petal and button lovingly delineated.

A friend of the Arósteguis, a painter named Omar de León, had the last two available Asilia Guilléns for sale, but prices have already gone into four figures, far beyond our purses. Ramón Osuna, our friend from the Honduras trip, had already warned us that this would be so. But he told us to stop at the little Museo Tenderí between Granada and the capital where he had bought a little pre-Columbian Nicaragua figurine the week before. I picked up a similar one ($15) and a splendid wooden horse-mask for half as much, but was sure I'd been stuck with the first when the "curator" murmured "Genuine pre-Columbian . . ." as she handed me the second. "Señora," I reproved her, "you know they had no horses. . . ." "Of course not," she giggled, "but it's old, very old!" (Ramón took one look at my figurine in New Jersey the following summer, laughed, and said "We both bought fakes.")

From Granada it is twenty-three kilometers to the Highway, where the road proceeds southward through Rivas and Virgin Bay to the Costa Rica border.

9 COSTA RICA

Save Panama, and that part of Nicaragua where Commodore Vanderbilt plied his lucrative trade, Costa Rica occupies all of the narrow part of the Central American isthmus, and this circumstance has affected both its past and its present. Because of the almost impassable mountains along its northern and southern borders, Costa Rica has been relatively free to develop peacefully. It had revolutions of its own, but at least it did not have to cope with its neighbors. This is a principal reason why Costa Rica alone is a model democracy today, and one of the very few countries in the world without a standing army. But Costa Rica's odd geographical configuration east-to-west and its racial homogeneity have also affected its happy isolation. Most of the people live in the rich highland valleys along the central *cordilleras*, and almost all of them are light-skinned. There were never many

Indians in Costa Rica, and today there are almost none. No Indians to exploit; no Indian problem. Quite a few Negroes settled along the Caribbean coast, but since there are no roads connecting this coast with the highlands, the "Negro problem" has been at least kept out of sight. Costa Ricans are neither racists nor isolationists, but there is just a trace of smugness in their happy homogeneous remoteness in this tidy hinterland.

We drove into Costa Rica after being "processed" with dispatch (and gratis) on both sides of the frontier. An hour past the border on a straight paved road that runs through cotton fields and pasture land with arid hills in the background, we came to a chalk works on the right of a small bridge that crosses the Colorado River. On the left, in plain view, is a waterfall with a splendid swimming hole at its base. There are even tire-tubes provided for timorous bathers, and picnic tables and benches made out of the local red cedar. This, not the "famous" beach of Puntarenas, 120 kilometers south, is the place to stop for a swim. We did visit Puntarenas in due course, two hours later, and found nothing to recommend it. The beach is on a spit of land extending out into the Gulf of Nicoya. The spit is just wide enough to contain (a) the road; (b) a railroad track built by United Fruit; (c) a string of dismal sulphurous factories; (d) an endless line of beach shanties, end to end; and (e) a strip of dirty black sand. There is no undertow, but the waves are thick with sticks, boards, splinters and bottles. If one is successful in dodging them, they wind up eventually on the beach, where the fiddler crabs and local beachcombers have a go at them.

Twenty to thirty kilometers south, we were told, at a place called Escarillo, there is a very *good* beach, but there is no road to it. A hundred kilometers still farther down the Pacific is Puerto Quepos, with the best deep sea fishing between Lower California's La Paz and Panama's Darién coast. The warm current sweeps in to shore along a deep, deep shelf, alive with marlin, sailfish and swarms of golden dolphin. But you have to hire an oil tender, unless you come in your own boat. And again—no road.

The Caribbean slope of Costa Rica is almost as inaccessible, though the principal port, Limón, can be reached by plane and railway, and the slow train through mountainous jungles is an interesting one. But Puerto

Limón has lost its function as the principal shipping place for bananas—
Golfito on the Pacific is now the focus of Costa Rica's major export—and
Limón's eighty percent Negro and English-speaking population feels discriminated against both economically and politically. "It's as bad as South
Africa," one indignant Negro said to us; "it's almost impossible to get them
to give you a railroad ticket to travel to San José—your papers are never
'in order.' They're so afraid of diluting or polluting their progressive little
white kingdom up there!" Exaggerated, no doubt, but a certain source of
trouble-to-come unless integration becomes more than lip service.

SAN JOSE: PARADISE WITH A TIN ROOF

We had driven into the capital directly, leaving Alajuela, Heredia and
Sarchí, home of the exquisite painted carts, for a later excursion. The highland country along the way *looks* richer than anything we've so far seen
in Central America, save Don Leo's little enclave and Guatemala's Cobán;
and probably it is. Every inch of rolling mountain-slope, including even
the *ditches*, is terraced and planted to coffee, bananas, pineapples, sugar
cane, vegetables—a wonderful variety of greens against the terra cottas and
burnt umber of the fertile soil. And the houses, uniquely for Central America,
are *frame* houses, well painted, spotlessly clean, and hung with ornamental
ferns and flowers. The Costa Rican's income is the highest on the isthmus,
but it still averages less than three hundred dollars a year. What a difference
those very few extra dollars, a tiny piece of land, and a good health, education, and public service system, make! This small farmer, obviously, has
some control over his destiny—or thinks he does, which is almost as good.

But we came here as tourists, not sociologists, and it is our sad duty to
report that Costa Rica has placed a rusty tin roof over its highland paradise.
With comparable sound effects.

Along with the Royal Dutch (best food) and the Gran (most luxurious),
the Europa is one of the three best hotels in a city crammed with good
hotels; but if it isn't the noisiest hotel in the world, it was the first night
we bedded down in it. Placed precisely at the capital's busiest intersection,
each room receives the full impact of the nation's *Toyotas*,[1] buses and
trucks as they rev up in low-low for a test run before assaulting the
mountains. At about eleven P.M. there was a slight de-crescendo. Then a

---

[1] Even city folk drive this Japanese version of the Jeep since it passes as a farm implement and
therefore sells tax-free.

male chorus of drunks in the street below, each member singing in a different key, opened up with the Costa Rican version of "Happy Birthday." "They must know that it's your birthday," Bill said. It was, too; but I was not amused.

Waking at six .A.M. we leaped simultaneously out of bed to see what the din was. It was raining, and we had our first view of what the rain was hitting: an entire city covered with rusting tin roofs. Since it was raining anyway, we decided to get with it and have a swim before breakfast in the hotel's pool. We were not the first pun-loving Americans, we were sure, to be delighted by the sign in the hallway: PISCINA POOL. Nor were we likely the first to be tempted at poolside by a sack of "pre-Columbian" gold brooches which an enterprising salesman dangled in front of our noses as we floated by. We were tempted indeed, but having already been told that these pieces are dug up mainly in the Golfito region, we decided to by-pass the middlemen.

After breakfast, we set out to walk to the cathedral, get our Panamanian visas and visit the Ministry of Tourism. The cathedral has a gray neo-Greek façade partially hiding what looks like a Victorian railroad station telescoping back 300 feet or more. Naturally it is covered with tin. But its ugliness is as nothing to what it faces in the Parque. This is a bandstand which is best described as a giant squatting tarantula about to give birth to twins—identical twins resembling Cobán's "Tortilla Smasher," very likely.

The better to be seen at night (we turned our eyes away when passing through the square after dark) its bowlegs are equipped with fluorescent tubes.

The Panamanian Consulate was working full time, predictably and understandably, to frustrate *Norteamericanos*. First, it had moved; no forwarding address. After an hour's search, we reached the new one by phone. "A visa will cost you double because this is a holiday . . . Monday? That is a holiday, too. George Washington's birthday." We hailed a taxi and told the driver to drive to the Presidential Palace—the consul was next door, he'd told us. Unfortunately the Presidential Palace had just moved too. By the time we reached the new palace and the new consulate, at one minute after noon, we knocked and a maid came to the door. "So sorry. The consulate is closed." Bang.

Ricardo Castro Cañas, Gerente of the Instituto Costarricense de Turismo, went out of his way to be helpful, promising to cover our board, arranging interviews with President Orlich and former-President Figueres, offering his own car and guide for trips to Sarchí and Turrialba. The guide, José Luis Gómez, left with us immediately for Sarchí. We had already heard of Joaquín Chaverri, one of the town's master craftsmen, and hoped to prevail on him to paint a pair of small beds in the gay style of the peasant carts, and ship them to us in the States. Carrying on in the tradition of his father, his grandfather and his great-grandfather before him, Joaquín closely supervises the work of his sons, and their apprentices. We finally arrived at a price of 400 *colones* ($60) for the two beds, and spent an hour admiring Joaquín's superb carts—some scaled to toys six inches long, at $3—and his superb hardwood salad bowls. The big cartwheels, with their interlocking diamond shapes painted red, yellow, blue and black would make any Op artist envious.

On the way back we stopped at the new jetport, which will soon be connected with the capital by a fifteen-minute straight road, and at the widely publicized *Balnearea de Ojo de Agua* for a swim. This bathing spot, off the Highway a little between Alajuela and Heredia, is rightly popular, but has been blighted, to our eyes at least, by the Costa Rican genius for uglification. The fabulous "Eye," a bubble of spring water which gushes six thousand gallons a minute and eventually supplies the drinking water for Puntarenas, here overflows in a cataract to fill a succession of swimming pools and a small boating lake. In its natural state, or even with the pools, this would be a visual wonderland. But everything, including the eye itself, has been sheathed in concrete, interspersed with picnic tables, dance floors, jukeboxes, bars, and overshadowed by huge signs in rusting tin advertising "Squirt," "Fanta," and "Orange Crush."

José Luis regaled us on the way back with an account of José (Pepé) Figueres' 1948 revolution, the decisive event in Costa Rica's coming of age. Calderón Guardia had then been in power and was ruling with an unscrupulous alliance of Communists and right-wing militarists. Great progress had been made in the early years of this regime, giving Costa Rica Central America's first social security system and minimum wage, as well as a liberal labor code; and in the wartime atmosphere of Russo-American friendship, even the Archbishop saw no objection to Catholic workers joining Marxist federations. But when Calderón's party sought to perpetuate itself in power by annulling an election defeat and then calling upon "Tacho" Somoza across the border in Nicaragua for armed support— "Well," said our friend, "on that day even Calderón's fanatics went over to Don Pepé, and not a single one of those Nicaraguans ever got back across the border." Figueres, a rich coffee grower with a moderate socialist philosophy, directed the revolution from his own *finca* near San José. When he came to power he nationalized the banks and dissolved the army, leaving only a police force for protection. But honesty and individual liberty were the real heart of the fiery little leader's program, and this was proved, our friend said, during a subsequent campaign for the presidency when Figueras had been asked at an open meeting to promise the country a new soccer stadium. "Soccer to us," José Luis said, "is like baseball to you—only much more so. I was at that meeting. Don Pepé stamped his foot and shouted 'Never! Not until there is full employment, social security, and peace!' There was a deathly silence. And then, little by little, spontaneous applause, rising to a great roar."

Changing the subject, we asked José Luis on the way into the capital whether it was true that prostitution flourished here as nowhere else. He threw up his hands. "Don José's best predecessor, President Jiménez, was once asked to 'put a roof' over their district and replied, 'I would have to put a roof over the whole of San José!'" Whatever truth there may be to this, there is no question at all that the women here are very attractive, with their high-piled black hair, almond eyes, and olive complexions—and very inviting.

There is no question, either, that the cost of living is very high in Costa

Rica. Political appointees like the Minister of Tourism may make $5,000 a year or more, but our guide (after we pressed him) admitted that his own salary amounts to no more than $120 a month. How could he support a family on that, we asked him, where the prices of everything except food are higher than in the U.S. The answer—as we'd found out in other countries —is moonlighting. José Luis works from eight to eleven every evening in a surveyor's office. Even so, he can't save any money. The only solution here, if you can find the money, is to buy a *finca*. Land is still relatively cheap, and the farther from San José, of course, the cheaper. As a travel folder puts it in the inimitable Central American Madison Avenuese:

> Beyond the Country Club is Santa Ana about which is an aura causing the casual visitor to start pricing real estate and the cost of building a home in this unusual quiet—even sleepy—little village which is at the correct altitude for Costa Rica's famous eternally springlike climate which uniquely smells like spring. . . .

THE GOOD AMBASSADOR

Raymond Telles, the El Paso-born, completely bilingual American Ambassador, was confronted with a Communist-led student demonstration a few days before our arrival. The demonstrators were protesting over our bombing of the Viet Cong supply bases in North Viet Nam.

Instead of staying indoors, as expected, and receiving the usual barrage of rocks, tomatoes and speeches from there, he sallied into the street in front of the Embassy and invited the leaders to come inside and discuss their grievances amicably and at length. Meanwhile an angry mob—angry at the demonstrators—had begun to close in, and a cop took a sandwich board from one of the Communist students—"leaving him naked," as Telles put it to us. The Ambassador took the sign from the cop and returned it to the astonished student. The leaders of the demonstration followed him inside and they talked for an hour. When they emerged the crowd was still there. Telles spoke to them briefly, telling them in future not to demonstrate but to talk to him—"any time. This door will always be open to you." Then he proposed a cheer. "Viva Costa Rica!" The crowd responded enthusiastically. "Viva los Estados Unidos!"—and before their Party leaders could object, the crowd shouted this after him too!

We asked Telles why Pepé Figueres had been able to dissolve the army while a leader like Villeda Morales had been helpless.

"Because," he said, "the army here was never an autonomous institution.

Every time a new president came to office there was a sixty percent or more turnover in the army's personnel."

"But why was this so here and not elsewhere?" Bill asked.

"Tradition, education, the predominantly Caucasian background perhaps."

President Orlich was doing a good job, he added, "But he's had nothing but fiscal trouble for two years—in the aftermath of Irazú's eruption."

THE BAD VOLCANO

We passed by Irazú on our way to Cartago, the ancient capital, and Turrialba. There are no signs remaining of the terrible damage. But Count Tattenbach, a planter of German descent at whose *finca* under the volcano's slope my friend Devin Garrity had witnessed the mating of quetzals five years ago, told us that the *finca* had to be abandoned: ashes had almost buried the trees. We passed over an iron bridge near Cartago that had been donated by Queen Elizabeth II last year as a gift to the valley that had been levelled by floods. These had been caused by the accumulation of jelly-like "dams" of ashes which eventually gave way under the tons of water piled up behind them by torrential rains.

José Luis described the prevailing climate in San José during the eruption —visibility almost nil, housewives on the tin roofs sweeping madly to keep the gutters from clogging up, pedestrians with handkerchiefs over their noses and ears, two years' coffee crops wiped out. "By a strange coincidence," he said, "it all began on that happy day President Kennedy visited us, and it had its very last fling the day he was assassinated."

The Cartago cathedral, with tin roof and domes, has a delightfully gay façade: outsize stone angels perched in every conceivable nook, and a Star of David in the center, lighted. There are two other interesting buildings.

One is the ruins of an ancient church with a bronze bell above its entrance and the interior devoted to a small park with flowering trees, goldfish ponds, and Costa Rican couples necking. The other is a clocktower on a street corner, with a public address system built in, constructed entirely of sheets of corrugated tin.

Turrialba, across the Continental Divide on the road that will someday reach Puerto Limón, is the seat of the Central American Agricultural School run by the OAS. We were disappointed to find it closed, and so was an old friend from San Pedro Sula in Honduras, Emilio López Mejía, who had come at the same time for the same purpose. We only got far enough inside the lobby of the handsome Swiss-chalet administration building to see a portrait of another old friend, Henry Wallace, who had written us to be sure to visit the school and talk to his friends, the directors.

We had better luck, re-entering San José, to find the Archaeological Museum open. This is one of the two or three finest collections of pre-Columbian sculpture in Central America, and by far the most efficiently and tastefully presented. It contains, not surprisingly, a collection without peer of the gold figurines and jewelry found in the Costa Rica–Panama region. Hundreds of these exquisite pieces cast from clay molds—eaglets, nose rings, ear plugs, disc pectorals of pure laminated gold, and figurines of extraordinarily intricate detail—are displayed behind glass on a big slowly revolving drum covered with black velvet. But the Museum contains, in addition to its priceless artifacts from the local Chorotega, Huetár and Brunka cultures, a fine display of Costa Rican birds, beasts and butterflies.

Doris Stone, only surviving child of United Fruit's legendary chieftain, Samuel Zemurray, who made her home in San José until this year, not only organized and endowed this museum, but wrote the most authoritative monographs on the art of the region. From all accounts she was, and is, a formidable woman, as formidable and eccentric as "Old Sam." We heard stories about her all over Central America. I liked especially the one about a convention of world-famous archaeologists that had met in Tegucigalpa. The Honduras government begged her to show them around Copán, and she agreed provided they would not reveal her identity. The tour was going well except that every time she would describe or date a stela, one old professor would complain, "But Doris Stone says. . . ." Finally, exasperated, she turned a withering glance on her tormentor and rasped: "*I* am Doris Stone!"

We had just time before dinner with the Tattenbachs to visit the studio of Jorge Gallardo, a superb draftsman, whose studies in sepia line ennoble poverty, fatigue and old age as easily as they caress youth, motherhood and the dance.

THE GOOD PRESIDENT

We had not yet called on President Orlich when Christian Tattenbach gave us a very clear statement of the case *against* the "Figueres dynasty." He began with a cogent critique of American policy in this part of the world.

"You *must* have supported both the Juan Bosch and Villeda Morales overthrows last year," he began, "at least passively, because your policy is to support whatever group is most anti-Communist regardless of whether the people like it or not. I was Minister in Honduras then, as I was in Guatemala under Arbenz. Arbenz was not a Communist in the beginning. In Villeda's case, you feared not him but his successor, who might have been friendly to Castro. In our country you give all-out support to the National Liberation party of Figueres, Orlich, and Orlich's sure successor, Odubar, because they are in power—which is also a dangerous policy in the long run. You *must* support them, of course; I recognize that, even though I am an Ulate man. But I think your diplomats should make at least a show of being impartial. At least you should socialize with the leaders of the other parties. Anti-Americanism is growing in the country, outside of San José and the rich central plateau, because America is associated with the monolithic party in power—just as in Mexico, only more so. We are moving away from democracy, toward a one-party state. The banks are a government monopoly, and all bank directors are appointed by the party in power. Business, increasingly, is divorced from political rivalry because it fears to offend the banks. Two million dollars was spent by the government in the last political campaign; from a population of a little more than a million, that is a fantastic sum."

The Tattenbachs see the Common Market—now embracing only a customs union, but eventually to encompass economics, education and political life— as the ultimate hope for Central America. "All countries must someday offer the same facilities to industry, the same minimum wage, the same cultural opportunities, if we are to survive." But President Orlich thinks along exactly the same lines! And in that common ground, that ideological closeness between the two major parties so closely resembling our own, lies Costa Rica's uniqueness in this ideologically embattled part of the world, and its untypical stability.

Francisco Orlich didn't tell us anything startling or new. He has a long, sad, wrinkled, scholarly face and the only time he smiled was when I asked him what Costa Rica needed most and he answered: "Money." His country was extremely lucky, he said, not to have an army. "The other Central American states put anywhere from twenty percent to thirty-six percent of their meager budgets into armed forces. Silly, isn't it? Our police costs us only eight percent and the result is we can spend the difference on education." He said that Costa Rica hadn't recognized the Dominican Republic's junta "because we don't approve of military *golpes*."

"But you recognize Guatemala," I said.

"They have made it constitutional."

"And Nicaragua—"

"The same."

"And Honduras?"

"No. . . . At least, not yet."

What really impressed us about President Orlich was not what he said but what he so obviously was: a good man. Unafraid. Friendly. Not trying to impress anybody. No guards frisked us, or ushered us in. Nobody asked for our papers. In his chamber the three of us sat and talked entirely alone. On his desk there was one telephone, a tiny bronze bust of President Kennedy and a tiny plastic figurine of a Costa Rica *campesino*. When we got up to leave, he got up with us and ushered us to the door. And that was that.

"IRVING GOLDSMITH"

We drove to Palmar Sur, close to the southern border of Costa Rica, in a little over five hours. This was the part of the Inter-American Highway that defied road builders and engineers for decades. The mountains are of surpassing grandeur. The road, from Cartago on, isn't paved yet, but it is broad enough and smooth; the conquest is all but complete. And since there are very few trucks and buses, dust isn't a problem. Very soon after Cartago, the Highway rises to its highest point (eleven thousand feet) and one is driving in and out of the clouds, with clumps of hydrangeas and calla liles by the roadside, and orchids in the hundred-foot-high trees.

Past San Isidro General there is a widening band of erosion: wildcat lumbering, but sometimes just plain destruction of the tree-cover for a cornfield or two—felled forest giants smouldering one across another up the charred slopes to the skyline. I thought of the smoking wastelands of Verdun, photographs that had terrified me as a child; and of William Vogt's gloomy prediction that Costa Rica might never recover from the Highway that was supposed to be its salvation.

Presently this deathscape gave way to jungle again, and then arbors of giant "goldenrod," countryside so fertile that the fence posts burst into leaf almost as soon as driven into the ground. But man cannot live by bread alone—or be satisfied to let the fence posts flower. Suddenly on our left loomed the showpiece of Costa Rica's architectural purgatory: a church built entirely of rusty corrugated sheets, its tower four tin boxes of diminishing size, its windows pale green laminated plexiglass. How is it possible, we speculated, amid so much natural beauty. . . . The gorges, loud with cicadas, gave no answer. Nor did our own visual contributions to the landscape: Gulf, Esso, Texaco and Chevron stations cheek-to-jowl at Buenos Aires.

The forty-four concrete bridges on which the Highway leapfrogs the canyons between San José and the Panama border are completed. To the left of the big one that crosses the Rio Grande de Terraba is a marvelous natural swimming hole at the base of a small cataract from one of the feeder streams. With hindsight of what awaits the traveler in Golfito, we would have stopped here to be refreshed. The lovely spot is 218 kilometers from San José: and three kilometers farther on (but to the right) is a three-hundred-foot falls, as delicate in its fine tracery as Japanese quillwork, or seed pearls racing down the seams of folded velvet. But quickly the terrain changes again. More dust, more smoke, more erosion; evidence of landslides, with only an occasional *frangipani* to soften the harshness.

"*Donde está 'El Chino'?*" was a question people had great difficulty or reluctance to answer in Palmar Sur.

Where is the Chinaman? We were asking the question because Mauro

Fernández, manager of the Gran Hotel and grandson of Costa Rica's great educator of the 1880s had given us a note to a Chinese bartender in Palmar Sur who occasionally supplies him with gold figurines from this region. After asking half a dozen villagers and receiving blank looks, we had lunch at the United Fruit commissary and picked up a local "guide." Fernández had been wrong, he said; "El Chino" lived in Palmar *Norte*, and there were *two* of him. We backtracked across the Terraba River to Palmar Norte and located El Chino No. 1. He had nothing, but waved us on to No. 2, many blocks away, who had one small, badly damaged piece for which he was asking forty dollars. He told us of another Chinese merchant, however, a certain Ezekiel Wong, who owns the local movie-house.

Wong greeted us and conducted us around his house. There he rather reluctantly opened a large padlock and let us in. The pergola is constructed of plumbing fixtures, covered with oleander, and surrounded by huge granite balls; its ingenious "furniture" consists of an I-beam and some battle-plate and air-stripping left around by the Seabees during World War II. We told Wong several times what we were looking for, but he had a disconcerting way of grinning and giggling at everything we said—and displaying as he did a mouthful of gold teeth. Finally he walked away and came back with two battered stone pieces. Again we explained, and again he grinned and backed off into his house. This time he returned with a greasy carton containing broken fragments of pottery. We explained again: "Oro, Señor Wong, oro!"—feeling a little like the gold-crazed conquistadors. Back he trotted, this time returning with two old Kodak boxes held together with rubber-bands. In each were three or four very small pieces. One, a quarter on an inch long, represented a monkey. The largest, almost six inches in circumference, beautifully chased, was of a turtle clasping emblematic "waves" in its front feet; the belly-plate was slotted and contained a rattle, as many such pieces do. We asked how much he wanted for these, and Wong went away again—"to consult my wife." He returned and said the monkey would be $75 and the turtle $820. We shook our heads and were about to leave when Wong said slyly: "You want to see the best there is?" We did. This time he came back with a large framed photograph of himself, his wife, and their five children. On the lapel of the oldest boy was a tiny

object. "What is it?" we asked. He shook with laughter. "Now I show you!" and away he went. Coming back with another dirty little box, he removed the usual bands and tissue paper. Our jaws dropped. Not even in the Museum had we seen such a masterpiece. It must have been fashioned for a king. Little more than an inch square, it consisted of twin crowned figures, linked in their intricate crowns and again at the hips, three-toed, slightly bowlegged, with women's breasts, and tiny penises erect. I knew the answer without asking, but asked anyway. "How much?" The wife calculated on paper for several minutes. "$2,010.75."

Ezekiel Wong waved us on to the next merchant, a restaurant proprietor in Villa Neily far down the road past the Golfito cutoff. From him I finally did buy an inch-high little man with ears as big as his hands and feet. If he turned out to be gold, he would be worth the $100 I paid for him; if he turned out to be pre-Columbian he would be worth more. Bill took one look at him, sniffed, and christened him "Irving Goldsmith."

GOLFITO AND BANANAS

In Palmar Sur we had managed to reach F. A. Hatch, Jr., director of the Costa Rica branch of United Fruit Company, over the company phone to Golfito. We asked him whether we might inspect the huge banana installations there, and whether the Balneareo Bella Vista in Golfito was the place to stay.

"Not if there are women in your party," he said.

"No women," I said.

"Who sent you?"

I told him that the de Solas had advised us to contact Doris Stone, but that Mrs. Stone had left San José some weeks ago. He was more cordial.

"You may stay at our American Club. I'll notify them to put you up. I'll be on the golf links by the time you arrive, but you can reach me at home before the movie show at the Club begins."

The dirt road from the Palmars to Rio Clara is very good. We covered it, driving 60–80 kpms, in less than two hours. The road is less good from there to Golfito (12 kilometers) but it isn't bad. United Fruit's plantations stretch on both sides as far as the eye can see, and every stem of fruit is in a cellophane bag to prevent premature ripening. We stopped at Balnearea Bella Vista, a ramshackle affair with a large concrete dancing platform, a jukebox, sleeping quarters 25 *colones*, $3.75 a day with meals), a couple of pools filled with opaque green and very warm water, and a beach area, palisaded against the carnivorous predators, which Bill promptly dubbed "The Shark Pit." Bill would have no part of the pools, but the 106° heat was too much to make me as reasonable. I let myself in gingerly. . . .

If Bill had followed suit, the heat would not have gone to his head and he would not have entered the American Club's parking area and impulsively backed the Volkswagen into a four-foot drainage ditch. We squeezed out the doors with some difficulty and contemplated the perpendicular vehicle with its front wheels gaily spinning. Bill hadn't joined in my laughter; in fact he was already inside the kitchen door looking for jacks, a derrick, or maybe only a basin of cold water. Less than a minute later he reappeared and looked at the Volks dumfounded: it was standing on all four feet as though nothing had happened. I thought of assuming all the credit and posing as a Samson, but our rescuers, four brawny schoolboys, were still in sight.

Golfito has all the appearance of a typical "company town," though unquestionably United Fruit has been a godsend to the area with its 7,500 jobs in the fields and on the docks, and its wages and social benefits exceeding those of any other enterprise in Central America. Miserable shacks, bars, gambling dens and houses of prostitution face the medium-gauge tracks along the waterfront. Until you reach the administration offices, Club, tennis courts and golf links, and then suddenly the road is asphalted, the houses move behind neat hedges, and the families of the six American administrators and perhaps twice as many Costa Ricans in the managerial posts next in line, are there watering their lawns. Later on we watched these solid citizens arrive in their best clothes for the Event of Golfito, the thrice-weekly movie, this night an Italian Grade C offering entitled "The Killers." We watched it in fascinated disbelief for half an hour while part of the 200 inches of rain that falls here every year battered the roof and we sweated inside.

We were "rescued" this time by Mr. Hatch's driver who picked us up for an inspection of the dock. An English freighter of medium size was being loaded with 14,000,000 bananas, packed in 90,000 cartons, 160 to the box, part of the bounty of Golfito's 28,000 acres, a planting exceeded in Central America only by Honduras' 37,000, and in the rest of the world only by Ecuador. An English-speaking foreman was at the table where every tenth box is opened and checked for uniformity. The foreman was peering down at this table like a surgeon or a priest. Under a powerful spotlight lay a single green banana with an ordinary rectal thermometer inserted in its flesh. The temperature (82°) proved right. The box received its blue "Chiquita" label and went back on escalators which carry the fruit from the two lines of freight cars (where a crew of eight to each car put them into the boxes and onto the belts after removing the cellophane sacks that cover each stem in the fields). After inspection the boxes climb steep criss-cross towers and slide into the hold. We asked the foreman what the workers receive.

"From $75 to $150 a month, depending on the amount of work, but we supply houses rent-free as well as food, social security and medical care."

"Then they save enough in a year to buy a small *finca?*"

He laughed. "For some reason, most of them spend every cent of it on wine, women, song, and lottery tickets."

We pursued this with F. A. Hatch, Jr., at his office in the morning. His version of where the money goes was different. He said that the rotting shacks along the waterfront were not workers' homes but belonged to those who moved in to trade with them. He denied that the wages were frittered away in the *cantinas*. "Our Savings and Loan Cooperative has 2,000,000 *colones* in it right now. The thrifty *are* saving for a rainy day."

We looked out the window instinctively, but the early morning rain had stopped. We thanked the Gerente for his hospitality, and took off for the Panama border forty kilometers southeast, humming the old song:

> I'm Chiquita Banana
> And I've come to say
> Bananas have to ripen
> In a certain way . . . [2]

10 PANAMA

THE PANAMA HILTON could be described by an ungrateful guest as a Stainless Steel Fleabag Without Fleas, but a description we preferred after a good deal of discussion was A Millionaire's Mousetrap—with ourselves as the unwitting mice. We stumbled into the Hilton in circumstances that permitted no quick retreat. And once we were there, we never managed to get out. We became the victims of our schedule which was so tight we never had time to repack and scram. In a way, of course, we were rolling with this dilemma: the four concrete tennis courts and the Lucullan swimming pool toughened our resistance.

We had taken an instant dislike to the French manager, M. Jean Berthelot at a conference after breakfast the first morning. His suave martinet's efficiency and patent-leather smile aroused my Francophobia from the moment he kept us waiting at his desk while he

promised his son in French on the phone that he'd have front-row seats at the pool next week to see the crowning of the Carnival Queen; and Bill had started drawing his cold blue eyes and pearly teeth even before we left his office. But there was no denying that Jean's minimal gesture in agreeing to cut the price on our room from twenty-four to twelve dollars helped us decide not to waste time bargain-shopping. If we didn't *eat,* we said to ourselves walking away from our benefactor's antechamber, we could swing it. And having thus eased our thrifty consciences, we descended to the dining room and ordered a second breakfast.

It all began when we lost our way entering the capital the night before. We had been driving off and on all day, following our eight A.M. departure from Golfito. The road from the border to David, and some distance beyond, was concrete. Then it deteriorated badly for a stretch of detour running through Soná and into Santiago, but we broke up this three-and-a-half-hour spell of intense heat, rocks, and dust, with a swim in one of the many broad rivers over which two-lane bridges are being built. To get to the river we chose, we had to roll under a barbed-wire fence and sneak past two rampant Brahmin bulls. The next detour, to avoid a charge of dynamite, brought us back to the state of discomfort the river had assuaged. But at Penonomé an excellent dish of *arróz con camarones,* washed down with ice-cold tamarind juice, revived our spirits for the last three hours on a good road to the capital. Nor did the five *casetas* at which our passports were supposed to be checked slow us up perceptibly, since one guard was asleep and two others failed to blow their whistles before we were out of range.

As far as the local people are concerned, the Highway is a success. Only the Indians of Chiriquí province on the Costa Rica border are reputed not to enjoy the *estranjeros:* they've melted away toward the two oceans, and they won't sell their knee-length embroidered shirts of unbleached muslin for less than $500. Most of the natives we saw were either using the road to herd their cattle, or as a hot plate to dry their coffee on.

Our trouble began when, perhaps from an accumulation of dust in our eyes, we overshot the capital by twenty-five miles, driving along the Canal almost half way to Colón. Not a pedestrian in sight; nor a car that would stop to give us directions though we hung pleadingly from the windows, waving madly. "Just like the U.S.A.!" we said bitterly. And in fact it *was* the U.S.A., for we were in the Zone. The city, when we finally did find it— thanks to some friendly Negro dock workers who spoke English with an English accent—looked (at night) like Cleveland or Cincinnati: all the American companies in spanking new skyscrapers, billboards mostly in English, oversize cars bumper to bumper, and girls (the first two we saw) with heads piled so high with curlers they looked like walking generators.

SAN BLAS: MATRIARCHY OF ARTISTS

Colonel Michael Petrosky, and his assistant manager, Philip Sladen, have none of Jean Berthelot's arrogance and resistance to good public relations. We were given their names by a charming employee of the Tourist Bureau, Señorita Manuelita de la Guardia. They not only offered to fly us to the San Blas Islands as their guests, but put at our disposal a launch which ordinarily rents at $5 the hour. The usual round-trip plane fare is $16.80.

We took off in the Cessna 185 "skywagon" at 8:30 and flew over the Continental Divide at an altitude of 7,000 feet. As we glided down the dense, trackless jungles of the northern slope, the Caribbean came into view, and the archipelago of 365 islands that Columbus had correctly guessed to be "as numerous as the days of the year." Here lie the most happily isolated and unusually protected tribe in the hemisphere; and the greatest concentration of natural artists on earth. For unnumbered centuries the Cuna Indians have lived here: Mongolian-seeming, with high cheekbones, slanting eyes and straight black hair, a race of great beauty and fierce independence. Except for a brief period in 1926 when, under the influence of an American smuggler, they seceded and formed the shortlived Republic of Tula, they have been part of the Republic of Panama, a reservation with a governor from the mainland, but with virtual autonomy and strict laws prohibiting any visitor to remain after sundown on those islands actually populated by Cunas. The society operates on matriarchal principles. The men do the fishing and work the islanders' farms on the mainland. The women keep the money, rear the children, make and wear the incomparable costumes. If a man on one island falls in love with a woman on another, *he* must follow *her*, endowing her family with his possessions.

The dress of these queenly women must be seen to be believed. Tight anklets of woven orange beads, a sarong of many colors sweeping to the ground, earrings and breastplates of gold or silver, necklaces of perfectly matched seashells, nuts and coffee beans. But the crowning glory is the *mola*, a blouse appliqued back and front with a design, sometimes figurative, sometimes abstract, and never repeated, in every conceivable superimposed color. One mola takes as long as a month and a half to make, and many of the women we saw were stitching as they walked. Except for the one she wears (and often won't sell, because it is the best) each *mola* goes into a stockpile under the eaves of the thatched hut—money in the bank. An occasional Paris or New York merchant has been known to carry off as many as five hundred in a single foray. We saw some selling at the Hilton for $29.95. As pillow covers in New York they bring more. Here the very best may be had for five dollars and the average price ranges between one and two dollars, but one must be prepared to bargain, long and fiercely, for this is what the San Blas woman expects and enjoys.

We saw none of this at Porvenir, the small island with a "strip" (of beach sand) between rows of towering coconut palms, where we landed. There is the strip, the governor's house, a place called Jungle Jim's Hotel, and that's it. We were told to be back here at four and we watched, with some misgivings, the takeoff into the fierce wind that always blows here, the pilot sideslipping just in time to clear the tips of the palms. Cipriano's launch took us first to Wachuguala, where three women gorgeously arrayed in *molas*, and brandishing more in our faces, attacked us at the dock like wolves. We took a picture or two from a safe distance, and fled. Stopping at Kort-Bisky to drop the proprietor of a copra factory, we sailed next to Pico Feo ("Ugly Peak"—but flat) and Nalunega, where the finest *molas* are to be found—and as happy, earthy and talented a race of women as could be imagined. At the last of these little islands where we swam in the translucent but urchin-perilous sea with pelicans flying around us, Bill made friends with the women by insisting that *they* photograph us. Very soon we were photographing them—and being invited to lunch in a big communal cooking-hut. They were delighted when we accepted, laughing, throwing their arms around us, letting us hold their babies, and serving us a most unappetizing meal of fried dehydrated fish and baked plantains dipped in salt. Three huge logs, crossed, made the central cookingplace on which pots rested. The smoke (*some* of it) sifted through the roof. A pail of water and a four-foot bar of soap had been brought to the table for our ablutions.

Once outside, the bargaining began in earnest. The charges and the
countercharges. The screams of rage. And the final dissolve in laughter.
Seventeen superb squares, our haul, including several complete blouses
"bought off the back" after a quick change in the nearest hut. But the great
golden breastplates, and anklets, and coin-bangles (as much as five hundred
dollars' worth on one Indian woman's breast, the governor was to tell us
later), are not for sale. For these, and the solid gold nose rings—forged
aboard ship by itinerant sea-borne jewelers while the Cunas wait ashore—
are what the women spend their money on.

"Do you have schools?" we asked one of the local beauties—(and my
God! the young are beautiful, with that blue line painted from the forehead
down the nose to the upper lip. . . .)

"Yes. Schools once. But for months no *Maestro*. . . ."

Many of the islanders, or their *caciques*, don't permit schools—except
for a stiff price. But if the copra cultivators don't work, out they go. So
said, at any rate, Juan B. Barragán, the gracious governor of the islands,
when we had returned to Porvenir. He offered us dinner and beds when
our plane failed to show up at four. He also told us that the Cuna language
is the only one in the world without *verbs*—an inflection of the voice being
sufficient. But just as he was telling us of *his* troubles—the lack of a launch,
or any radio or telephone to alert the mainland in case of accident or sickness—our petty one ended and we were off, wishing now that the plane
hadn't made it, that we'd had time to visit Jungle Jim (pronounced Yungle
Yim) and his "Hotel," and again and again those natural artists, who put
all abstractionists, figurative or geometric, to shame.

THE ZONED AND THE UNZONED

The problem of the Canal is so complicated in its factual background and so overheated in its emotional crosscurrents that to attempt to discuss it rationally invites derision. At a time when the French had failed, when most Latin American governments did not represent their peoples and could be bought, and when there was no one else to build the necessary link, was our highhanded seizure of the Zone justified? It was unethical and it was realistic. . . . Skipping half a century (the Canal was completed in 1914), who was responsible for the bloody riots of 1964? Three parties. First, the United States, not for any specific act, but for its continued presence, its failure over the years to nationalize or internationalize the installation, and its psychologically inflammatory operation of the Zone as a sort of American Country Club with economic and racial privileges for the management. Second, the Panamanian ruling class, the Twenty Families or *Rabiblancos* (white-tailed birds) as they are called, who have consistently exploited popular resentment over the efficiently run Canal to cover up their exploitation of the Panamanian people and their failure to develop Panama. And third, the Communists, Russian, Chinese and Cuban varieties, who will always turn a molehill of legitimate grievance into a bloody mountain to discomfit their rival for mankind's salvation.

We had a taste of the smoldering brew at a sidewalk cafe in downtown Panama before visiting the Zone. An otherwise well-educated and mild-mannered Negro, who had worked in the Zone and who liked *gringos,* told us that if he saw another mob attacking with rocks he'd have to join them and throw some himself. Why, we asked him. Because Southerners almost invariably are hired as civil administrators in the Zone, and "because the authorities don't want us niggers to get out of hand, you know, or ask more than thirty dollars a month wages." He admitted, when pressed, that Southerners haven't been in the majority for years, and that Panamanians pay domestics less than Americans, but it didn't matter. "It's an emotional thing, I guess. . . ."

The defense of Frank Baldwin, the Canal's chief information officer, whom we called on next, was just as predictable.

"The Canal," he said, "is the scapegoat for all the troubles in Panama. But American newsmen are also to blame. They invariably compare our way of life in the Zone with the *slums* back home—never with the homes of Panama's own rulers which are far more luxurious than anything here.

Fifty years ago, to be sure, there was segregation, and we paid in silver and gold.[1] The average Zonian is not from the South but from the Middle West, and many of us are married to Panamanians. Only fifteen percent are second-generation Zonians like me.

"The trouble began," he continued, "when we backed Egypt rather than the English and French in the Suez crisis. 'Egypt got *their* canal,' was the immediate reaction here, 'so why can't we?' There are thirty thousand Panamanian unemployed in the capital today and this is twenty-five percent of the total labor force. The proportion is much higher in Negro Colón which, since a road was built across the isthmus, no longer produces anything. There are fourteen thousand employed by the Canal, ten thousand of them non-Americans. The base-scale for pay is the same for we pay an average twenty-eight percent income tax to their seven to eight percent, so the take-home pay is about the same. Sure, things here are cheaper, but Panamanian import laws make it so! Domestics? We pay $45 plus room and board, they as little as $15 or $20.

"Panama is controlled by a few families, all of them intermarried. There are more millionaires proportionately here than in any American city. Their government was very weak and chaotic under Chiari, so talk about their 'rights,' and the old treaties, flourished. Riots hid the reality. But the Twenty Families woke up when for four days last January the National Guard failed to stop the looting and burning and it began to spread to *their* stores and homes. Presto! it stopped. And now they fear the *loss* of the Zone which brings Panama ninety-three million dollars a year in direct benefits. Does the Canal lose money? If our military defense of it is included, we lose forty-five million dollars a year. Neither the U.S. nor the Panamanian employees here are worrying about the future—they're protected by pensions; but what will happen to the wholly dependent Panamanian economy?"

The embattled Mr. Baldwin was really steamed up now; we couldn't have stopped him if we'd tried.

"Why do stores in Panama City pay only nineteen dollars a month 'to clerks? I saw the payroll last week at one of them. Why don't the Forty Families cut their profits? Well, under Robles, and thanks to the Castro threat, they are paying slightly higher wages here and there. And we are changing, too. Five years ago only five percent of the comptroller's office staff was Panamanian—today forty-three percent. But apprentice training is

[1] Silver for Negroes, gold for whites.

very difficult in Panama. Panama itself—in fact all of Latin America—has no schools for skilled labor. Even for plumbers! In our Zone schools, Panamanians drop out after one or two years and start their own businesses.

"There was not one case of disloyalty among our native employees during the riots."

We asked him where, since there are few consumers in our sense, and the rest of the country is undeveloped, the Panamanian millionaires make their fortunes.

"You've seen the slums here? Wait until you see them in Colón! All the slums are owned by the Forty Families. They keep it that way since the buildings are all amortized and the rents are gravy. Like Harlem. But the Zone is 100 percent integrated; there's even a Negro on the governor's staff. But among *them*, it's different. The *Rabiblancos* hate the *Rabinegros*, and vice versa. The Negroes had to be brought in to build the Canal, but when we prepared to send them back to Jamaica and Barbados, the *Rabis* yelled: 'Don't! We need them as servants, as buyers of our groceries, as inhabitants of our slums'—though of course they didn't say 'slums'. . . . Do we Zonians ignore Panama City? If we did their whole economy would collapse. A few here, but a very few, are so burned up over the riots they refuse to leave the Zone or are afraid to. But just look at the number of black license-plates outside! And who's spending the big money at the Hilton and the other hotels? Do our schools prejudice them? Hell, no! We teach them exactly what their Department of Education requests us to. Panamanians say: 'But you *could* raise tolls and give us more money.' If we did that we'd be damaging every other nation on earth."

But deeds speak louder than words, and hearts than heads, and love than anger, and perhaps the one man in the Zone who is doing most to reverse the slide into disaster for all concerned is the man who is just doing his job well, because he loves it, and loves people.

We sensed the quality of Fred Berest, guide to the Miraflores Locks, long before we talked to him—in the obvious respect and affection with which he treated the lowly Panamanians in our group, in the intensity of his interest in what we were all looking at. As we walked out on the observation platform of the control tower, a Liberian freighter 624 feet long, the *Olympic Star*, was being pulled into the locks by ships-guide cables attached to small electric engines ("mules") on both banks. A single man in a rowboat had done the attaching. This tanker, Berest told us, pays about eight thousand dollars for its passage, and is guided entirely through the canal by a Zone pilot who takes over from the ship's captain—here and here only. Only the largest flat-tops are too large for the Canal. Berest had often seen the *Missouri* go through—"with only nine inches clearance and hardly a paint scratch."

As we watched the water being forced out of the first of the two locks which lower the ship fifty-four feet at this point, we noticed a pigeon swimming about frantically, its wings too saturated with oil to fly. "It will make it," Berest said, adding with a catch in his voice, "probably. Even rowboats, even kayaks have gone through."

"At what cost?" we asked.

"A dollar and a half, Colón to Balboa; every ship is charged according to its cargo. A thousand go through every month."

As we watched, the great hollow steelplated gates opened softly, guided by a long arm attached to a geared wheel, and this in turn to the forty horse-power motor no larger than a Volkswagen's. The pigeon floated through!— followed by the *Olympic Star*. Inside the control room there is one one-hundred-foot panel whose red and green lighted levers repeat in miniature the entire operation. The single gray-haired operator flipped a switch without even looking out the window. He glanced at a blackboard with its latest news of ships and tides, and resumed his conversation with an unarmed guard, the only other inhabitant of the efficient mechanism.

When the ship had passed and the sightseers had gone and dusk was descending, we sat on a bench with Fred Berest, and I asked him what had brought him here. He had graduated from New York University in 1930, becoming, shortly after, that college's youngest instructor—in drama. During World War II he'd served with the infantry in the Aleutians. Then he'd become an associate director of the Pasadena Playhouse. There he had joined the Bahai, and because they had asked him to carry the faith to Panama, he'd applied for a job in the Zone. "They saw my background in drama," he said with a smile, "—and made me a lock guard. But in 1954 I'd suggested that explaining the Canal to visitors might be a good policy, so I was the first one hired to do this."

"How long do you expect to continue doing it?" Bill asked.

"All my life," he answered.

"There may not be a canal that long," I said.

"Quite possibly. But there will be a Bahai faith."

We asked him to explain Bahai to us. "Imagine," he said, "seven or eight glasses being filled from a pitcher of water. God, holding that pitcher, may be conceived of as pouring the Holy Spirit from age to age. Every five hundred or a thousand years, you know, religion takes a new name. If the first glass contains Krishna, the second Moses, and so on through Buddha, Christ and Mahomet, we come finally to the Persian seer, Baha'u'llah (1817–1892), who taught the oneness of *all* faiths and of all mankind. A progressive revelation, we call it. Just as the Indians of San Blas and Darién grasp intuitively the oneness of nature, so we in the larger world must reestablish this principle and break down the barriers of nationalism. Each in his own way, to the best of his ability."

We had no doubt, driving out, that Fred Berest is doing more than his share of what most of us are not doing at all.

"My God!" I broke into our reverie, "I was so moved I walked away with his pad!"

"He's lucky you didn't walk away with the locks," Bill said.

We were still in the Zone and the Zone was showing its best face—impeccable engineering, calibrated lawns, golf courses, Little League baseball diamonds, every road clearly marked and banked, and even a store selling bananas by the bunch—the first we had seen in Central America.

Bill, the *Puertorriqueño*, looked at it all and sighed deeply. "Do you know," he said, "that the phrase 'civic pride' doesn't exist in our language?"

A PEEK AT DARIEN

We flew over the jungle-clad mountains that stout Cortés never saw, in the company of a friend, Jim Zonnevylle, who had to check on six shiny new Esso tanks at a place called La Palma. It is 120 miles southeast of Panama. From there we flew fifty miles farther south to Yaviza, which is not very far from the Colombia border. This is virgin territory for Esso: It is doing business with the savages whose idea of heaven is to have an outboard motor and really move their banana and coconuts to where the money is. The money, we were soon to discover, makes wonderful necklaces. It is virgin territory for the Inter-American Highway, too, for surveyors have already hacked their way through on foot, and in a few years expect to complete the last link of the long road linking Alaska with Tierra del Fuego. Rich as it is, the Panamanians have never touched Darién. But Cortés was of a different breed, and if it had served his purpose to go beyond Honduras nothing would have stopped him. As a matter of fact, the first thing we saw in

Yaviza was a ruined fort built by later *conquistadors*: tapered gunports in two-foot-thick brick walls lowering above the village on the steep banks of the muddy Tuira, Panama's biggest river.

We were happy to land, not from any fear that our pilot (the same one who had hedgehopped us to San Blas) would dump us in the climax forests that cover every inch of mostly flat Darién, but because the assault on the ears from the open radio-communication in all these small planes is devastating. Why earphones aren't used, was a question we felt in no position to ask, though we wanted to. A dugout canoe ferried us across the river and soon we were sharing our sandwiches with two Chocos Indian women on the keel of an overturned canoe that served them as a table. These buxom but shapely aborigines wear only a sarong-like loincloth, but they embellish their necks with such a mass of chains, shells, bangles and coin that their breasts are scarcely visible. Their stiff long black hair, with bangs in front, is as bristly as a wire brush. Their Eskimo-like faces with splayed nostrils and very Oriental eyes are well set off by pendulous earrings—American dimes and other silver coins alternating with half-moons of thin silver. We noticed scars on their necks (from the pendants of these half-moons?) a feverish spot of rouge in the center of each cheek, and good old American nail polish on every fingernail. But there was nothing up to date about the tattooing on the face of the only male we encountered—red and black lines defining the nose and chin, and an intricate bridge-pattern over and below the lips.

There is nothing picturesque about the village itself. It is as spindly-poor as Haiti's Jérémie, and its children, mostly Negro, play in the dirt and garbage. The village store is as full of American cans and cheap textiles as any in the remoter parts of New Jersey. A Shell sign hanging from a crook on "Main Street" was its only decoration. And a political slogan stencilled on a wall provided the only visible connection with Panama's top-heavy prosperity:

DICKY ARIAS

Austeridad y Miseria? No!

Prosperidad y Bienestar? Si!

We flew over the gulf of San Miguel on the way back. Here, at Piñas Bay, a fishing club and a $180,000 home has been established by Ray Smith, a multimillionaire Texan, who flies in weekend guests "at cost" ($300) from Panama City. Piñas Bay is already said to be supplanting Peru's Cabo Blanco as the hemisphere's most posh fishing camp, and it boasts eighteen world records in black marlin, sailfish, seabass (up to 400 pounds), whale sharks, killer whales, bone, and red snapper. But the skindiving, we were told, does not compare with that at the San Blas Islands, where the underwater visibility is sixty feet, and you're in submarine heaven unless you pick up a stone fish ("death in 4 minutes") or get cut by a piece of fire coral ("piss on it, or that can bring death too!").

With islands and shadows of clouds glinting below us in the half-light, we finally caught a glimpse of the end of the Canal, Fort Amadór, with its more up-to-date formula for quick death, a missile base on the ultimate promontory.

SOCIALIZING

Considering the limited amount of time (four days) we found ourselves with by the time we arrived in Panama, it was astonishing to us how much of a variety of social life we seemed to fall into.

We managed to play tennis twice, and both times in a foursome that included Ed Kelley, an army captain at Fort Sherman, who is in charge of counter-insurgency training for all Central Americans interested in combating their Castroites. Kelley is short, musclebound, and so fiercely aggressive that when he went for an overhead near me I held up my racquet lest he miss and split my skull; off the court, but presumably not in the jungle range, he is the gentlest of men. Once, while we were playing, there was a noise so deafening and prolonged that it was impossible to hear the score. I asked whether there might be a fractured steamboiler in the hotel, but Kelley said, "No, cicadas." A waiter by the pool confirmed it by bringing an upside-down specimen about the size of a small hand-grenade to our table. "By coincidence," he said, "we found this one in the kitchen." He was a Negro and we at once developed an intimate, joking relationship with him—the sort of relationship that's almost impossible with a Latin.

The Zachrissón family is an exception. I had seen some of Julio Zachrissón's magnificently grotesque etchings in Guatemala and wanted to see more of his work. Julio was in Spain, but his brothers Boris and Ivan, and their friend Carlos García de Paredes, a short-story writer, and their wives, showed us Julio's paintings and drawings, and entertained us with wine, songs and stories all of one memorable evening.

Ceci Heurtematte, whose brother had gone to school with me and later to Yale, was another exception. I hadn't seen her in years and she had lost none of her vivacity and beauty. Her family is one of the Twenty (or is it Forty?) and she gave a graphic description of the panic in those upper strata when the rioting began to get out of hand last winter. She came up to our room to see the *molas*—to our surprise she'd never visited either the San Blas archipelago or Darién—but when we looked for "Irving Goldsmith" he was nowhere to be found. Irving had already led an active life in Panama—visiting the Archaeological Museum where he was pronounced a fake, a jeweler's shop where he was assayed as solid gold, and the best curio shop on the isthmus (Mary Harnish's) where an expert gave him a completely clean bill of health. Apparently it was too much for him. We searched the whole tennis court area with Ceci by flashlight but I accomplished nothing except to rip open a pair of pants on a wire frame that had been erected to support tomorrow's carnival queens. ("Irving" popped out of my overstuffed suitcase the day we flew back to Guatemala).

But Carnival Day, our last, out-socialed everything. It began with a luncheon party at the exclusive Club de Golf de Panama where a *Comparsa* was in progress. Ladies in *Polleras* and men in *Montuñas* were dancing the *Tamborito* and we were joined at the Zonnevylle table by Lolita Parsons Arías, a *Rabiblanco* of ample beauty, to watch the crowning of the Chinese and the Zone "Queens." Lola's headgear, a collection of family heirlooms dating back more than a century, was spectacular. Her hair was live with

golden wires studded with pearls and other gems. Between the ear and the corner of each eye was glued a half-inch, thin, circular gold plate containing a pearl. Dozens of strings of pearls and gold chains containing placques and fifty-dollar gold pieces hung from her neck, and at the throat a tight velvet band supported a golden fish; and from her ears, of course, dangled equally elaborate gems. It had taken her servants all morning to dress her, she told me. "A woman's wealth," she added, "used to be gauged by the number of petticoats she wore under her *pollera*"—who counted them, she didn't say. While we were dancing I commented on the beauty of another of the *pollera*-wearers, but Lola looked upon this late-comer with a glance of withering pity and said: "To wear a diamond tiara, or *any* diamonds, for that matter, with the *pollera*, is to desecrate a tradition of great antiquity and beauty. She should know better."

We had to leave this glittering affair at two-thirty. Mr. Baldwin had insisted on sending a car and a guide to the hotel at that hour to show us the rest of the Canal. The only part we really wanted to see now was the "ghost" city of Colón, which was reputed to celebrate the carnival in a bizarre if not ferocious style of its own, but Mr. Baldwin was not to be denied, so we plotted to lure Teófilo, his driver, into Colón, skipping all the locks we could along the way. As we descended the ramp at the Hilton with him he pointed to a limousine with one passenger coming up. "That's Rubén Luis García," he said, "head of the press syndicate and a Communist."

The present "anarchy" in Panama began, Teófilo reminisced, when José Antonio Ramón Cantera, a strong-man president, was machine-gunned at the racetrack. The confession of the dying man implicated the *next* president and he went to jail. They had both, it seems, been mixed up with a narcotics ring, and American gangsters had been responsible for the killing. We asked whether the Canal itself had been dug in this atmosphere.

De Lesseps, Teófilo replied, had been personally honest, but scandals had come to a head toward the close of the French fiasco—digging a ten-mile ditch only 105 feet wide had cost them 30,000 dead and $260,000,000 —and De Lesseps had gone mad. The American effort that followed owed its success to the brilliant engineer John Stevens who had masterminded the switch from sea level to locks.

We passed (after Miraflores) the San Miguel locks, eighty-five feet above sea-level and walked to a high hill to look at this eight-mile section which took nine years to dig. Three hundred trainloads a day, each carrying four hundred tons of rock, with a cost of ten thousand more lives this time. I expressed surprise at the jungle we were now beginning to drive through. "This is our water insurance," Teófilo said. Very soon we were crossing the tracks of the first transcontinental railroad (1855) built by a private American company to carry a billion and a half dollars in gold ingots from the California fields to the Atlantic.

Teófilo, as Bill put it, is more of a one-hundred-percent American than Goldwater himself. The Panamanians, said our Panamanian friend, could never run the Canal. "Why not? I'll give you one example. Under the De la Guardia government a small schoolhouse was built in Chiriquí province for three thousand dollars. Under Chiari it was *repainted* for four thousand." When I remarked that he spoke of "Chombos" (Negroes) and Panamanians as of two separate nations, he said "It was a great mistake to give the Chombos citizenship in 1948. But then tenement-owners protested against our proposal to send them home to the West Indies. They hate us; and most Panamanians dislike and distrust them. Today twenty percent of all the people in our country are Chombos, and the percentage is always increasing."

As if to confirm his words, we were now driving into Colón, its outskirts a jungle of dilapidated shanties on an oily lagoon from which old tires and dumped truck-bodies protruded. Teófilo grimaced as I got out to photograph this nightmare. Soon we were at the waterfront and there was the Washington Hotel, a decayed pink plaster relic, once the pride of Central America. We also passed the absurd bronze of Columbus protecting an Indian maiden—gift of Empress Eugenie—and the burnt-out administration buildings of the Canal Zone where thirty thousand pounds of bulk milk intended for Panama's poor went up in flames last year while snipers from nearby roofs picked off the Zone police. Why? we asked our guide.

"Because," Teófilo said shrewdly, "when anyone gets anything free, doesn't he always hate the giver?"

Now, as we turned into Bolívar Avenue, an unforgettable sight met our eyes. And in very little time, despite our guide's dismayed injunction to return to Panama "and see the real thing," we were a part of it. And so, for all of his rational protest, was Teófilo himself. The long street and all its overhanging balconies, were jammed with celebrating Negroes. Not to mention East Indians, Polynesians, Arabs, *gringos* with beards, and a few

"slumming" Panamanians. Thousands by the minute, in trucks, even in Jeeps and four-ton transports loaned by the U.S. Army, were augmenting the disorganized, wholly spontaneous parade. Haitian Mardi Gras was the only thing I had ever seen to compare with it. Naked "savages" painted with blue and yellow spots, red "devils," masked Bat Men, honey-colored Mulatresses of great beauty with hair dyed red, a prisoner in black-and-white stripes, his number "6705392" on his back, drummers and bull-horn men and iron-beaters and auto-horn blowers, and whip-snappers. Improvised "Bazooka" teams were covering everybody (including us) with white flour. A man in an intricate house of mirrors stopped the show, posed for a photograph, and vanished. But the costume to end all costumes was worn by a thin man in dungarees that must have belonged to a 300-pounder. The belt-loops were filled with an iron hoop, hung from suspenders and bouncing up and down at every step, a foot away from the bouncer's torso in red jockey-shorts. A blue bandanna under a dirty straw hat covered *all* of this character's face, but he never faltered as he snake-danced down the avenue, bowing almost to the ground in front of every pretty girl.

Only once, when I stepped up to a Jeep-load of musicians to photograph them with my new Yashika was there any sign of the hostility that might have been expected. "No! No! No photographs, you!" But the protestor was rebuked, and severely, by the bandmaster; and we rejoined the march, dancing and singing our way down that wonderful thoroughfare that was the fitting end to The Road to Panama.

EPILOGUE

We're back in the U.S.A. again—at least we're on a Pan American flight heading north, Hertz having agreed to drive our impeccable Volks back to Guatemala for us, and we're about to be served lunch. Breathless anticipation. What will it be? We'd been away from American food long enough to relish the thought of ham and eggs, Southern fried chicken, or a fat slice of apple pie à la mode. The lovely hostess leaned over us and set on our laps two nine-by-five-inch plastic "coffins" sheathed in cellophane. We pulled the cellophane off gingerly and peered inside:

1 salt and 1 pepper, in pin-size cartouches
1 wafer of Nestlé's chocolate
1 corn muffin
1 wedge of Elysian cheese in tin foil
1 black olive
1 green olive
1/16 of a pickle
3 bite-size ham and cheese sandwiches
1 paper shot glass sheathed in aluminum, ½ full of peanuts
2 factory wrapped pretzels
1 toothpaste tube of Amora French aromatic mustard from Dijon with the legend "M'aimez-vous ainsi, présentée en tube?" (5 grams)
1 napkin
1 package of toothpicks

"Will they serve any liquid with it?" I asked Bill.

"Tear gas," he said.

The passenger in the third seat suggested that if opened at an altitude over five thousand feet, the tube of mustard might explode, covering our faces with tiny olive spots.

"There's a remedy for that," Bill said. "On all future flights a small altimeter will be attached to each tube. It's the sort of service we provide so well."

INDEX

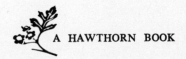